Nina Lyon has worked in a Bu[...] in Scotland, written contraband[...] helps run the HowTheLightG[...] philosophy festival near her home in Hay-on-Wye. Her essay 'Mushroom Season', inspired by youthful psychedelic misadventures and the mountains behind her home, was published by Random House in 2014 after being chosen as runner-up in the Bodley Head/*Financial Times* Essay Prize. She is currently completing a PhD about nonsense and metaphysics at Cardiff University.

Further praise for *Uprooted:*

'An unusual, digressive and timely piece of writing that pulls on many threads . . . But just as the meaning of the Green Man hides behind the foliage that sprouts from his mouth and eye sockets, it turns out that the true purpose of *Uprooted* is also hiding in the undergrowth, waiting to be discovered.' Paul Kingsnorth, *New Statesman*

'This quirky but engaging book describes Lyon's quest to track down as many examples of [the Green Man] as she can . . . Ultimately the book is less about the Green Man and more about the author's search for meaning in her life . . . Lyon is a witty and insightful writer and her account is filled with self-depreciating charm.' Ian Critchley, *Sunday Times*

'[Nina Lyon] has a sociologist's – or perhaps a taxonomist's – eye for human tribes, and *Uprooted* is liberally seeded with passages that neatly skewer British behaviour and mores.

Her description of Clun, with its rival "cloaked people" and "cagoule people", and her sardonic assessment of the didgeridoo-wielding types at Avebury, are delicious.' Melissa Harrison, *Financial Times*

'What is most remarkable about Nina Lyon's stylish and eloquent book is the way she has mapped extraordinary things – ley lines, mythological figures, alchemy, magic – onto ordinary modern experience in a way that enhances in both directions . . . [It] is a major triumph which enables you to see the unfamiliar with new eyes.' Bernard O'Donoghue

'Not only is it wonderful – sharp and beguiling and stuffed with the beginnings of tangents – but reading it together with my partner has been the strangest thing; an almost continuous sense of weird brought on by finding a book containing the same thoughts she and I have been discussing for a while.' James Holden

Uprooted

On the Trail of the Green Man

NINA LYON

FABER & FABER

First published in the UK in 2016
by Faber & Faber Limited
Bloomsbury House, 74–77 Great Russell Street
London WC1B 3DA

This paperback edition first published in 2017

Printed in the UK by CPI Group (UK) Ltd, Croydon, CR0 4YY

A CIP record for this book
is available from the British Library

ISBN 978–0–571–31802–5

FSC
www.fsc.org
MIX
Paper from
responsible sources
FSC® C101712

2 4 6 8 10 9 7 5 3 1

For Felix and Lara, and all who
lurk in the undergrowth

Contents

ONE

Kilpeck

What seems to be the white noise of the wind is, on closer listen, both polyrhythmic and multi-tonal. There is a single background hum and, weaving around it, the rise and fall of other winds: sidewinds and crosswinds and eddies. The house is on a hill, or, to be more precise, on the head of a ridge running off a hill into the Wye Valley. You can therefore, on a clear day, see down the valley in both directions, and across the valley to the Hergest Ridge and, behind it, the Radnor Hills, which are sometimes dusted with snow. Behind the house's promontory is Little Mountain, which is not really a mountain, but a big hill.

You can see everywhere, and the wind can get everywhere. Perhaps because it comes from everywhere at once, channelled down the broad valley but refracted through many other places, it creates a cacophony, always altering, never resting. While the patter of windless rain is calming in its soft consistency, there is something rousing about the wind, which is not relaxing. It is like a restless chant.

It was after another white night of wind that I drove, sleep-deprived and in a condition not suited to adverse road conditions, along the length of the Golden Valley as it follows the path of the Dore down from the hills that loom above the Wye. The road was, in its better parts, a conduit for water flowing from one field to the next and, when it sloped, a waterfall. This was a good thing, for the movement of the water meant that it did not pool deeper. Red mud coursed along past abandoned cars left in last night's floods, which had, for the moment, subsided. The static bodies of water were the scary bits, because you did not know where they would end. There were fewer of these, but the road had been carved away at its edges, which fell aside like glacial moraine, and the road, like the washed-out cars, looked fragile. An unremarkable journey alters when its success cannot be taken for granted. The water was winning.

We live in an age controlled by humans and human technology. One current assumption, the pessimist's, is that human technology is so efficient and invulnerable that it will, eventually, kill off the planet. The optimists take a different line, which is that human ingenuity will evolve to solve all problems regarding human survival. Both rest on the assumptions that human ingenuity is unique, for good or for bad, and that human technology is more robust and powerful than nature. It took a month of angry storms to make me consider this more critically than before.

There was something about the surfeit and force of elements that made me want to go back to Kilpeck, which is where I was headed. I felt as though the aggressions of the weather might make more sense there, or perhaps that Kilpeck would make more sense in the light of the storms.

Kilpeck is a village in Herefordshire, about twenty miles away from my home near Hay-on-Wye. The village itself might have come straight out of *The Archers*, a westerly Albion of rolling hills and well-kept pretty cottages and a smart-looking pub with good food. At its edge are two noteworthy things: a motte-and-bailey castle and a church, which is not really, to my mind, a church in any conventionally understood Christian sense at all.

In the eleventh century, the parishioners of Kilpeck would have been trying to understand their landscape and the weather that altered it as an expression of a greater will. As human endeavour moulded the land, with clearings and mounds and buildings, so it was moulded by the land, existing in conflict, and in symbiosis, with nature.

Our rational belief in a mechanistic world of things enables us to find effective ways of operating in it, and our ways of operating in it further build that belief. We seem to be very adept at shaping the world to our will, and think little of the idea that the will and the ways of humankind might fall prey to any entity other than our own self-destruction.

But this sustained attack from untamed nature together with a big cultural wave of environmental doom-tales had made me question our narrative of human progress, our sense that comfort can be gained from our capacity to build and improve our world. It all seemed a bit anthropocentric. People looked small on stormy days. Once upon a time, the storms would have been attributed to a pagan deity of some kind, or an angry Old Testament God.

When I was seven, I was politely excused from Sunday school on the basis that being a vociferous atheist was fine but poorly suited to its aims – a gentle dismissal that leaves me with a residual fondness for the Church of England. I am not inclined towards religion, or superstition, or anything much that can't reveal itself empirically.

I was not in a mood for finding God or redemption, or, for that matter, its pagan equivalent. I was interested more in how to simply understand a relationship with nature and the land in which both were considered to be alive, and not just alive but conscious. I wanted to get into what I had come to think of as the Kilpeck headspace. There is a sense

3

of godliness revealed in nature that characterises the architectural decoration and, I would venture, would once have characterised the creed of the Kilpeck church. I was starting to wonder if taking a worldview which encompassed the idea of a will that is everywhere, whether of God or object or ether, might actually be a more practical way of understanding the things that modern-day scientism sometimes doesn't.

The rain had stopped and the wet road, lit up in the first sunshine for weeks, glared its path to the village. The church stood, calm and flesh-pink in the new light, as though the storms had never happened. Behind it, through a yew-lined uphill avenue, the ditch around the castle motte had flooded into a moat, cutting it off apart from a foot of raised track. Rather than concealing the structure of the space, the water clarified its depths and heights and the even circle of the motte. Now that the rain had stopped and the sky was blue, its bright reflection shone in the flash moat.

Behind the castle tump, above the spiky tips of a pine forest, loomed the massif of the Black Mountains. Today the mountains were not black, but white with snow. As I drove back down the Golden Valley later, the snowline looked as though it were painted on in one vast stripe along the Cat's Back. Birds sang from above the village. Beneath us, I thought I could hear a distant hum, or roar, and braced myself for revelation, but it was the A465.

The most famous thing about the Church of St Mary and St David at Kilpeck is probably the Sheela-na-gig carved among the corbels that encircle it. A woman baring her dilated vagina in an aggressive fashion is not the stuff we are led to believe that the Church, however early, is made of. But to see the Sheela-na-gig in isolation is to fall prey to our own post-Victorian prurience at such things – she sits in a line of extraordinary carvings of animals and men, song and dance and food and love that look like a pagan celebration of the stuff of life.

The Kilpeck Sheela-na-gig is seen as a warning against the sins of the flesh. It is true that, with her bald head and staring eyes, she looks bellicose rather than buxom, as though she'd glass you after a few drinks. But in the context of the other corbels it is very hard to see her as an aberrant warning against sin, because none of the others have that function.

As a point of comparison, the Abbaye d'Arthous is in the French Basque country, close to the Pyrenees, much in the same way that Kilpeck lies in the last flattish part of the Welsh Marches before they ascend into the Black Mountains. It was built at the same time, in the late twelfth century, and its corbels are similar in their Romanesque style and carving technique to those at Kilpeck. It is thought that the Herefordshire School of stonemasonry that graces Kilpeck and, somewhat less after desecrations and rebuilds, the nearby churches at Eardisley and Shobdon, consisted of a number of local craftsmen overseen by someone who had trained in France. There are, however, substantial differences in the subject matter.

The corbels at the Abbaye d'Arthous are clearly about the Christian conception of sin. There is a man either drinking from a barrel, or vomiting over it, as though the ambiguity links cause and effect. Adam's modesty is covered with a fig leaf; a wolf seizes a lamb – it is sound biblical stuff. The corbels at Kilpeck include a Green Man presiding from his pillar across the main south entrance, two people either dancing close or getting amorous, someone playing a rebec as though warming up for a party, a number of animals – rams, pigs, fish, something like an armadillo – and, of course, the Sheela-na-gig. The Church that oversaw these could not have been the same in character as the Church that decorated the Abbaye D'Arthous.

And this is why the Kilpeck church had always intrigued me as a place, for how it showed how little we understand of the mindset of what must have been a fragmentary Church in the early Middle Ages, and how little we know of the old religions that pre-dated it. It takes the form of a church, and it is known and recorded as being one, but its character and location make it feel far more like a pagan site judiciously taken in by the Church.

It is easy, in an age of scandals deriving as much from its obsession with maintaining institutional face as from the endless abuses of power by sexually wayward priests and sadistic nuns, and conscious embrace of the AIDS pandemic for fear that women might gain bodily autonomy, to think of the Catholic Church as driven by a unified doctrine at all costs. But its development in the Dark Ages belies the etymology of its name: it set itself out as a universal Church, one that could take in a breadth of existing beliefs and rituals. The sense of 'catholic' as liberal and all-embracing is more developed in English than in other languages, and at the wild outer reaches of our wet and windy island, far from Rome, there was greater room for compromise.

Just as the early Church adopted pagan festivals of Christmas and Easter into a chronologically reshaped Jesus myth, so it took in bits of pagan iconography. You can see it as a simple cost-benefit exercise: on the one hand, you want to grow and maintain universal rule over a vast and diverse congregation; on the other, you want to preserve doctrinal integrity and get them all to toe the line. One option happens at the expense of the other. If your institution is in a growth mode, you let them keep their sun-worship Sabbath and their parties. Austerity and heretics can happen later.

And so the Church of St Mary and St David was built, its axis from chancel to nave following the line of a stream arising from a holy pagan spring, its altar beneath four half-heads of green men or something like them, and its exterior ornate with idolatry. It was at this altar, with its holy quaternity that bore no obvious physical or numerical resemblance to Christian doctrine, that the inchoate sense of God-in-nature I had always found here formed into something more concrete. Maybe what troubled me about the storms, and the journey, and the strangeness of Kilpeck, were all the things tied up in the Green Man myth.

The Green Man is a twentieth-century name given to the many carvings across Britain and Northern Europe that bear the image of a man whose face is made from vegetation, or who grows it from his mouth or beard or hair. He is a sort of forest-god, an emblem of the birth-death-rebirth cycle of the natural year. He was worshipped in hope of good harvests, and guards the metaphysical gate between the material and immaterial worlds. He is the entry-point to Faerieland and the Small Folk of British and Nordic myth.

He is also a reminder of the superior force of Nature over human enterprise, that Nature will, in time, consume us all. This underlying power – the quiet threat of force that makes power power – is something that haunted the storms. Those Kilpeck stonemasons and, I'd wager, the priest and congregation, were not about to give up on their Green Man. They gave him godly stature in that church, and I bet they didn't only pray to Jesus for their crops to grow and the long, wild, wet winters to end.

I walked around the church again, to the spot at the edge of the graveyard that marks out one of Alfred Watkins's first leys, and looked out across the land. It was a secure spot to stand awhile, as though the church and castle tump had got your back. You can see for thirty miles or more, from the line of Offa's Dyke across to the softer hills of Herefordshire. It is the sort of place where invading forces of Welshmen or weather can be viewed coming in like distant waves. Pagans understood location.

In the meantime, in our time, people were getting cross with the Environment Agency for not dredging undredgable places or removing floods from the flood plains they lived on, and with trains that were not running, and with the schools that had just re-opened. From my bedroom window a fragmented ribbon of water sat across the broad Wye Valley where the river had broken its banks.

The water had settled, and was silver rather than brown. Over the course of the day it retreated, leaving the land scattered with oxbow lakes and ponds, changing by the hour. In the sunlight, the day after the biggest of the storms, the water looked benign. It sprayed up into rainbows when you drove through it, and the background rush of spontaneous streams and waterfalls underscored all other sound.

Driving back down the Golden Valley, my earlier trepidation about the state of the road dissipating along with the falling floodwaters, I did not thank the Green Man, because that would have been a credulous thing to do, and I was not, or not yet, in credulous mode. I did think about him, though. I was going to meet him again – and another storm came.

Someone on Twitter mentioned that the Peterchurch road was closed again. I had intended to go out Green Man hunting – Dore Abbey, Garway Church, back to Kilpeck and home. Instead, I watched sheets of rain tear down the valley, and then there was a knock on the door, because water from the garden was overflowing into the boiler room, a shed on the side of the house.

Not long ago a brook flowed through the garden, providing the water source and outfall for what the house had of plumbing. You could tell, because the water had re-appropriated its old path. I dug a drainage trench while my landlady cleared leaves from the ditch by the house and mopped the water from the floor. The rain soaked through my coat and stuck my hair across my eyes, and the water level in the ditch rose and fell as more mud fell in and was scooped out, and at some point it fell beneath the doorstep and stayed there, and I went back inside.

When I got inside, where it was warm, because the boiler was still working, I was not at all sure that I wanted to be inside. The obvious thing to do was to strip off the layers of wet clothes – denim, leather and wool, all the worst things to wear in the rain – get warm and dry, and get back to work. But it didn't feel particularly like work: what is reading about late-Victorian metaphysical disputes compared to digging a ditch? I never did proper work now; when I lived up the mountain and there were logs to bring in every night, and external plumbing that needed fixing through thick undergrowth or at the bottom of waterfalls, and snow to clear for a couple of months every year in order to get the kids to school, I did enough of it to have no need for more. And there was no point in pretending that a bit of emergency scrabbling in the mud was anything more than a fantasy

9

version of hard physical labour, in much the same vein as Marie Antoinette's toy farm at Versailles. I was not of the outdoors, even if I was more of the outdoors than my contemporaries back in London who found it exotic to walk fifty metres with the compost every day and considered an umbrella to be rainwear.

The satisfaction of being purposeful in the rain was both a rural fantasy and, as I considered it further, related to an unusual sense of the fragility of our bubble of creature comforts, and an urge to preserve them. I generally preserve my quality of life by staring at a screen, as I am now. The interventions that result in capital are virtual, immaterial, as they are for anyone whose place of work is a desk. They are not real in any concrete sense. Many of us exist in a state of privilege that places few demands on physical labour. There are systems out there to create and maintain the infrastructure of comfort, and we pay for them with bills and taxes. Sometimes, on the mountain, the phone line would be blown down in a storm and there would be no Internet, which seemed terrible and perilous, and then a few days later some men would arrive and would interface with real mud and hardware to make the virtual world reappear. I marvelled at them.

Right now, across the country, tens of thousands of people were bailing out their homes with buckets and building makeshift sandbag dykes and reappraising their sense of urgency in a way that I could not imagine. Bricks and mortar and all the sturdy technology that feeds our normal lives can fall apart pretty quickly in a storm. Meanwhile, my brush with the edge of comfort was over, and I was back in my warm kitchen, beneath an expensive lamp that mimics the colour of natural light, and not really working in any sense, but reading about the Green Man.

The term 'Green Man' was coined by Julia Hamilton, Lady Raglan, in a paper published in the journal *Folklore* in 1939. The paper consisted of a set of observations regarding foliate heads on a number of churches across England, Wales and elsewhere in north-western Europe. Raglan talks about the fifteenth-century Robin Hood cult, which she sees as a corruption of Robin of the Wood, an anarchic celebration that troubled all factions of the Church.

A half-century earlier, James George Frazer's *Golden Bough* had forged a new and comprehensible way of looking at the rituals of the past: the central theme of death and rebirth that unified creation myths, whether pagan or Christian. It was part of the birth of anthropology; as an exercise in comparative religion, it was also heretical. Frazer's account of the Crucifixion was judiciously removed to an appendix, and an abridged edition was released to suit late-Victorian sensibilities. By the 1930s, folk mythology was all the rage. Lady Raglan's aristocratic husband FitzRoy Somerset took up anthropology while stationed in Sudan and published a well-received book about hero myths. Educated feudalists were ready to take their ritual ground back from an enfeebled Church. Green Man studies flourished.

One of the controversies around the Green Man myth is that Lady Raglan's account is seen as being pretty mythical itself, in the sense that it is an under-evidenced speculation about things that we know very little about. There is no such thing as a simple stock image of the Green Man, for starters. There are subsets of Green Men – the foliate head, covered in oak leaves, and the disgorging head, where foliage sprouts from the mouth and, in a more grisly variant, all facial orifices. These are sometimes elided with the ritual May Day figure of Jack-in-the-Green, a man dressed in leaves, sometimes resembling a moving Christmas tree and with an effect more comic than awesome.

There is something compelling about a partial account, where there seems to be ground for a story but it is incomplete, so that the gaps to be filled bear the possibility of an openness of interpretation. So it is with the Green Man myth, which is not one myth, but an interconnected and fragmented series of images from various times and places, all riffing on a common theme. It is difficult to ascribe any single story to the foliate heads: there is only the fact of their imagery, and speculation about their role.

These figures adorn churches, but there is no doctrinal account of their genesis or existence. It is easier to say that there is no hard evidence for their pagan function than it is to suggest a credible Christian alternative. And it was the Church that had the monopoly on the written word back then, and that therefore guarded written history.

If the best information I could find about the Green Man was speculation, then the only response was to speculate further, and I needed a forest to do this in. It was time to go for a walk up the hill.

The footpath to the top of Little Mountain, where kites and buzzards circle on calmer days, passes through the boundary of a wood that falls sharply away to one side, on the left if you are headed uphill. From here, in the crook of a rocky outcrop, you can see down to a waterfall carved deep into a ravine. Today a vast ash lay across it, perhaps fifty metres long, snapped at its base like a trodden stick. The wood was light and healthy; the path itself was crisscrossed with the corpses of rotten trees, their cores orange-brown with mould, some of them less recent to the floor, their bark thick with moss. It looked as though the upper part of the wood had been knocked by the hand of a petulant child. It was a mess. The wood could have done with a guardian spirit. If the wood had had a spirit, you'd think that he or she would not have been happy.

There is a big flat rock that juts out above the steep fall of the ravine, and I sat there, surveying the damage. It is the sort of place that you take your children for a picnic while they still believe in fairies, but are big enough to be trusted not to fall off the edge. It didn't look too idyllic and it occurred to me that part of the reason was the lack of obvious signs of life: the badger setts with no marks of fresh exit, the absence of green undergrowth, the graveyard of branches.

Humans have a talent for anthropomorphising things in the world. If the basis of our ability to think is about forming patterns out of information and using them, the patterns we like to recognise best are those that reflect ourselves. We do it today with our apparently insatiable need to front all information with the recognisable face of celebrity. I wondered, briefly, if the celebrity pantheon fulfils a role similar to the Mahabharata, or the exploits of the Greek gods, in mirroring earthly virtue, vice and frailty in a series of interlocking, entertaining morality tales for the mortals.

Intangible concepts, like the processes of fertility or regeneration, or love or war, might seem as though they resist a simple line-drawing until you embody them in a character whose face and body tell the story with something approaching clarity. All the early animist rituals and beliefs that we lump together into paganism or the Old Religion reified these sorts of processes into godly objects. An easier job still is to embody things that you can actually see into a god – the sun, the moon, the sea. And it is not as though some bright pagan spark came up with the idea of marketing ideas as gods; a fearful deference to the entities that mattered so critically in day-to-day human lives needed to be enacted, and became ritualised, and then the rituals needed to be communicated within tribes and communities, and were institutionalised, and the outcome of this was the godheads.

I gazed out across the wet, broken forest and wondered what it would look like embodied in human form. A strong, injured man or woman – there was no obvious gender judgement to call here – sleeping in silent recovery. If you found this person, you might want to leave them something while they slept: food and water, or a blanket.

Today we have so little forest that we manage most of what is left. You could get the humans in to amputate all the damaged stuff, and clear the strewn branches from the floor. But in an age long before chainsaws, when trees were bigger than people, the best consolation might have been psychic, symbolised in the ritual of offerings to the forest-god.

It is this idea of psychic communication that is so far removed from how we think about the physical world now. And yet, if you lie on a rock hanging over a forest, as I did – in a state of slight discomfort because my coat was not quite waterproof and becoming less so by the minute – and give it time, a strange thing happens that is eerie, in eerie's original sense. You need to lie in silence, and allow the sensation of lying on a rock, breathing and listening, to expand. I suppose you could call it a meditative state, but there is no real need to, because it is only the ancient art of lying down for a rest.

After a time the silence is less silent. Beneath the distant, constant rush of the waterfall there are, in fact, sounds, but sounds whose patterns are too muted or too long to be heard as you tramp across the ground. They are not sounds that we tend to acknowledge or talk about. It is not clear which part of life in the forest they come from, but they are the sounds of life, of earthly process. They are merely patterns of waves, from undefined sources, and because the sources are undefined it feels as though the whole forest is breathing, which, in a sense, it is. The longer you stay there, the longer the detail builds.

Something similar happens if you find yourself trying to work, or sleep, next to a field of sheep. We describe their voices as a reductive 'baa', which is a pretty effective ono-matopoeic description. If you hear them for an hour or so, distinctions emerge: there are deep-voiced sheep and higher-pitched sheep, some sounds like a dark bellow or cough, some plaintive, and some strident and bossy. It is our human reduction of the vastness of the world that creates the assumption of simplicity of non-human things. There is nothing intrinsically simple about any of it.

Back in the forest, I was getting seriously wet, and it was not conducive to attempts at communion with nature. I brushed the mosses off me and walked back down the hill. One of the few fairy-tale aspects of the stormy weather had been the proliferation of rainbows that you get with per-petual fronts of rain, and now one emerged, faintly, out of the curve of the hedgerow along the line of the hill. As I walked, the rainbow moved east along the valley with its raincloud, so that by the time I got home it had made a good ten miles from Clyro to Bredwardine.

I thought about the forest, and about the way that it is possible to hear it, and about the idea that things that are too small to see have a spirit. Panpsychism, the philosoph-ical position that all matter has consciousness, is not short of adherents who are otherwise held to be in the sensible mainstream of thought. If you want to bridge the apparent reality of the material world and its capacity to behave unpredictably, it is a position that works.

In the late twentieth century, a reaction against the dangerous superstitions of organised religion led to most spiritual woo being cleansed from Western ideas of how the world works, and with it the idea of will across all scales, large and small. It was the most anthropocentric of times.

What if the pagan conceptions of the forest were about an idea of a mutual consciousness, so that while it might not be possible to literally feed the forest-god with an offering or sacrifice, the ritual itself might exist as an acknowledgement of the forest-god's will, and of the goodwill of man? It would then be a meditation on the connectedness of man to forest, and of life to life.

And so all of the messy possible meanings of the many and varied Green Men, who may not have been called Green Men at all, seemed to me to be indicative of these sorts of meditations: meditations that could sit unthreateningly on a church altar as a reminder of the God in all things, and of all the things that could be God.

Sometimes, when you see something unencumbered by prior knowledge or expectation, it can feel like a truer representation than those framed by other people's stories. It was in this way, with a carved sandstone image of a head, that I had become attached to the Green Man myth, or had somehow constructed my own. I'd got to that point that people of faith get to where you want to believe. We could do with a reminder that humans are fallible, and finite. We do not think enough about the fragility of our strange, sanitised reality. If ever there was a time to rekindle a Green Man cult, it is now.

TWO

A Beginner's Guide to Starting a Cult

May, the blossom of the hawthorn, smells of sex and death. This is neither hyperbole nor poetic licence: it contains a substance called trimethylamine that appears when bodily tissues and sexual fluids decompose. Perhaps because of this, and perhaps because of religious opposition to its ritual use as a portal to the otherworld, a folkloric fear of hawthorn exists in living memory.

At the concentrations found in fresh air, the may smells sweetish and faintly musky. Its five-petalled blossoms are lined and spotted with pink before they fade. Shamans and druids and people who are into trees see the hawthorn as having a male and female aspect, and it is the female that comes into play in the may. The autumnal male aspect, thick with berries, forms the foliage of many medieval Green Man carvings, second only to oak as an adornment.

Now it was May, the month of may, and we were at peak blossom. Hawthorn, previously invisible, was everywhere. Within a week the blossom would brown and fade, and the trees, which now made swathes of white across the hills, would disappear into the landscape again. The blossom went over the week before the Whitsun Bank Holiday, in line with the waning of the moon and the fading of the month, and I was reminded of a deadline.

In my moment of pseudo-shamanic revelation in the woods, it had seemed that the revival of a cult of the Green

Man was a good and desirable thing, and I had decided to try to make it happen. It all had a sense of urgency, lashed by wild weather and a revelatory sense of doom at our deluded addiction to growth and progress. We had been admonished and needed to make amends fast.

But then the rain stopped, and so did the doom-tales. The swell of rage on Twitter, wondering if anyone was going to change anything to sort it all out for next time, subsided with the rivers, which went back to where they were supposed to be, and the insurance companies paid up and the trains started running on time.

I moved to a house where there was no radio reception, and, for a while, no phone line, and the world was better for it. Easter came, and with it the sun, and I lay complacent in my warm garden, and scythed the nettles in my woods, enjoying the view. In cold, northern places like ours, the scarcity of sun means that when it does hit you it does so in a wall of beneficence, and nothing seems to matter very much.

I was also distracted by other things. For ten days every year I run a philosophy festival, which, for a philosophy festival, is big: there are hundreds of events and tens of thousands of people passing through them. As festival-time draws near, it is like a vast wave of activity that subsumes everything into its path, and any intention of escaping seems futile: you just have to go with it.

One of the things I had learned over the course of its growth – which began five years ago, with five people doing everything themselves, and has evolved into one person managing a team of five hundred people via various managerial channels – is that doing things yourself is the strategy of martyrs and narcissists. It is far more sensible to delegate everything as quickly as possible. I was able to make quite a lot of stuff happen while the festival itself was happening, but that power was as ephemeral as may-blossom, and I needed to use it while it lasted. This thought struck me, but without much urgency; there were too many other things to do.

When the rain returned, with it fell a realisation that weeks had passed, and they would not come back, and that opportunity would soon slip away too. I had left it all a bit late. This was partly due to a digression, a week of taking a false path that had, nonetheless, proven to be illuminating.

One of the few things that everyone seemed to agree on about the Green Man was that he was connected with leaves, which was pretty obvious when you looked at a picture of him. Another thing that people agreed on was that leaves represented fertility, and also, in medieval visual culture, the fleshly material world, and by extension the bodily pleasures of sex. Mindful of this, and of the central story in *The Golden Bough* about how all religion is basically a fertility cult, I conceived the obvious idea of starting a sex cult.

The traditional May celebrations are a sex cult too, or always were before they were neutered by the Victorians. In some places, not too far away, they still are. In my mother's village in Austria – in Carinthia, the traditionalist, ultra-Catholic south – the whole village celebrates May Day. The tallest birch in the village is cut down and carried to the ceremonial ground overlooking the saddle-shaped valley. It is trimmed of bark and branches, adorned with garlands and hoisted up into its hole. The mayor of the village, a laconic man, gives a speech in which he urges the young people of the village to go out and dance and make merry for the night, for the village could do with more children. It is an only partially veiled exhortation to engage in the sorts of activity that led the Church, at least on our island, to banish such Satanic pursuits, until they crept back in reincarnated as an exercise of ribbons and little girls.

We inherited our maypoles with the Saxons, and developed our own forms of the weaving dance around it. The Teutonic way involves fertile youth getting it on beneath a vast, phallic pillar, the bigger the better. The infantilised Victorian version I sometimes watched, bored, as a child on the village green in suburban Kent, is retrospectively creepier for it. Given the Victorian patriarchy's predilection for little girls, the idea of substituting them for marriageable youths in a ritual celebration of the phallus hardly cleans the whole affair up. It makes Aleister Crowley look positively respectable.

I went to see a friend, who we'll call X. X was big into Crowley, and magick in general. At some point a year or two ago he was talking about making a film about a sex cult in a sleepy Welsh village, and I had no reason to think that this was for shock value, or that the film would be entirely fictional. X had been wildly successful early in life with a rapidity that led to great feats of excess, and he had, therefore, seen a lot of things in his time. Now he sat up a mountain reading about magick, like an unholy sage, and left intermittently to do things that made unmatchable anecdotes upon his return. He would have some ideas on this.

We met for tea as usual in a hotel in town. The conversation rapidly became unrespectable. Walkers and book tourists came and went in the lobby, and X periodically lowered his voice for the best bits. The best bits were so good that they'd be unreportable anyway, because nobody would believe them.

I had asked X about magic before and was philosophically

untroubled by his description of it. When you think about it, it is simply an intervention. It is the event of a change in state, the making of something into something else. In societies that believe in magic, it is not considered strange, because it is a mode of getting things done. Our materialist model of getting things done is not something that we see as magical, even if the cargo cults of the South Pacific might see bits of our ordinary technology as magical. Magic is technology of unknown mechanism. Much of experimental physics is technology of unknown mechanism; so is neuroscience. If someone can turn people into toads in a demonstrable fashion, I am happy with it. If only the magicians would be more empirical, and then everybody could get on.

X was pleased that I was finally showing some interest in this. He reckoned I was a witch anyway; this, from X, was high praise. He gave me Crowley's *Book of the Law* and Peter Carroll's *Liber Null*. He was broadly approving of the sex-cult idea, but thought that it needed the correct magical skillset in order to work. We were engaged in an increasingly interesting discussion of Crowley's advanced teachings on sex magick when I had to go and pick my children up from school.

I thought it through a little in the car. I didn't know how I was going to make a sex cult work on a practical level. I lived in a very small town. I was a school governor. Everyone could wear foliate masks, I supposed, but I couldn't imagine the anonymity would last for very long. I could recognise people from their shoes, the car they drove, the way they sneezed from across the street. Maybe if you imbued it with religious significance people would be more into it, though. If environmentalism was the new religion, folk round here were more devout than most.

I did some early market research at the school gate. It was inauspicious, although I suppose that was what you would expect.

'It would be destabilising,' someone said.

'But everyone ends up having affairs anyway,' I said, 'and those are far more problematic because they last. Get it all done out in the open four times a year and it wouldn't be a thing. It might even be a chore.'

'I find having to do the deed with my husband hard enough work,' said someone else.

'But that's because he's your husband.'

'You wouldn't be able to avoid people afterwards.'

I conceded that this could be awkward. That was, apparently, why the swingers' club in Hay had died out – the inevitability of bumping into each other too soon afterwards. And, when you came to think of it, it was the young, unmarried people who got paired off in all those May rituals. I was chasing the wrong demographic.

I consulted a friend in her mid-twenties, who, after X, was probably the most debauched person I knew in an environment otherwise lacking in competition. She now had a boyfriend, whom she liked, and had nothing useful to offer me. The dearth of young people in rural areas is well documented. There are plenty of rosy-cheeked teenagers all desperate to leave, and there are the thirty-something returners and incomers, who arrive to raise children. There's a big gap in-between, a life-era that one might call, after the academic fashion of stretchy decades, the Long Twenties, that period from university to childbearing that takes place in Bristol and London and Cardiff and other elsewheres.

These were the people I needed, but they were not here now. They would arrive at festival-time, though, in their hundreds, bright-faced among the damp cagoules of middle-aged Middle England.

When I got home I saw that X had texted me the key lines from Crowley's *Book of the Law*, which now lay on my bedside table: 'Do what thou wilt shall be the whole of the law. Love is the law, love under will.'

There is a truism out there that your political position is, when you dig deep, emotionally motivated rather than being based on rational thought or some external morality. On an anecdotal level, looking around me, this seems credible. There are people who are naturally kind and caring, and they are natural socialists, whatever their environment. There are people with a sense of entitlement who, if they are born into wealth, become conservative and, if born into poverty, adopt the clothing of socialism but for different reasons than their bleeding-heart comrades. Then there are the liberals, in the classical libertarian sense, who are affronted by the idea that anyone should dictate how anyone else should live.

You can see these behaviours in tiny, unsocialised children at a playgroup: most are self-interested, and seek to keep or grab their toys. A surprisingly sizeable minority is unduly kind to them and each other; some just go off and do their own thing in a corner.

I fell into that last category. I don't like being told what to do, and I am uninterested in telling others what to do. I am not in natural possession of much empathy – enough to get by and raise my children without, I hope, turning them into sociopaths, and to be reasonably civil to those around me. I am not often moved by the plight of others, but can't see how reciprocal altruism, in which people treat each other kindly and fairly, can fail to be a good idea, for fortunes turn, and we all find ourselves at some point at the mercy of others.

Put like that, to those of my mindset, at least, Crowley looked like good common sense. Do what you want, be kind, be in control of your faculties. I tried to think of any further necessary principles and got nowhere. I warmed to the Beast.

Then I read on. The rest of it was so ridiculous, the prose so purple and engorged, that it became impossible to engage with it in any way other than critically. Crowley fancied himself as a poet, and was terrible at it. The revealed text looked like an ingenious mechanism for spewing out a lot of bad archaisms that even the most ardent Kabbalist would find trying.

The introductory pages, which are written in prose, are inoffensive enough. He sets out a description of the world and the modes of experience and agency in it, in the form of a basic reappraisal of ancient Egyptian metaphysics. He provides his famous Law of Thelema: 'Do what thou wilt shall be the whole of the Law. Love is the Law, love under will. There is no law beyond Do what thou wilt.'

Then the possession by Aiwass, his higher being or super-ego or *deus ex machina* kicks in, and the *Book of the Law* begins in earnest. It is written in lines that are short like verse and numbered, as though breaking it down into discrete little chunks makes more sense of it, or as though it merits scholarly formatting. He refers to Egyptian entities and deities by name and epithet, clearly entranced by the Orientalism of it all. He throws in some random utterances, which, to the seeker of Hidden Truth, can mean whatever they are desired to mean. It all goes wrong a few lines in when the sub-poetic aphorisms come spewing onto the page in frenzied glossolalia, things like 'The Khabs is in the Khu, not the Khu in the Khabs.'

There is a sweet spot in the construction of nonsense where, if there is the right amount of coherent story, and the right amount of nonsense, the presence of the coherent bit convinces the reader that the nonsense must make sense too, if only they can dig deep enough to find it. This is the gnostic model. It is how magazine horoscopes are written.

The *Book of the Law* would be less irritating if it contained only the first three short chapters, or indeed those three tenets that are, theoretically, the Whole of the Law until all the other stuff about Horus and Aeons and hidden doorways gets going. Crowley makes a claim for simplicity, openness and individualism and then uses it to construct a cult obsessed with hierarchy, arcane ritual and its own institutional status. The extent to which Crowley undermines his own supposed principles, even in the same document, is an extraordinary example of cognitive dissonance, in which two or more mutually conflicting stories are held at once.

If you want to get pop-psychological about it, you could generate theories in the vein of R. D. Laing about the conflicting and impossible expectations placed upon all people, but particularly gay men, in Edwardian society, and conclude that the construction of other realities was the preferable course of action. Or you could go down the DSM route, and pathologise it as a bad case of narcissistic personality disorder. It is no coincidence that the presence of 'magical thinking' is part of the diagnostics for the latter. The act of seeking salvation in nonsense, and imposing one's own magical thinking onto it, is a narcissist's task too.

Whatever the validity of these speculations, some certainties can be drawn from Crowley's life and works. Crowley really wanted to have his own cult and to dress up in robes and have a load of people standing around him being impressed. Crowley also really wanted to have sex with lots of men and for this to be OK. He is described as bisexual but I suspect that, in another time and place where it was acceptable to want to have sex with men for its own sake, he may not have felt the need to throw women into the equation.

Crowley wrote the *Book of the Law*, or claims to have done so, under the dictation of an ancient Egyptian archangel called Aiwass. He did this on his honeymoon with his first wife, Rose, after a trip that had consisted of sleeping in a pyramid at Giza and testing her extensively on her knowledge of Egyptian deities. When Rose had proven herself capable of performing Crowley's chosen brand of nonsense, she was able to pass instruction onto him via Aiwass: go to your room and write this down.

A bisexual man in love with his new wife would probably have not spent their honeymoon doing these things. He would probably have been having sex with her. Crowley doesn't rate that sort of sex, though: his magick is all about the boy stuff, specifically semen, and is weirdly hierarchical so that anal sex – surprise – comes out top. It is hard not to assume that Rose was already so sick of having to listen to her husband pontificate that she sent him off to write alone instead, so that she would at least have a few hours of peace.

His marriages existed to bear children, but don't otherwise seem to have been of much importance. Even the child-propagation bit seems to be narcissistically driven. There is, apparently, a thing that magicians can do if they are old or sick where they find a woman, get her pregnant, kill themselves, and take possession of the soul of the foetus. It is a crude metaphor for the reason that narcissistic people have children in the first place, which is to populate the world with themselves.

I wished poor Rose had had more balls, and had pricked her husband's swollen ego before he had had a chance to ejaculate his nonsense into the world. I came away from the *Book of the Law* a bit disgusted by the whole premise and also by the contexts that led someone like Crowley to develop a worldview matched only by the great Abrahamic religions in its silliness.

Having written off Crowley, I felt that I needed to do justice to X, who I like and find to be a broadly sensible person who makes rational decisions about things, so I started on *Liber Null*. The title is appealingly apophatic in itself, and chaos was a paradigm I felt I could work with. Its opening pages bore weird faux-Egyptian diagrams and a flow chart of woo feeding a river of nonsense from Gnosticism through the Knights Templar and Alchemy and Rosicrucianism to the Bavarian Illuminati and the Hermetic Order of the Golden Dawn, but, for all that, it basically made sense.

Peter Carroll takes the line that shamans, Buddhists, and most pre-twentieth-century Western philosophers do, which is that the material world is illusory and mediated by human experience, and that behind it lies a reality that is not normally accessible to us. It is a position that is controversial to contemporary Western materialism, but contemporary Western materialism is an anomaly in the history of thought.

It is hard to resist slapping on the labels of philosophical terminology here, which are as unhelpful in describing what Carroll thinks is going on in the world as his own occasional recourses to jargon are. Carroll sees the reality behind day-to-day human experience as unlimited and powerful and possessed of, or made out of, a greater consciousness. Again, there is nothing new or unique about this sort of thinking – it became very unfashionable in the early twentieth century, but a few decades previously had formed the main thrust of discussion in Western metaphysics.

The Society for Psychical Research – which concerned itself with exploring all of this, orchestrated seances for empirical purposes and intermittently became embroiled in controversies regarding fraudulent spiritualists – was founded in 1882 and is still going strong. Among the luminaries who took on its presidency are Bertrand Russell's Cambridge mentor, Henry Sidgwick; the Conservative Prime Minister Arthur Balfour; the founder of pragmatism, that most common-sensical of philosophies, William James; and the Continental philosopher Henri Bergson. It is hard to find a prominent late Victorian who was not involved in some way or other with the SPR. Arthur Conan Doyle led a mass resignation in a spat over spiritualism. And set against the Theosophical Society – its more extreme rival organisation led by Countess Helena Blavatsky, the occultist, mystic and author of *The Secret Doctrine*, *Isis Unveiled* and *The Voice of the Silence* – the SPR seemed quite reasonable.

The key underlying belief that most of these Psychical Researchers share with Peter Carroll, and, if you unravel it from the bullshit, Crowley, is the idea of everything being made out of a great universal consciousness. This position, it seemed to me, was one compatible with the idea of the Green Man as arbiter of a will beyond the human sphere.

Carroll calls this Chaos. He introduces various intermediary mechanisms, such as the Aether, by which Chaos can be used to create interventions in the world. His particular terminologies do not disguise the fact that his grand metaphysical map is broadly similar, for all the variations in rhetoric and intention, to much of the stuff published on metaphysics and the philosophy of mind in the late Victorian era, and earlier Eastern philosophies that are, in part, responsible for it.

The common predilection of magicians, madmen and philosophers for constructing Grand Theories of Everything had not passed me by. I once wrote my own, during a period of voracious drug-taking and otherwise unproductive unemployment in my early twenties, which situated evil as a desire-based process of emergence within an institutional ontology. Nobody ever really got it apart from me. The thought crossed my mind, on a number of occasions, that this might be an excellent opportunity to have another go at it, in the guise of a Green Man-ifesto or suchlike, and I had tried to do so in the form of bullet points, essays and even biological diagrams, but to much irritation and little success.

This frustrated manifesto-writing exercise led me into a second digression, one that appeared at first glance to be fruitless. It was a hot afternoon, the first in a while, the ground still muddy with weeks of wetness. The sun was a novel thing, and felt good, and I took a scenic route to spend more time in it.

Cusop Dingle, on the English edge of Hay, falls down to the Dulas Brook, the border between England and Wales, on both sides. It faces north, and is steep-banked, with Cusop Hill rising behind it to the east, so that the water wins out over the sun. There is a lot of water, too, with the Dulas Brook rising between Cefn Hill and Hay Bluff and feeding off all the little tributary springs and brooks along the way. These merge deep in the Dingle, in a rainforest-like place where there is a long, high waterfall and a short, wide waterfall, impassable unless there is a dry spell in March, when it is sometimes possible to scramble down the bank without falling, and when the brambles and bracken have not yet sprung.

Accounts of the folklore of Herefordshire present Cusop Dingle as haunted with fairies and will-o'-the-wisp, making the dark, steep forest all the more fearful for those who had to pass it. On a sunlit day, in our under-forested times, nowhere could be more idyllic. If you were inclined to tree and water worship, here was a temple to it, tantalising in its proximity and guarded by banks of thorns.

There was a reason, beyond this, to be here, though. It was on the way to somewhere: I had some negotiations to do, and advice to seek, up the hill. H, the person I was negotiating with, was better at negotiating than me, which troubled me. He was also the father of my children, which made the need to ask advice slightly irritating, a little like an act of deferral. He was also, in the context of the festival, my employer. These details distracted me from the forest floor, which was now lit with sun towards the top, and from the flat, slippery rocks of the upper High Waterfall, and I slipped and nearly fell.

Within living memory, the children of Cusop would have made this walk every day, because the old schoolhouse was two fields above the Dingle. Half of it still stood in semi-ruin, thick with nettles and the north wall crumbled away to nothing, the other half reconstructed into a grand, high chapel of a room that faced west to the Bluff.

I scrambled up the first steep field beyond the wood, re-treading the steps of my reasoning. There are various modes

30

of getting stuff to happen in the world. Some people are authoritarian and like to feel that they are in charge and issuing orders. Some people like following orders, or do so naturally because that is where they perceive themselves to be within the human wolf-pack. Some people are naturally anarchic and resist being told what to do.

If you are explicit about wanting to make something happen, you alienate the first and last of these categories. It may be the case that they account for a smaller part of the population at large than the wolf-sheep in the middle, but you are then vying with them for power. The solution to this is to create a situation in which the bossy, authoritarian people and the stroppy, passive-aggressive people all think that the desired outcome was their idea first. They then put it into action or adopt it themselves, and the results emerge with relatively little fuss. The effort is all in the planning.

I had noticed for a while that certain conversations with H had translated into various events at the festival. By way of late-night conversation, after the children had been put to bed, a chapter I had been writing about the metaphysics of satire had turned into a series of panel debates, and so had another about process philosophy and desire, and so, more latterly, had another about paganism, environmentalism and contemporary belief.

This last category kept growing and growing. Call it synchronicity, or cause and effect, events kept popping up with names like The Great God Pan and Pagan Gods over the weeks that the framework for this book was conceived. I didn't even have to do anything apart from talk about it. Ideas, or memes, or whatever you want to call them, are all borrowed and cyclical anyway, and we should be grateful when good ones prevail by whatever means. If the Green Man and what he stood for was due to return to the popular imagination, the signs seemed auspicious.

And if these sorts of ideas had been in circulation all along, it just went to show that the notion of intellectual property is merely a silliness of late capitalism. Nobody, apart from a blip in the twentieth century, ever lived off their art or ideas without a sponsor. It is a naturally feudal exercise, as was the matter of getting ideas out there into the public domain again.

The world is a naturally feudal place, too. People fall into their patterns of behaviour, and fighting them is often counterproductive. Perhaps the way to make a cult happen is to let the people who like performing do the rituals, and to let the people who like to be in charge deliver orders, and to let the people who like to resist instruction feel like they are rebelling. There was a whole organisation here that had somehow started doing what I wanted it to do, without the need for much intervention on my part. It was ideal.

There was one thing missing, though, a ritual. Ideas are all very well, but unless you can deliver them in concrete form they won't get you very far. I needed a fertility ritual to take place.

I had been given a book, the poet Laurence Whistler's *The English Festivals*, that, despite being better written and organised than Frazer and all those other early anthropologists and myth-makers, had fallen out of print. It is a lovely edition, with musical instruments beneath a maypole on its cover, and mine had all sorts of old newspaper cuttings about the history of Easter and corn dollies stuck into the inside cover by its previous owner.

Whistler makes his feelings about Church and Establishment known at various points within the book, quietly delighting in acts of anarchy against them. The Whitsun Ales, and the pamphleteer Philip Stubbes's enthralled outrage at them in the *Anatomie of Abuses*, a proto-*Daily Mail* tirade against the turpitudes of sixteenth-century England come in for particular focus.

At Whitsun, a Lord and Lady of the Ale were announced and set up with a bower, throne and entourage on the north side of the churchyard, considered unholy in popular and Church superstition. A gang of morris dancers in cahoots with the churchwardens would plan an evening's entertainment in which they appointed a Lord of Misrule, their king for the night, and would dress up in green silks, ribbons and bells, bearing hobby-horses, as his attendants. A band would be summoned up, with drums and pipes and bells, and the gang would approach the church as noisily as possible before bursting into the evening service and, finally, partying until dawn in the yard. The week that followed would be spent in a blur of feasting, drinking and sex. Stubbes was unimpressed, querying why the revellers 'should abstaine from bodily labor, peradventure the whole week, spending it in drunkenness, whordome, gluttonie, and other filthy Sodomiticall exercyses?'

The bank holiday over which the festival falls is the Spring Bank Holiday at the end of May, and the school half-term always follows it, no matter how close to Easter. This was once the Whitsun holiday, and the week after, to which Stubbes refers, Whitsuntide, a week off from the otherwise frantic cycle of agricultural labour as midsummer approached.

33

Whitsun is the Christian festival of the ascension; there is no known pagan antecedent pre-dating it, for it falls between the great Beltane fire-festival and the summer solstice, and is thus too close to both. The hijacking of this most holy of holidays for purposes both rowdy and heathen was in its most grass-roots sense a celebration of sex for pleasure and fertility. It offered a better argument for the intrinsic human need to worship the desires made by nature than any neo-pagan attempt to reconstruct old bits of druidry. The Whitsun Ales are the opposite of sacred, for nothing is being taken seriously, or done because it is divinely intended, or taken as unassailable historical fact.

I acquired a second copy of *The English Festivals* and tied it up in a ribbon. It had nearly fallen out when I tripped on the waterfall, but it was still intact, and it was time to make an offering, if not directly to the Green Man himself. I stopped beneath the row of tall ash trees that marked the boundary of the second field and looked down the valley to where I had come from. From the top of the Dingle you would have no idea of the depth of it, or what it contained: there were the tops of trees, and, just beyond them, Hay, a small grey blot, with the Radnor Hills rising in a rolling wall beyond.

H was in his studio by the old schoolhouse, his gaze oscillating between a spreadsheet and the profile of the great mountain beyond. The huge glass desk was strewn with programmes annotated with incomprehensible scribbles, half-full water glasses and dried figs. He asked me what I wanted.

I gave him the book. He eyed it suspiciously, but opened it, and made a pot of tea. We talked; I mentioned, as if in passing, that I was supposed to be starting a cult. He laughed and said I should be chairing the paganism talks. I said that

I thought that would make my intentions too obvious, and that I wanted the cult to be an anarchic cult that rejected hierarchy and dogma, and realised in doing so that I did actually think this.

It is a tragedy that most attempts at anti-dogmatic cults eventually turned into religions themselves. I would, for example, describe myself as pro-Jesus and anti-Christian, in that I approve wholeheartedly of the principles espoused by the man, which were all about overthrowing the legislative dogma of Talmudic Judaism and engaging directly and ethically with being. But I don't approve of the institutional power wielded by the blind adoption of his name as a tag for those principles, which was exactly what he was trying to avoid. As soon as you describe your belief as identical to someone else's, you diminish its infinite complexity into a simplified and more concrete form. The process of engagement ends.

The act of writing beliefs down into words is a disastrous exercise too. The process by which the Bible cements whatever it was that Jesus actually said and did into a text, and the institutional processes by which people agreed its meaning, and that text became sacred, and in doing so became treated as something concrete, a Truth, is how the principle of love for the world gets turned into holy warfare. As soon as Jesus' disciples began to think of themselves as disciples, the game was up. They were following something that was True, and therefore they were right, and by implication those who did not share their Truth were wrong. Truth is a divisive, deadly notion. Writing it down was the nail in the coffin, with one honourable exception.

The famous opening line of the Gospel of John is the Bible's closest attempt at expressing this in the written word:

'In the beginning was the Word, and the Word was with God, and the Word was God.' It is a brilliant exercise in ambiguity, and presents the most concise account of the shifting, relational quality of language, and belief, that we've seen since. The Word itself becomes the Trinity, a Trinity that exists only in relation to itself: it is itself, it is the relationship between itself and God, it is God. In the 1960s it became fashionable to query the ineffable ways in which meaning springs from language, and everyone got excited about Derrida and Deleuze making very similar points to John 1:1, but it had been with us all along.

The King James translation of John tiptoes around meaning. What it doesn't do is present the Word of God as a concrete object – it is anti-dogmatic. Zen goes further than being anti-dogmatic: it tries to undermine not only religious or philosophical dogma in favour of a pure engagement with being, but to undermine the structures that language imposes on being. Early writings on Zen are strings of surreal aphorisms and anecdotes, called koans, which are stories about Zen sages outwitting novice monks by revealing their desire to follow rules and accept information as futile and ridiculous, sometimes by extreme means, like slicing off their fingers. This violent rejection of religiosity makes Zen, to my mind, the best of all religions. The koans are written like dark, nonsensical jokes, with the intention of undermining the process of reading them, and of undermining the notion that language has anything at all to offer in making sense of the world.

I was talking about this with H, whose grand theory about the world is as close to Zen as you can get: the world is infinite and open, and we have to close it into discrete bits of experience in order to get our heads round it. It was one of those cyclical conversations you have and replay with people you have known for a long time in which little of the conversational content is new, and the variations in position of its various interlocutors provide the focal point and novelty. It had always been H's schtick and I was now adopting it, thereby validating his long-held belief that he was right about everything if only we would all come to see it.

This was not, however, helping pin down a manifesto. I knew that if I asked for advice at this point in the conversation, it would only become more impenetrable, and he would get going on the paradox of saying the unsayable, and I couldn't face that. I sought distraction. There was a copy of *The Wicker Man*, and we watched the beginning of it.

The pub where Sergeant Howie, the film's earnest protagonist, arrives on Summerisle, the fictional pagan Scottish island where the film is set, is called the Green Man. The sign outside it presents the Green Man in somewhat demonic aspect, Pan via Falstaff, round and beardy with a glint in his eye. This look is recreated by the men in the pub when they gather round to sing their bawdy song about the landlord's daughter.

The things that are shocking at this point in the film are that the song is primarily sung not by the young men, but by the old; the landlord's daughter, far from being slut-shamed into coyness or embarrassment, regards the whole thing as a pleasurable ritual and dances flirtatiously with all of them; the landlord is proud of his hot young daughter and finds the episode amusing. The pub episode highlights all the dark puritanical corners in our own supposedly over-sexualised culture – none of these things would ever happen. Old people, and, for that matter, middle-aged people, are not supposed to be sexual, and we are disgusted when they are. Parents have

37

tacitly reinterpreted the patriarchal desire to conserve the virginity of daughters as a need to protect them from some kind of broader 'objectification of women' that will damage their self-esteem, or some other immeasurable entity.

The ingenuity of the film is to make the policeman so tediously pious and unlikeable from the outset that this act of rebellion seems fair game, so that the alienness of Summerisle's paganism is offered up against a joyless, authoritarian counterpart. It is no accident that the explicitly religious policeman is an agent of both State and Church. Lord Summerisle is the epic hero here, just as Satan is in *Paradise Lost*. And just as *Paradise Lost* – which supposedly sets itself out to 'justify the ways of God to Man' but is more successful at justifying Satan's rebellion – might be seen as taking an ambivalent, or even satirical, line on Christian dogma, *The Wicker Man* is basically a satire on Christian puritanism couched in a supposed horror movie about paganism, in which paganism comes out looking significantly less weird.

I hadn't made much progress, though. The theorising hadn't stopped, only shifted, and it was getting late. When I set off back down the hill, the sun had dipped behind the Begwyns and the pink sky was swathed in bands of grey cloud. A clutch of early glow-worms marked out a small constellation in the long grass at the edge of the top field. By the time I reached the Dingle it was dark in there, and I stopped, eyes shut, for a minute or two to improve my vision in the murk beneath the trees. I heard the rustle and shuffle of creatures large and small, and the roar of the water, and inhaled the warm damp smell of summer in the wood. I could tally little of the sound to anything visible when I opened them again: there was too much hidden life, there but not visible, moving too fast to be fixed.

Worried about losing light entirely, I picked up my pace, and broke into a jog, placing my feet carefully along the narrow, sloping path, which fell steeply down to a ravine on the left. The ground was wet and uneven, strewn with damp leaves, treacherous. The green of the canopy grew darker, the sky blacker, and I ran on. An owl called, and another called back, in a hoot and a shriek. I was made of breath and feet and sweat, and slowed only at the very bottom where the track was wet mud a foot deep, and some thought was required in crossing it.

The paved road that made the rest of the journey into town had always seemed tiresome, but there was comfort in it now, the Dulas Brook roaring away and contained in its place beneath the road. The wet tarmac reflected what little light there was, and then there were streetlights, orange and dirty and comforting, and then the car, and home.

A week later, the production office, which is an office only in an institutional sense, for it is really just a shepherd's hut with power, was over-full of people and laptops, each marking out their space with printouts of their name along the wall. A sense of urgency veered towards panic, and back again, and the hum of voices in earpieces underscored all attempts at thought. It was the festival's first, and worst, day: rain fell in great relentless waves, the site, so pretty when it went up, churned into mud, faces marked by stoical persistence despite it all, hooded and hatted.

The weather mattered less as evening fell. The aesthetics of mud versus meadow faded with the light, and, more pertinently, everyone got drunk. At some point, late in the evening, a procession of robed figures with the heads of wild beasts – eagle, hare, horse, deer – snaked out of the green room, waving hobby horses and chanting. The hobby horse, which was a child's hobby horse, beige and cuddly and without an air of sexual menace, needed improvement. Outside, though, the crowd barely noticed. They cheered the procession on, following it with claps and jeers, dancing behind it in the rain. The rain fell and fell, and nobody noticed as they followed the procession through the mud and into the old Methodist chapel and out again.

The broad pagan fertility cult exercise was, on the surface of it, going splendidly. What was missing from it was the Green Man and an act of true ritual significance. I tried the institutional avenue, calling a meeting, and requesting the inclusion of a leaf-based deity for the replay the following evening. Someone pointed out that the Jack-in-the-Green was a May Day presence, and not right for Whitsun. I queried the elision of the Green Man and Jack-in-the-Green. Someone else said that it was all a construct anyway, which was an inevitable thing to say. Someone muttered that it was all empty ritual, no better than Catholicism.

I interjected, remembering an incident the previous year. The editorial team, disinhibited by months of overwork, sleep-deprivation and a French intern with an impressive personal pharmacopoeia, had all disappeared into the woods by the river and engaged in revelries that could be described with unstinting accuracy as an orgy.

All that was needed, surely, was the same exercise, done with intention. It would be a social experiment: they just needed to be mindful of trees, maybe take a few branches of oak or may back afterwards, something that sealed a union with the plant world.

We had an oak tree on site: surely we could capitalise on it, so long as it was in line with the environmental health regulations concerning external noise after 11 p.m. I suggested this, and, taking it as a licence to shed their worries for the night, they discarded their headsets and left the office. I called after them, requesting written feedback on their experiences with the Green Man, but no one was listening. I went home.

They all came in late the next day, which seemed auspicious at first. They were pallid, glassy-eyed, as though moved by something. When the morning rush had lessened, I attempted conversation. I had no desire for gory details, just an update on whether any psychic engagement had been made with trees, or in any broader sense with an underlying immanent Being.

They looked at me with a mixture of irritation and pity, and pretended to be having radio conversations. The latest latecomer entered. He did not have his earpiece in. Here was an opportunity.

'So – about the trees, last night. Did anything noteworthy happen to your understanding of the oak, or the hawthorn?'

'I am trying to write my speaker briefs. I feel awful. Please don't talk to me unless it's urgent.'

'Can I just clarify – do you mean that you were not, at any point during last night's revelries, aware of a universal consciousness, or mind, or whatever you might wish to call it, that pervades all things?'

'Fuck off.'

Even when weakened by sleep loss and suspected chemical imbalance, their dogged materialism showed no sign of abating.

'So you haven't renounced Badiou?'

'No. Leave me alone.'

He put his earpiece on. I considered remonstrating with him, and desisted. The power balance was all wrong here. Having made assertions about how I wouldn't want power anyway, how the responsibility of it would be an exhaustion best avoided, how the only truly revolutionary social move-ment is the anarchic anti-cult, I was disappointed. Getting people to follow my will, simply by virtue of their recalcit-rance, became desirable.

People started to trickle into the field. The preparations for the midday talks were called. When the production office emptied out to other venues, and no one was looking, I took *Liber Null* out of my bag. It had been an implicit part of the deal with X that I should actually do some magic, and not just write a critique on the particulars of Crowley's own sex cult.

Liber Null provides step-by-step instructions on sigil ma-gick, where you get into a trance-state which, I suppose, engages you with Chaos or the Great Immanent Being or whatever you want to call it, and you then draw your desires into an increasingly stylised set of diagrams with the out-come of an abstracted symbol of your desire, whatever that may be.

X had said I should try a sigil, that it was freaky how effectively it would work. I couldn't text him now for moral, or immoral, support – he was somewhere in South Amer-ica, hanging out with voodoo witches, and his phone wasn't working. I was alone. Perhaps all true magicians operate alone.

There were lots of things that I would have liked to manifest right now. I was irritated with the recalcitrant ma-terialists in the editorial team, and their hangovers. I was irritated with the stewards, who, every year, just stood there. There had been a joke that we would sacrifice one of them. I wondered if it was a joke.

A queue of people snaked into a yurt. Events began; the disembodied voices faded from my earpiece. More rain came, a tentative smattering on the roof of the shepherd's hut, becoming more regular. There was a brief pause now, a twenty-minute gap in which nothing much would happen out there in the material world with its material speakers debating materialism and all its attendant paradoxes. I accessed my trance state.

I took a piece of paper out of the printer and drew without thought: an oak, or something like it, and beneath its broad branches some stick-people. I drew some arrows, indicating, I think, mind control on the part of the oak. I wanted them to obey the oak. I wasn't sure what it was the oak wanted, and I couldn't get away with talking to it, not now with all the people everywhere. Someone came into the office, wanting a meal voucher. The magic subsided. I scrunched the paper up and hid it in my pocket.

And, besides, I couldn't shake Doctor Faustus from my head; karmic comeback haunted me. Even if we're just brainwashed to be afraid of exercising power, my brainwashing was complete enough to make me suspect it would enact its own grim psychological revenge tragedy. So much for magick.

What was really needed, and what I had so far tried to justify my avoidance of, was leadership. I needed to get out there and make it happen myself. I needed to make sense of what needed to happen, though, and why, and what I thought was going on with it all. A cult needs a story to adopt, and it was time to generate one.

Later, at home, I went into the garden, which was over-grown and untended from weeks of distraction. The walk-way along the edge of the garden was thick with vines and elder, and when the rain came full pelt the leaves took it all so that the path beneath was damp only from the resid-ual wet in the air. The lawn was now a meadow, clumps of daisies and buttercups springing out of it. The only things that did not grow were the lettuces, which slipped away into the ground as though they had never existed, and the peas, which had needed some sort of attention that never came, and waned around the edges of their frame. There was a small tree too, a foreign acer, which bent double one morn-ing under the weight of Welsh weather, and never really recovered from it. The things that were supposed to grow grew, and the things that weren't didn't. You had to be fatal-istic about it.

Maybe, if you were a good gardener, and a patient one, and did all the things you are supposed to do, lovingly, you could bend nature to your will. Looking at how well the things that grew grew, and how rapidly those that didn't failed, it seemed like a pretty pointless exercise trying to get anything to happen that wasn't going to anyway. The gardening interventions I could actually do were destructive in character: mowing, strimming, weeding, turning over the soil. The channelling of other entities into a form you not they desire is a perverse thing to do, when you think it through.

Human existence arose from exactly that, though. We stopped being ape-men and became men in the process of developing agriculture and having enough of a surplus to create societies and technologies and think. We were men because we could subordinate nature to our will, at least some of the time. But we still needed nature to be on side, to respond with some measure of predictability, to deliver the goods.

Around the time those first green men were being chiselled into being in the English churches, the balance of power between man and nature was, some would argue, close to equilibrium. There were technologies that enabled humans to communicate and farm and do basic medicine, but all on a small scale. There were significant limits to human population and endeavour.

The unity of Man and Nature, to a religion that privileged the human sphere over all others, and an eternal afterlife over the impermanence of earthly existence, was both threat and weakness. The threat lay in the force of nature, which could work for human ill as well as good, at a time when human technologies were few, so that human existence felt fragile and ephemeral in a way that it may not to most rich Westerners today. To attempt to counter nature's power by appeasing it, in the manner of the old pagan religions, would be both idolatrous and futile, for earthly life was time-limited, and the act of idolatry would make for an afterlife in hell.

The extruded leaves and poking tongues of the green men in English churches also alluded to another facet of nature and the bodily world: the analogue of sex – the sins of the flesh. Here, the connection between nature and fertility embodied in all the old religions was acknowledged and transformed into human frailty, so that the power of desire became an earthly delusion, a trap.

I think that this was what the Church had in mind. However, the variation of representations of the same trope and the variation of emotional tone that they convey – all those different sorts of faces disgorging different sorts of foliage, all those different sorts of faces peering out from different leaves, and all the differing expressions on them – indicates a variation of understanding among the sculptors who made them and, we must assume, the congregations who perceived them.

The Church needed to remind people of the path they were supposed to be taking. It needed to both keep its congregation and contain the congregation's interests. It would have been a sensible strategy to provide a reminder of how best to view superstitions about nature, and an acknowledgement that these superstitions were there. As I would discover in the process of exploring the ancient churches of Archenfield, the strange old border kingdom of the Marches, these superstitions would often be alluded to over the north doorway of a church, the unholy side, so that they were kept in house, and didn't need to be sought elsewhere, but subjugated to the naughty step.

Now, in our most material of worlds, the balance of power between Man and Nature had shifted. We had got better at having our way with the world, so much so that it seemed as if there wasn't much world left to be had. Whether or not you believed in the Cartesian notion that humankind was somehow uniquely special and deserving of privilege, and whether or not you saw the rest of life as being sentient and deserving of consideration, it was getting harder to argue that the other life forms out there were going to last much longer in the face of human onslaught. The critical change that had made this happen was technological: we had developed all manner of interventions into the material world that were effective at making changes in it. We had nailed alchemy.

Or so it seemed. There was the inconvenient issue of unintended consequences, of man-made climate change, of storms and floods that broke human worlds now as they did in the Middle Ages. The fear of human technological power was both of its rampant erosion of all the resources that sustained us, and of the unpredictable backlashes that it might invoke. You could couch the backlash in chaos theory or animism, but the fear remained the same.

And that was just for starters, for the people who still believed in humans being special. Descartes had a lot to answer for. What if humans weren't special – what if will was not limited to our willingness to see it? Most eastern philosophies found will everywhere, and so did the the various New Age beliefs that had started to flourish in the West as the power of the Christian Church began to wane. The grisly spectre of the Green Man in transition from humanity to nature took on a radical new meaning.

We needed reminding more than ever of the ephemeral nature of life, of ours and of all other life. We also needed to rethink human privilege, and whether we really were alone in our conscious existence, and whether our mechanistic models of the world still worked. The Green Man was supposed to have some kind of shamanistic function, perhaps derived from the Sufi figure of Al-Khidr, the Green One, who may have been the inspiration, at least in part, for the foliate heads brought over at the time of the Crusades. Just as human flesh, in its impermanence, would cede to other forms of life in time, so perhaps would human consciousness.

This was probably the most heretical bit, the bit where the conventionally religious and godless alike would roll their eyes. But, it seemed to me, the tide was slowly turning.

Ex-atheists and Methodists and Catholics found Zen and Tao and Tibetan Buddhism, in which the world was made from a great immanent consciousness. Clever cosmopolitan people with multiple university degrees got into the theory behind yoga, and did not find it silly. People were gradually laughing less at Prince Charles.

And, starved of foliage in overpopulated cities, people fetishised trees and waited years for allotments. Nature, in its friendlier incarnations, had acquired a rarity value. The new morality was a National Trust morality, a new, green conservational conservatism. It was not cool to not recycle. Air miles needed tempering with carbon-offset penances. There were carbon footprint apps. Carbon was a moralised commodity. Some people were calling these sets of beliefs a new religion. I was inclined to agree with this analysis. I also found a common thread to it: a belief of the human as the guardian of the world. That, it seemed to me, was precisely the problem. For as long as you believe that humans are special, you cast all activity relating to life at large as an act of largesse on the part of humankind. There is nothing necessary about it.

What was needed was a renunciation of the Enlightenment idea of humans being special. We needed to get over that. We use 'awesome' casually now, denoting something good. It once meant fearful. Awe indicated an appreciation of the power of the thing that inspired it. This would be a power imbalanced against the human subject. We needed more awe in our dealings with the world.

And so, strangely, the image of the Green Man had nearly come full circle. We needed him again, for some reasons that were, in a way, the same, and for some that were radically different. His role in the architecture of the Church had been inverted: he was now a reminder that we needed to get out of the man-shaped Church and post-Church head-space, with its man-God and the men made in His image, and all the stupid things they did and do, all giddy with power to abuse. We needed to get over ourselves and find ourselves again, our smaller selves, entwined with the selves of all other things.

THREE

The Trail

I had made it my mission to go and find Green Men in whatever form they took, and it happened to be that some of the oldest and grandest were also the closest to home, prompting a new and pleasing mythology about the magical qualities of where home was.

The part of Herefordshire bounded by the Monnow and Wye, from Ross to Hay, was once the old kingdom of Archenfield. Formed from its more ancient predecessor, Ergyng, Archenfield was a border state that was neither English nor Welsh, though Welsh-speaking, and a centre for early Celtic religion based around its administrative centre at Kilpeck.

The Domesday Book lists special dispensations given to Archenfield, which had dated back for centuries: in return for providing carriage and translation services across the border into Wales, and backing up the king's army if necessary, the border people were left alone to rule themselves. Offa's Dyke does not pass through it, presumably because the arrangements worked.

For hundreds of years the hill-people of Archenfield were left alone to live as they wished. Even the Normans treated them carefully, and although they were not immune to raids from the Welsh, Owain Glyndwr, greatest of all Welsh warlords, is thought to have died there at peace. When the castle at Kilpeck was razed to the ground by Glyndwr's men, the church remained untouched. The area was incorporated into Herefordshire after the Act of Union in the sixteenth century, but retained its language and character into the early nineteenth century. It was too far from civilisation to be civilised.

People who lived in Archenfield now agreed that there was a magic to it, the way that it was dotted with mysterious mounds and standing stones, the strange carvings you would find next to a spring or well, the way it never got pervaded by respectability like other places. I found meaning in road signs: Wellbrookside, a row of social housing in the otherwise unremarkable village of Peterchurch, was, of course, the place by the holy well, and when you tracked the holy well down on the map, in the corner of someone's garden, there was a carved stone face by it, and leading from it an old trackway through the fields bounded by hawthorns.

Most of the people who got excited about Archenfield had chosen it, or would see themselves as chosen by it; the ones from ancient farming dynasties, who are notoriously unromantic, just laughed. There were all sorts of overlapping mythologies discovered by people who arrived at derelict hill farms in the seventies and ate the magic mushrooms there, and the people who were spiritual but not religious and had realised this at raves in the nineties, and came back to have their children there, finding the energy special; all these people were, in their own way, sane and sensible and enamoured of their home, which is how it ought to be for everyone.

Having decided on a largely emotional basis that the key to the Green Man lay in Archenfield, which we either lived in because it was magical, or was magical because we lived there, I crossed the Wye to Hereford to find books and inspiration, and found that both were plentiful. Every municipal library has its local history section, crammed with underused books written out of private loves and interests. Each of those little-read authors found their inspiration in a local place or tale, and each of them, no doubt, would have liked the world to find the magic of it. Hereford library, perhaps like every other, has a huge space dedicated to all these intricate mythologies that never managed to escape the local shelves, with issue slips untouched from decade to decade.

I read about the history of the Marches, and the religious histories of England and Wales, and the most promising title of all, *A History of Archenfield*. I read Alfred Watkins's early lecture to the Woolhope Naturalists' Field Club on 'Early British Trackways, Moats, Mounds, Camps and Sites', which would turn into the book that birthed leys, the *Old Straight Track*.

The metamorphosis of Watkins's thesis, that in a preliterate, pre-map age it would have been useful to be able to identify routes to important places from the ground, was a compelling digression in itself. The Archenfield-identified population of Hay would say, if you showed a hint of interest in its psychogeography, that it was all about the leys, that it was criss-crossed with them, even more than Glastonbury, and the conversation would conclude there unless further magic was suggested.

That wasn't Watkins's intention at all – he assumed that at a time when holy sites would form significant meeting places and have markets and other places of commerce nearby, linking them by identifiable routes would have been necessary just as it is now with roads and railways. Watkins suggests that leys take in prehistoric religious sites, and pre-date churches, which would have been built over the old sites so that they were accessible. Many Herefordshire churches are built in the middle of a straight path through the sites that would once have formed the ley.

Watkins's ideas about leys were grounded, and of the ground. The process by which leys then took to the skies and became conduits of spiritual energy is more mysterious, and might have something to do with the practice of dowsing. After Watkins located the first and most obvious leys using his eyes and a map, the idea of lost tracks became an idea of hidden tracks, opening up infinite speculative avenues.

Dowsing, in its way, works in the material and ethereal spheres too. It is demonstrably useful in locating water, for example, and it is quite common for people experiencing problems in siting boreholes to bring in a dowser to help. The engineers are fine with this, and accept its efficacy. Some dowsers are engineers. Maybe it is true that whatever perceptory skill is harnessed in dowsing for water can be used to detect other things too – things that, if they are not exactly hidden, are not the things that we privilege or notice in our day-to-day lives, much in the same way that people who train in neuro-linguistic programming can learn to read the fine detail of non-verbal communication that most of us rarely see.

Where it looks like there might be things that are not concrete, there will be the desire to locate subliminal forces, and for them to have a particular meaning. I read John Gibson Forty's promisingly titled *The Interconnectedness of All Things, from the Perpetual Choirs of Britain to the Present Day*, which posits a case for the soul of a vast wonky decagon made of leys residing in an oak tree at the foot of the Malvern Hills. Its author was far from being alone in this belief, and a number of previous books had been written on the subject. It took in dowsing, Hawaiian linguistics, Reichian character morphology and the Knights Templar, an irresistible common obsession of all who veer towards magical thought.

One of the earliest and finest green men in England was commissioned by the Templar at Garway Church, which prompted me to call a friend who, I knew with telepathic certainty, would be up for a Templar road trip. S knew everything about everything, a fast-talking human encyclopedia who could hold forth on medieval Welsh history, herbal medicine, and the strange fates of Herefordshire's old sacred sites.

Lots of people make claims about the strange fates of suppressed sacred sites, and many of them are drunk at the time, or exist in social worlds too isolated and sketchy to query their assertions. S made complete sense on less controversial stuff too, and was basically sane, and when she mentioned in passing conversation that she had befriended Pan as a child and then felt a bit violated when she saw him with a huge erection after taking mushrooms a decade later, it seemed like an entirely reasonable anecdote.

S was good at mythologising. She made art from photographs that she took on her iPhone, manipulating images with reflections and filters until they reached a middle distance of abstraction in which you could see that the tree was a tree, but it also looked like a giant, and a doorway, and a chapel. I bought that one and put it on the wall in the study: I suspected that the Green Man lived nearby.

On the road she told me about how she had been born, illegitimately, from a teenage gypsy and a lapsed Norman aristocrat, and adopted by Methodists. The aristocrats wouldn't accept the gypsy girl, whose family were showmen and stole chickens as tax when they left town. Perhaps it was S's gypsy blood; perhaps, as X would say, approvingly, she was a witch; perhaps it was long days being alone on a farm up Dorstone Hill, up there on Watkins's first ley beside Arthur's Stone and a spring that may or may not have been sacred that made seeing fairies, elves and Pan something that just happened to her.

There is no such thing as an objective truth where personal histories are concerned. They are retellings of unverifiable stories, and the most exciting bits of speculation are the ones most likely to be transmitted down the line. After a few drinks I will tell anyone who's listening that I am distantly related to Karl Marx and had an ancestor who was burned as a witch, but if your family hails from Trier, or the German Rhineland, it is an unremarkable claim to make. It all depends on how you define distance.

A bit of romantic embellishment has its uses. It adds some magic to the world. It makes humdrum things come alive, and gilds all stories into being momentarily special. I was in the process of lining up conversations with sensible people who were extensively referenced by other sensible people in proper institutions, the sorts of people who wrote books about agreed facts; and I had an inkling that they would stamp on the romance soon enough, and so it seemed right to make the most of it while it lasted.

For those who are minded towards the conspiracy theories of the Knights Templar, and they are many, the obstacles that beset us on our way to Garway might not have seemed entirely accidental. There was the sudden ravine that dropped, cliff-like, off the side of the road from Pontrilas, and there was the point, further on, where that road was impassable, closed completely, unannounced. We wove our way back, past the tearoom on a hillside in the middle of nowhere advertising Fairy World, which, S said, was a vast barn adorned with magical fairy scenes that, over the years, had been eaten by damp and were lit with fluorescent strip bulbs. Perhaps we should have stopped; perhaps it was a distraction, a decoy from the places of real magic.

We drove past another closed road and navigated tiny lanes, dark with foliage, and pulled over while roadworks commenced, as if by magic, just behind us. When we got to Garway the road there too was a zigzag of torn tarmac and diggers. I asked a man the way to the church. He denied any knowledge of it. The turning to the church was in the middle of the roadworks, hidden behind a digger.

We saw the church then, its tall tower rising squarely out of the top of the valley, and walked along the lane to it. The churchyard, through a wrought-iron gate constructed of delicate floreate crosses, was wild and overgrown, in that midsummer-jungle way, with grasses and meadow flowers that consumed all but the highest gravestones. We found ourselves by a plaque marking out the location of the original round church, an early Templar design, and wandered round the building.

Most churches in Herefordshire are built on hilltops and ridges, so that they are the first thing you see from a distance, but here we faced down a long valley with little in it: the church, its strange round dovecote with its famous 666 nesting holes, and between them some terraced land that now formed a smart garden to the top and an idyllically weird courtyard below, with an iron sculpture of a man-horse and a large boat, far from the sea. Then there were just fields and trees, and nothing beyond them.

Inside the church was painted pink, blotched with ancient damp, the ceiling of the nave marked out with twenty-four white stars. The stone archway to the chancel was striking amid the pinkness, carved with the same zigzag technique as Kilpeck. The Green Man, who sat upon the inner left-hand capital, was horned. He was rumoured to be Baphomet, a Satanic figure whose name is a corruption of Mohammed from an early medieval attempt at Islamophobic populism, and which, unintentionally, spawned its own occult cult centuries later. He looked rather like Pan and peered out across the nave, serpentine-roped vines spreading from his mouth, a sole face among the waterleaf carvings that adorned the other capitals.

Nobody knows what he is doing there. He, like the rest of the arch, dates from around 1200; he is one of the earliest of his kind in Britain. He is stylistically similar to the Green Man at Kilpeck and at the Church of St Peter at Maxey in the old diocese of Lincoln, both of which predate him by several decades. The Green Man at Maxey chokes foliage from his mouth, eyes bulging; the church, like Kilpeck, is surrounded by bestial corbels. In all cases it seems as though the work was at least overseen by imported stonemasons from somewhere Mediterranean, although the work at Kilpeck, by the celebrated Herefordshire School, is the finest.

The altar-stone at Garway, magnificently huge like a sacrificial slab, was engraved with five crosses in its corners and centre. Above the piscina were a crudely carved fish and lamprey, and between them a winged cup with a cross on it. S said the Holy Grail was, in some rumours, supposed to be buried beneath the dovecote.

We went through the churchyard into the neighbouring

garden to try to negotiate seeing the dovecote. The house next-door had a garden wall embedded with beeboles, square recesses in which skeps, straw beehives, were kept by the Templar to make the beeswax and honey they sold. The garden's owner emerged and took us round the church and into the locked tower. He showed us the engraved coffin-stones that had been reused in repairs with their motif of a long sword and round eight-pronged cross. The tower was hung inside with bells and a ladder, backlit from the slit window, and in it was a vast chest, several metres long and triple-locked, carved from the trunk of a single oak for strength, in which the Templar moneys were kept.

I had a vague idea of who the Knights Templar were and a vague sense of their reputation. I had read the account from the Magick camp, Crowley and his ilk, who credit them with developing various sex rituals. And then there was the Crusade story. Nobody likes a holy war, not when it is distanced from their own time or religion, anyway. The Templar were the people who carried out the brutal military conquests of the Crusades, in the guise of securing the pilgrim route to Jerusalem; their counterpart organisation, the Knights Hospitaller, looked out for the pilgrims and ran hospitals, and still do, and were supposed to be the good guys. Therefore, the story goes, it was fair game when all the Templar estates were seized in 1310. Garway was one of them, transferred to the Hospitaller minus assets under the command of Edward II.

Inside the church, a book written by a retired local schoolteacher detailed the politicking more fully. The Knights Templar were set up by the Catholic Church to wage holy war. This huge, well-trained army was fed by the impoverishing effects of Norman primogeniture, whereby non-inheriting young men had to find an institution to keep them. With their own power to raise money they soon became a military and economic powerhouse that threatened to rival the Church itself. They set up the first European banking system and lent money to its monarchs. Garway was one of many Templar industrial estates, producing honey and beeswax and wool, and keeping all the money locked up in the hewn-oak safe in the tower, money which would be collected quarterly and sent to London.

Philip IV of France, deeply in debt to the Templar, did for them because of it, choosing a time when their reputation had subsided after losing the Holy Land to Saladin. Various rumours about initiation rituals, sexual dissidence and strange idols had been doing the rounds for a while anyway, and to the illiterate peasantry of northern Europe this secretive institution of men with their cosmopolitan ways and foreign images must have looked suspicious. The Church, irritated by its offshoot's power, would have been relieved to rid itself of a military and economic rival.

Pope Clement had been trying to merge the Knights Templar and Hospitaller for a while, for the internecine rivalries between the various Christian factions in the Holy Land had not worked in the Church's favour. Investigating some complaints against the Templar in the process, he passed an information request to Philip. Philip seized the opportunity. He had previously asset-stripped and exiled the Jews as a money-raising scam, and his people loved it, so why not rouse some outrage against the Templar?

The accusations against the Templar were presented on a three-metre-long scroll, listing all manner of sodomitical perversions, abnormal kissing, devil-worship involving arcane rites – you have to suspect that Philip's accusations were responsible for unintended consequences, for the continuing draw of the Templar myth is all tied up with that supposed occult stuff, the devil-worship. The *Ordo Templi Orientis*, precursor to Crowley's *Thelema*, is based largely on Philip's slurs. It is not short of enthusiasts.

There were carvings on the external wall that we'd missed before: a gryphon, a hand, a reverse swastika. The cohabitation of all these images was strange, though perhaps no stranger than the corbels at Kilpeck. If they took in Stars of David and the swastika and the Green Man, or whoever he was supposed to be, I wondered how much enthusiasm the Templar could arouse to play at warfare with other religions.

Here was an institution set up by the Church in order to do its work, and which selected in its dangerous nature the more adventurous and enquiring of men. They would have found themselves at a junction of worlds at Jerusalem, and must have been immersed in its competing stories about the world too. It might have been hard to go back to Europe and not feel at least a bit heretical.

What would it be like, to fight for the rights of a Truth that turned out to be one of a number of competing Truths? Wouldn't your sense of God's one true will dissipate a bit, far from home? The bits of the Templar conspiracies that made a little more sense in this light were the idea of hidden religious rites and symbols, and perhaps scraps of borrowed philosophies that needed to be kept quiet too. Maybe travel broadened the mind too much to keep fighting for what took them out there in the first place.

The idea of this Green Man, in his horned form, as an imported Eastern symbol seemed very unlike the Robin Hoods and Jacks-in-the-Green, all those northern forest archetypes that Lady Raglan made him out to be related to. I was tiring fast of Lady Raglan. This process was hastened by a trip to Llangwm, her parish church whose foliate heads inspired the idea of Green-Man-as-archetype, an uninteresting building and impossible to find in a corner of Monmouthshire whose hills were unremarkable and villages bourgeois, and to which I had to make a return visit to find the Green Man, well-hidden beneath some masonry of indiscernible function. Outside the main entrance, which was covered loosely with iron mesh, a wooden cross lay propped up against the wall. Even the congregation of Llangwm couldn't be bothered with it. It was time for something new.

I went in search of misericords, but found them dull and lifeless, foliate gargoyles of a grim, repressive faith. Looking for more from the Kilpeck stonemasons, I went to see the font at Eardisley like everyone said I should, and the depressing kitschy wedding-cake of a church that replaced the interesting old one at Shobdon, and the bits of stone that remained there, and I was unmoved. The stonework, if you are into that sort of thing, is, no doubt, impressive, but it concerned itself with conventionally biblical interests and didn't tell me much about what was going on for the people worshipping there, if that was where they worshipped. I went further afield.

The train to Birmingham from Hereford takes ninety minutes and straddles vastly different worlds within that time. Flat, marshy fields are intersected by rivers, brooks and channels, the railway lined with hazel and elder, units of view lined with trees and marked out by intermittent houses. The eastern side of Herefordshire is made of a dreamed England: a land of endless orchards, bent against past winds, cows grazing rolling meadows and a patchwork of greens reflecting whatever arable crops happen to be growing. The county boundary is marked out by the serrated ridge of the Malvern Hills, so that from its western edge, at Hay, it lies along the river's spine, enclosed by hills on all sides, a map of itself.

From Ledbury and Colwall uneasy reminders of civilisation creep in: advertisements for commuter deals to London and private schools, indications of capital that you don't see up in the hills because there is little of it and those that have it keep quiet. The houses are larger and more plentiful. The station gardens are manicured, and ox-eye daisies line the cuttings rather than the raggedy mix of cow parsley and thistle before.

At Great Malvern fast-talking teenagers from the international school got on, and the sleepy world behind was no longer accessible. Leaving Herefordshire made me feel slightly mournful, as though a source of something that mattered had gone. There were times, on rainy days, where nothing could be better than the rush of synthetic novelty in the world on the other side, but today the summer was present and so was the noisy, inchoate life inside it, and there was something about the presence of these other lives that seemed to stamp on the summer's energy.

The train went past places where the green had been sliced off the side of the land as though with a giant blade, leaving red mud and, in the exact same shade, red boxy houses in unblinking rows. There were canals and mock-Tudor streets where children in private-school uniforms disembarked.

And then there was Birmingham, which was made entirely of humans. In the middle of a busy Saturday, the Bullring had its own ferocious velocity. There were crash barriers sluicing people up and down the correct escalators, preventing turbulence between opposing human tides, and in these channelled streams of bodies free will was a delusion. You had to keep going until the people thinned, and by then I was entirely lost. It was like being consumed into a mighty capitalist organism. The force of other bodies and the desire to escape them was met by the force of things designed to shine and lure. It was not somewhere to think.

Outside, it was newly hot, and the streets were dark and unpretty, and entirely unlike the Bullring's illuminated surfaces, despite the kinder light of sunshine. There was an old, red-brick church whose spire divided the sprawling view, a continuous entity that might have consisted of rooftops, warehouses or concrete slabs, with no discernible pattern in it. Beneath the silver-spotted swell of Selfridges, where all ideas are brands, and all brands subsumed into a single mucoid slick of consumption, buses went past to places called Maypole and Druids Heath.

I was looking for a Green Man in all of this, which seemed unlikely. The church was adorned with gargoyles, and if it had been in a grassy field sixty miles away they might have seemed remarkable, but here they just looked cross, like the face of the nearby boy trying to start a domestic on the street with his girlfriend, who was carrying their baby. Everywhere were people, with whom making eye contact did different things than it did at home, so that I found myself wearing glasses and dipping my gaze in order to not pick up the gaze of men, and, looking at the girls in hijab with their long robes and immaculate makeup, and the fierce girls in packs in crop tops and attitude, I felt pretty feeble.

Down Digbeth, past a market selling everything, past street preachers of varying denominations and the same urgeful soul, past closed shops and car parks onto a huge, long road with endless Irish bars like aircraft hangars built to contain the dewy-eyed and drunk, one bearing that other Green Man, the leprechaun, on its side. Painted billboards advertising club nights and a sign offering commercial graffiti indicated a change of population, a hipsterish quarter of repurposed warehouses, and down an alley populated by cafes and vintage dummies stood a huge Green Man, about fifteen metres tall, out of place but in it, made of iron and concrete with a shrub for manhood.

When I arrived at the foot of the Green Man, I realised that I had, in fact, seen him before. I once worked, for a brief and disastrous period, for the man who commissioned him, an episode that began with unreasonable hopes on both sides and ended with a glass of wine being thrown at him and his child. He declined to be interviewed; let us call him B.

B was a dab hand at writing job ads, the fount of the only magic on Gumtree. They boasted fairies and waterfalls. He made his living, in a fashion, by way of mythologising spaces and then selling them, and had originated the trend for regenerating old industrial sites by putting artists in them long before it became a hipster cliché of the Nathan Barley era. When London got too pricey to do it properly, he moved his sights to Birmingham, and when I worked for him the Custard Factory was the go-to place for the young and cool there. He had commissioned the Green Man a few years previously, from a still beloved ex-girlfriend, and his properties are rich with mythical beasts which may serve a similar purpose to those at Kilpeck, and those other old places of magic and ritual.

There is a type of visionary who fancies himself as Lord Summerisle. I have every sympathy for them: Lord Summerisle is hot. Perhaps for that reason, I have met several men like this in my time. They are better at understanding the power of images and ritual than other people – even if it is only by allusion, thrown in to better adorn daily life – and they understand too that you can make a place magical by ridding it of the things that make it ordinary. The Green Man was an inspired choice there: the old symbol of the human head, reclaimed by the anarchy of nature, became the symbol of the old institution reclaimed by the creative anarchy of the people who moved in there. It was the same story about death and regeneration, cast onto a human and urban scale.

Through an alleyway was a courtyard made of an ornamental pond with a band playing gypsy jazz by a music shop in the far corner, and set back behind the colonnades across the way the slogan THE CITY IS A WORK OF ART was painted in blue letters. A doorway was adorned with a bronze lion head. Above it, a big dragon crept up a wall.

Whether or not the city is a work of art depends on where you see art coming from. You could see art as intentionally misdirected activity, made solely for its own sake. You could see art as the aesthetic display of goodness, the beauty of something that is true, or that works. In the first way, it is the act of play rather than the city it takes place in that is art. In the second way, the city is a work of art, but more than that it is a work of life, the fossilised concrete presence of the passing lives that make it.

The city is like art in that both form a material surface for the desires within them, things that are not in themselves concrete. The extent to which it was possible and OK to make material the desire of God was always the hotly contested issue of religious art. Christian art, at least within the Catholic tradition, was broadly thought of as cataphatic, in making concrete representations of godly things. Muslim art, by contrast, is broadly apophatic, avoiding images that might lead to any reification of the divine in favour of intricate geometrical patterns that you could see as an account of godly processes, rather than their fixed endpoint.

The hardline Protestant traditions of northern Europe took a similar line, destroying all adornment where they found it, Taliban-fashion, somewhat misinterpreting the point of apophatic theology in the process. The idea was to avoid any fixed idea of what the divine entailed, and the dogmatic abuses that might follow. It should have worked as a safety-catch for monotheism, preventing any singular image from setting itself up as the authoritative sole Truth, but the human desire for fixity is powerful.

Once you get into the idea that making a representation of something with intention is a religious activity, most art seems to take on that character. The next Green Man on my list was a labour of love that took a year to make, and was rooted in its own magical belief-system, which, if you lived according to the weird norms of Hay, often appeared to be more common locally than old-school monotheism.

I had already heard about G. For years he was the man behind the big autumn event here: other, lesser towns had their Guy Fawkes fireworks on 5 November, and we had Hay on Fire, G's Samhain spectacular. This involved a procession and a show, a pageant involving vast burning sculptures. New to town, I saw a child outside the ice-cream parlour on the square carrying a staff topped with a sheep's skull, and had an early sense of the strangeness of the place. The procession made its way through the town to a long, sloping field on the inner bank of a bend in the Wye, where everyone sat to watch it turn into an enactment of old myths and fire-breathing dragons, and this was all entirely normal here.

Then G got ill and had to take a few years out, and re-appeared again for a bit before getting divorced and moving to a caravan at Penpont, a country estate outside Brecon where he had built a maze. When I stumbled across the existence of the maze via search terms along the lines of 'biggest Green Man sculpture' I wasn't particularly surprised to find the largest depiction of the Green Man on the planet close to home. As G later pointed out, you can see it on Google Earth, just to the right of the A40, if not quite from space.

It was a day in which bands of spring weather, of hot sun, cold winds and warm rain, each imposed their own significance on the moment. As I left the house, twenty minutes away, I wore a hat and coat and threw a second jumper in the boot. By the time I reached the layby where I wondered if I had gone too far, the sky was cloudless. Just beyond it was the sign for Penpont, written across the Green Man's face.

To the left of the long drive was parkland, immaculate and sun-dappled and all lit up with bright new beech leaves; to the right, lawns swept down to the Usk. I pulled over in front of the big house and followed the instructions to the campsite parking, over a cobbled yard with brightly painted outbuildings and past a barn with a gypsy caravan and then across the river and along a stonewalled lane to a spot beyond an apple orchard in full blossom. The place was so overwhelmingly picturesque that it was surreal in the same way that a film set is, as though the cinematographer fancied himself as an artist. It was composed like a formal painting, everything aesthetically correct and in its proper place, but without the symmetry that you get at some grand houses and which sterilises them.

G was waiting by the gypsy caravan, wild-haired and in an orange necktie. He was selling the caravan, which he had restored and repainted. I had seen it in town a few days previously; the one we were headed to now was old and blue and tucked away beside the river near the bridge. The path to it was lined with various sculptures: little wicker people dancing and waving and doing things like sun-worship, and a sleeping metal dragon the size of a large car.

Inside the caravan, we talked about the Green Man. There was an image of one in the roof light. The bed was laid with a cowhide and on it two folders, thick archives of Green Man-related things. G made coffee. A white piebald pony pottered back and forth along the edge of the field behind, a few feet away from the window. He asked me about the book, and how much research I'd done on it, and I said I'd been reading a bit about Archenfield, feeling that this should initiate me into the club of people who know about such things, and he corrected my pronunciation – the 'ch' is hard, Anglo-Saxon – and my ignorance was made clear.

If you get stoned enough, you can observe the conversations of others and make out patterns in their emotional or social shape. If you were the pony, watching through the window now and attempting such an endeavour – and let us suspend disbelief and assume that the state of pony consciousness is somewhat like that of a stoned human – you would make out, beyond the mannered Englishness of it all, a competitiveness emerging between the over-educated, under-informed young woman and the old eccentric who made huge, strange things there. On his turf, he defended the balance of power. She might have come to raid his space for information, but what she left with would happen on his terms. There was a minute or two of conversation that was characterised by this unspoken turbulence, and then it passed, and the situation was resolved, and, on the back foot, I listened to him.

G used the word 'archetype' a lot when talking about the Green Man. It operated as an explanation – it's an archetype, stupid. I asked if the Green Man was a thing in the sixties and seventies art-school scene. It wasn't. This was how I would have expected it to be. There was something about the Green sensibilities of the nineties and the way those later Summers of Love on the rave scene had merged into New Age culture that seemed to fit the recent history of the Green Man better.

We went out to the estate, back past the pony and the wicker men and the dragon and the bright river. We bumped into V, the owner, carrying a wicker tray of produce from the gardens, which she stored in an outbuilding with an image of the Green Man, or possibly Pan, or possibly both – it was, they agreed, ambiguous – overlooking the basket-fuls of vegetables on the shelves. It would be inaccurate to call this outbuilding a shed, because it had been plastered and painted inside in a fashion superior to most houses, and looked like the sort of place a fashionable organics business would stage a photoshoot for *Country Living*.

The Green Man sitting at the top, between the beams, had been made by her husband and had foliage for hair which came down in a mane of leaves behind each pendu-lously lobed ear, with more of it disgorging from his mouth. He had a long, bulbous nose and a sharply curved brow and slanting eyes, and looked a bit cross. There was a Green Man sign in the middle of one of the shelves, too – an old pub sign, or like one, with a smiling foliate face of oak and gold lettering above it, like Good Cop to Pan's Bad. A corn dolly hung in the doorway beside a long garland of flowers.

We swept on, past a courtyard with a tree adorned with bits of mirror that sparkled in the wind and a terracotta Green Man planter on the wall, and, everywhere, plants in pots and corners and old Belfast sinks, and through a kitchen the size of a house with a fireplace the size of a room and into a great hall, and out again to a huge, high glass orangery in which another Green Man, handmade in little mosaic tiles, presided over hothouse plants.

We climbed a sunny bank of grass towards the maze. To get to the maze, you had to cross a ha-ha, which was a recent ha-ha redug over the site of an ancient ha-ha, or what was supposed to be one. G had also built a bridge, whose position had been chosen in accordance with the sacred geometry that dictated the possible locations of an entrance to the maze. It happened to lie across the stone foundations of the old bridge, which he showed me. I described it, somewhat inaccurately, as synchronicity, and he agreed.

Across the bridge, the root structure of an oak stump sat in the pond that formed the Green Man's mouth. The shape of the roots of trees has its own geometry, a regularity that is not entirely symmetrical but that follows a predictable pattern. I had never thought to consider it before, and saw the magic of it. We went on, up the Green nose and into the maze proper. In it there were topiary people, dancing, and menhirs that came from a quarry, high up on Hay Bluff, that he used to have a share in and that I, as a relative incomer, knew well for the strange raves that happened up there when it changed hands. The maze ended at the Man's pineal eye, which was marked with a tall stone. I was invited to embrace it, and did. It was warm with the sun.

We went to see the sacred grove: a birch, an ash and a

tall female yew, doing a sort of handstand into the sky. I do not know where the sacredness of it came from, but it was convincing. The management of the parkland, and the trees in it, was a marvel in itself. Britain is full of old estates with swathes of parkland, and much of it is either over-managed, sparse or a bit unloved, so that broken branches are left stabbing the ether, and clumps of nettled undergrowth pop up here and there, breaking the smooth line of the grass from tree to tree.

The woodland at Penpont was eerily lacking in imperfection: every tree was beautiful, every tree felt necessary. Where a tree had fallen, or been felled, it was logged, and the logs trimmed and stacked, in a way that was as aesthetically fitting as the stones in a Zen garden. The woodland was dense but not overgrown, so that the floor beneath the trees was a forest floor rather than a lawn with some trees on it. A few branches lay on the ground near the old yew, and it emerged that they were there to protect a rare plant which I had never seen before, a mass of white bell-shaped flowers that grew off a long, straight stalk, a strange and ancient-looking thing.

As I was about to leave, the rain came, and we stood under a lean-to watching it while G told me a story. His son, an accomplished musician, played in a world music band that collaborated with the Central African Baka tribe, whose animistic relationship with the forest had sparked the interest of various anthropologists.

The Baka live in small nomadic villages of about fifty people and, as you might expect of a people dependent on the forest's beneficence, have a belief-system in which Jengi, the forest-spirit, is accorded a deep and fearful respect. There are other spirits too – Emboamboa, a clown-like character, and a moving pantheon of lesser spirits who come and go and can be bought and sold as commodities. The spirits channel a deeper supreme being called Komba, and the villagers regularly hold rituals in which they thank and appease them.

These rituals involve a group of men dressing up in foliage and grasses, each embodying a spirit. The women sing and dance to bring out the spirits, and by the time the trance-state of dancing has taken effect the embodied Jengi has the spirit of the Jengi in it, and must be approached with the greatest caution. The Jengi oversees the initiation ritual of the young men, without which they are not able to go into his forest safely.

An anthropologist who had worked with the tribe and observed this ritual organised an event in England, in a wood somewhere in the Cotswolds, to recreate it. G, with his existing interest in it, attended. It happened at nightfall, the magical time. The drumming and chanting started and as the trance deepened the dancing Westerners experienced visions: tiny flickering objects appeared in the trees, and then shadowy characters emerged from them too. The Baka forest-spirits had made themselves known.

It was all convincingly shamanic. As he left, G saw the black-clad people in the bushes and the fairy-lights, and was furious at the anthropologist, and unable to fathom how the whole escapade could have been a good idea. The Baka appoint one of their own to become Jengi, and a man who performed myths for a living being affronted by the performance of a myth seemed, on one level, rather odd. But perhaps it was the idea of it being done in bad faith, its method disguised, that G disliked. If so, I could see it too. It reminded me of the Victorian fashion for seances, and all the smoke and mirrors that went into the audience's need to believe.

There is something distasteful about channelling credulity by artificial means. But we could call music artificial, the beat of a drum, the creation of a space designed to invoke wonder, the priestly robes. It is not clear where to stop. It is where religions fall out with each other over the correct method of meeting their god.

Nobody can agree on the genesis or meaning of the old bits of iconography you find in Norman churches, either. It is remarkable how much the idea of a coherent Green Man archetype has caught on, given the forceful opposition to it on the part of today's academic folklorists.

There is no oral-formulaic record of the Green Man in folksong or story-telling. Jack-in-the-Green is a relatively recent phenomenon, emerging in the sixteenth century, and there is no evidence to suggest it is related to the medieval foliate heads. The folklorists do an effective job of demolishing Lady Raglan and her contemporaries but don't offer much in the way of a replacement.

The historian Ronald Hutton, regarded as the authority both on prehistoric Britain and on the emergence of neo-paganism, rejects the notion of present-day druids and witches being part of a thread of inherited authentic paganism that was simply suppressed for centuries by the Church. Hutton describes neo-paganism as a contemporary British export, more likely to be birthed in nineteenth-century Romanticism than the standing stones and barrows of pre-history.

If neo-paganism arose out of a Romantic desire for a closer connection with the rhythms of nature, it might also have gained a sense of urgency from the march of industrialisation and the increasingly serried character of industrial society. It didn't seem accidental that a religion of the woods might arise at the time when industry bit hardest into life.

And for centuries, even if daily life was left alone, a monolithic power structure guarded the communication of imagery and information. The desirability of occult knowledge makes more sense in that context than in our own. It ran counter to the thuggery of the controlling Church and needed to be kept quiet to avoid the violence directed at heresies. Today information is infinitely available and a secular society finds the dwindling congregations and internecine spats of its established Church openly amusing.

It is easy to see why certain images, strange to our eyes, might be understood as implying something mysterious or problematic in their relationship with the churches they adorn. If you have a hellfire- and heresy-based account of the medieval Church, everything in it that does not relate directly to a passage from the Bible looks subversive.

The alternative story is of the Church being a more open place than we think, one that kept its flock together with a plurality of stories, and a plurality of images that might be thought of as deities, or as embodiments of a single power. I needed a churchman for help on this. By a Panglossian stroke of good fortune, a friend had a friend whom she described as a 'pagan priest', whose parish churches were in the heart of Archenfield. He performed solstice rites, the story went, and encouraged nature-worship. He went away from time to time on shamanistic wanderings, where he spoke to the animals and stones. I called him.

The vicarage at Madley looked exactly as a vicarage should: a large, square Georgian building, austere respectability softened by the swing on the lawn and the assortment of wellies on a rack by the front steps. L answered the door, intense and bright-eyed in a white linen shirt. The hallway was full of art, his drawing room dominated by comfortable chairs and an overflowing wall of books. The place felt collegiate rather than ecclesiastical, his profession indicated solely by the selection of cassocks in white, black and blue hanging behind the door.

He had done all the things people do in their youth, the partying and meandering, and had then come to the land, farming in the hills and working as a ranger in the Elan Valley, a wilderness of vast man-made reservoirs high up in the bleak middle of Wales. There, alone, with little to do apart from walk and read, he found the Bible, and a calling.

Now, fifteen years on, with a number of parishes and their respective flocks to manage, he engaged critically with his Church. He had a fair amount of space to do this in – people within Anglicanism were 'doing things', he said, with contemplative movements like the Iona community and Oxford's Stillpoint. He could help his congregation pursue a meditative style of prayer, and create a space for silence and silent thought.

He wanted to go further, though. He had just been on an all-male death lodge in Scotland, where you fast and stay awake for forty hours. He wanted to take his flock out into the wilderness, too – a bit further out there than even the Anglicans would probably allow, and certainly too far out there for his current congregation in Herefordshire, who needed continuity and predictability, a Middle England ministry. There was no doubt that he was a Christian, but it was the Celtic tradition of Christianity that really fired him up.

In the late Saxon period, somewhere in the seventh or eighth century, the English Church council elected to follow Rome rather than the Celtic tradition. Archenfield, or its predecessor Ergyng, remained largely Celtic in character; pockets of the Celtic Church kept going elsewhere, too, for in wild rural places, then as now, there was less central control of religion as of life. Even where there was institutional change, or attempts at it, local practices persisted: institutions were never at their most effective in forests or on hilltops.

The Celtic Church was communitarian in character, and not given to hierarchies like Rome. It was non-authoritarian and non-ascetic: the Bible was regarded as a source of inspiration rather than proscriptive rules, and the facets of earthly existence that we see much of today's Church as set against – song, sex, celebration – were regarded as holy things in themselves. The non-human community, to borrow L's phrase, was looked to for theological insight. Communication was expected between people and animals. Rather than seeking to deny the physical world in order to ascend to some higher spiritual plane, the Celts embraced it. It was as though God was the name of the life force that inhabited all things, and in worshipping them you could access it, or him.

I thought, again, of Kilpeck, the centre of the last Celtic stronghold before Wales. It made more sense in that light. The Celtic story, and meeting someone like L, who, in his own way, embraced the Celtic tradition and saw something that was God in the infinite multiplicity of the world around him, collapsed the rather simplistic notions I had held about what the Church was and what paganism was. I had conceived of a Church that was monolithic and power-crazed in the way of medieval Rome, and whose rule was monolithic too, without exception. I had an idea of everything that lay outside of this as some kind of pagan heresy hidden in plain sight. The more textured reality of L's world was probably closer to the churches I had been to, and the people who had made them.

The holy world of the Celts was a full and round place, and they built round sites to celebrate it. The original churchyard at Madley is round, indicating an early Celtic site, but Madley has a further significance to the Celtic church as the birthplace of St Dubricius, or Dyfrig in Welsh. His Normanised name, Devereux, still persists in the churches and population of Herefordshire.

It wasn't a hopeful start in life: according to successive editions of Alban Butler's *Lives of the Saints*, his mother, young and illegitimately pregnant, was thrown into the Wye by her angry father, Peibio Clafrog, King of Ergyng, but failed to drown. The *Book of Llandaff* hams the story up further. Peibio Clafrog means 'Peibio the Leprous' – the king suffered from either leprosy or some kind of skin condition, and his daughter's role, pre-drowning, was to wash his head. Returning one day from a fight, Peibio ordered his daughter to wash him, and noticed her rounded belly. His fatherly response was to have her tied into a sack and thrown into the Wye, but she was persistently washed ashore, and the drowning venture failed.

Undeterred, Peibio attempted to burn her on a pyre, but the waterlogged princess failed to catch light, and was found the next day nursing her newborn child. Peibio reconsidered his position, and requested to see the child. His condition retreated, and he bequeathed Madley to his grandson. An image at Madley commemorating this incident is recorded in the mid-nineteenth century, with all deserving charm: a rheumy old king, spewing pus from his mouth.

Dubricius fulfilled his early promise, hanging out with St Illtyd – whom I was sure someone, in an Archenfield mode of speculation, had claimed to have been Sir Gawain's Green Knight along with all the other things like founding Llantwit Major that normal people agreed he did – and establishing an early Celtic monastery at Moccas. Moccas is derived from the Welsh 'moch rhos', the moor, or meadow, of the swine. The legend is that St Dubricius had a vision in which an angel instructed him to find a white sow nursing her piglets, and, upon identifying the correct scene at Moccas, he founded his monastery there.

I had high hopes for Moccas after that. A friend came to stay and we spent the weekend drinking tea and walking, stopping at Bredwardine on the way. We went along a lane lined with arching beeches and the white stellar flowers of wild garlic, past fields dotted with apple trees, pink with blossom, the grass sunlit and, behind it, darker, Merbach Hill. We opened the gate to the church on its little mound, past a vast yew that must be as old as the church – a huge, tall, twisting tree with bark that felt like peeling paper – and past the entrance too, because it was covered by a mesh gate that looked like the barriers you find secured over shop windows in rough streets. We went round the other side instead, and there found the bricked-up north door, and over it what we were looking for.

The Sheela-na-gig at Bredwardine has hair braided across her crown and wound above each ear like Princess Leia. To her left is a creature seemingly carrying a crook and with a long nose or beak that made us think, simultaneously, of Horus, although, unable to recall the correct name, we called it the Crazed Bird-God until we got home, and there is something to be said for that. He could, with a bit of imagination, be Cernunnos, the Celtic Horned God, although Cernunnos didn't have a beak. I had hoped that there was some occult elision of Horus and Osiris out there, so that the figure next to the Sheela-na-gig could be said in good faith to be a Green Man, but there isn't.

As it was, the red sandstone was so worn that you could make out the overall shapes of the features of both figures, but not the detail within them, and the Sheela's vulva was roughly pitted into the stone as though defaced in some earlier moment of prudery. The indentation, if it had come about from being over-petted, as if in hope of bringing fertility, would have been smoother and more symmetrical.

Sheela-na-gigs are generally quite grim-looking figures, sexless apart from the giant splayed vulva, like her bald, eye-bulging sister at Kilpeck, but this one was quite foxy. Maybe that was too provocative. In the church, there was some description of her as a monkey figure, interpreting her hairdo as giant ears, and distancing sex from the human sphere, but the only detailing that was quite clear was the braiding.

Beside the yew tree on the churchyard slope was a holly bush, even and pointy and tall, and I speculated, fleetingly, that the indeterminate object held by the Crazed Bird-God might be a holly club. We wandered down the lane to the river. Cow parsley had sprung up along the hedgerow in zig-zagging six-foot stalks, and the hedge grew ferally into the road, interspersed with white may. We pondered the circularity of hawthorn-may as genesis or derivation of May the month, and got nowhere; we reached the red-brick bridge across the river.

The river at Bredwardine curves around the grounds of

Brobury House on the opposite bank, and its mannered gardens look strange, dark and over-curated against the willows and haphazard apple orchards on the Bredwardine side. Today the water was high so that the usual stretch of gravelly beach at the edges was buried beneath black, swirling eddies, the sort that can do for an amateur canoeist. The night before I had been woken up by the rain, which felt not so much like rain as warfare, hammering onto the roof so hard that I checked for debris in the morning. The time-lapse from rainfall to river height is less than you might think, a matter of hours, and the Wye rises and falls quickly, so that the unwary can get lassoed by it on a floodplain.

But now the rain had cleared and the sun cast tiger-stripe shadows of willow-leaf across the ground, which was patterned into indented cobbles by some recent stampede of sheep and scattered with apple-blossom. We stopped to look at a tree that I did not know, its leaves furrily silver on the underside, and went back to the church, where we picked some wild garlic for lunch and made our way on to Moccas.

The relentless bands of weather from the west were doing their pathetic fallacy thing again, imposing a capricious emotional picture over each scene, and they did not favour Moccas. I don't think I did, either. The church at Moccas is set within a private estate that makes its privacy clear in a semiotically unfriendly fashion. A sign reads: 'Private Drive: Church Access Only'.

This private drive is lined with wooden fencing along each side, so that the vista across the flat plain towards the church and estate is carved up by straight lines. Bored cows lay around an oak, whose trunk had been fenced off too. Each tree had been boxed into its own discrete plot, no doubt to discourage the deer who, allegedly, populated the parkland across the road, although it felt as though they too might have been the victim of some terrible hygiene campaign and obliterated for being too unruly.

The drive turned left towards the big house, all perpendicular in Barratt-red brick, and left again, past an opaque pond, to the church. We parked the car by a barbed-wire fence. A field had just been ploughed and its mud was a purple red, like torn innards. I tried to superimpose sunshine on the place, to speculate if it would be nicer, and thought about how inadequate language is at conveying the emotional responses we have to physical spaces, as though it all comes back to sense again, and how sense resists being dismantled into logical constructions and words.

I hadn't read up on the church at all. Various people had mentioned it in passing when I told them what I was up to, and it was only when we got to Bredwardine that I'd deduced that if there was a Sheela-na-gig there, the Green Man must be at Moccas. The church was very old, and the same shape as Kilpeck, and made of a strange, cratered rock that looked as though it belonged in a volcano or on the surface of the moon. We walked past the north door, worn away to nothing apart from its capitals, which must have been carved later, and of a different rock than the brown-red sandstone which flaked away in our hands as we touched it. The tympanum over the main door wasn't doing much better.

Inside the church was pretty, and although it was weeks after Easter there was still a little branch decorated with brightly painted eggs by the helmet of a sleeping Norman overlord, whose feet rested on an improbably small lion. The candy-coloured eggs and the irregularity of the branch seemed an unlikely centrepiece in a space otherwise bound by symmetry and the darkness of a wet day. Here was the

Church, doing the thing it had always done of recycling old rituals in its own fashion, just as it had done when the Tree of Life was still freshly painted across the south entrance and the standing stone outside was incorporated into its wall. A Green Man, a new one, gazed down through oak leaves from the roof.

Not all of the trees in the parkland outside were caged up like animals in a zoo: some had fallen in a storm and lay around like corpses. Francis Kilvert, the churchman, diarist and indefatigable walker who habitually made his way by foot to the various parishes he served, many miles apart, around Hay and its surrounding hills, described the trees at Moccas as 'those grey, gnarled, low browed, knock kneed, bent, huge, strange, long armed, deformed, hunchbacked, misshapen oak men that stand awaiting and watching century after century.' That was in 1876; perhaps the character of the place hadn't changed. We went home and ate wild garlic on toast.

Back in Hereford with overdue library books a few days later, I stopped at the cathedral where there is a Green Man on a lintel, a famous old and inaccurate map, an alleged secret Sheela-na-gig revealing herself in a dark corner of the cafe, and, I had heard from a Green Man enthusiast, some gilded green lions, which seemed too good to be true.

The cathedral was quiet and museum-like, a steady trickle of people heading over to where the Mappa Mundi was, admiring all the gilt and grandness of it all. I wandered around for a while before going to the information stand and asking a man called Bob for help in finding the lions. Bob knew nothing of them. A woman in a black cassock paced up and down on the other side, serene and purposeful.

A hush fell, the sort of hush that precedes the act that should, theoretically, have caused it. The woman in the robe climbed up into the pulpit and introduced herself as the dean. She invited people to talk to her, and requested a minute's silence to consider the world's troubles. This seemed reasonable. I stopped, and looked up at the high ceiling, searching for the lions, thinking that I could at least use the time wisely. Then, when the minute passed, she began to recite the Lord's Prayer, and so did everyone else.

I hadn't recited the Lord's Prayer since school. In fact, I can't imagine having gone along with it then, at peak teen atheism. I don't think I recited it at any of my grandparents' funerals. It would have been hypocritical to do so.

There is something, though, about the directed energy of a large group of people in a space designed for that purpose that has the strange effect of overriding the individual will. The content of the words seemed irrelevant; the desire to be subsumed, for a moment, into that greater will was the compelling thing. And there was something about the layered noise of the various voices, dotted about the vast nave, making the same sounds at the same time, and the little variations in echo that gave each its own strange resonance, so that joining in had a childish, kinaesthetic quality.

Immersed in this swell of sound, and moved by it, I reconsidered my position on the Lord's Prayer. I had previously thought of it as a silly patriarchal fiction, something that no self-respecting atheist could go along with in good faith. But maybe the magic of ritual, of joining in with the same thing that everyone else in the space was doing, of going in the same direction as all those other wills, was something that, in itself, was beneficial to us sometimes. It left the same trail of feeling as when you are moved by a beautiful piece of music, with everything soft and filmic and revealing the good within it.

It didn't take long to find the lions after that. There were two of them, in the east transept. It would be inaccurate to describe them as 'green' – they were gilded, and they had manes that, while curlicued, were not of foliage. I went back to see Bob and told him this. He was satisfied.

I drove south out of the city, past the road that would take me straight back home, and past the Kilpeck turning, and headed to Dore Abbey on a whim. The lane to Abbey Dore, for the place name inverts its genesis, seemed endlessly long. The prayer phenomenon in the cathedral had put me in a strange mood, and the drive was the heavy-machinery equivalent of shamanic walking. I was entirely in the moment, my peripheral vision embraced by hedgerows and all the constituent lives that made them, waymarked by twisty oaks, a mind-cleared meditative state. The road was as empty as the sky, which was for the best.

At Abbey Dore, I parked at the roadside and saw that the abbey was closed for a recording. Crows called from a tall tree, but otherwise the whole site slept. There were no vans or people about. I opened the gate and walked down to the abbey, past a long wall trailing four-petalled pink flowers and a meadow of buttercups that were too high to be respectable. At the door, which was ajar, there was another printed sign. I could hear nothing. I looked through the gap and saw a studio rig laid out in the middle of the nave, with microphones and amplifiers and a portable heater. I walked round the side of the abbey, past the arched buttresses and the pillars that once held more of it, and slipped into the back doorway, which was open.

In the back room a mixing desk had been set up and I knocked, to see if anyone was there, but to no reply. Silence, when you are expecting noise, has its own presence. The plastered walls, painted with the Ten Commandments, were pale gold. The Commandments had faded into the ghosts of commandments, and were disembodied from their use.

There is something sinister about writing instructions on walls – it is an exertion of control over the space, forcing a behaviour generated somewhere other than the individual will. The beauty of a ruined abbey is in the death of the institution as much as the aesthetics of its structure. Faded commands that have been neglected and left to crumble might even seem poetic.

The pragmatist philosopher William James describes religion, in the subtitle to his great book on it, *The Varieties of Religious Experience*, as a 'Study in Human Nature'. For James, religion is as religion does: its nature cannot be determined from its history or dogma, but from the individual practices of the people doing it. James was after 'the feelings, acts, and experiences of individual men in their solitude, so far as they apprehend themselves to stand in relation to whatever they may consider the divine'.

All those disparate Green Men, the horned men and the leafy, the smiling and the sad, and all the mythologies and crumbling theories about them and what they stood for were immaterial, so far as James was concerned. All that mattered was how people felt about them, and what they did about it.

Along one side was a corridor with a long, warped bench made from a single oak, perhaps as old as the abbey. Beyond it, at the end, beneath a window, lay various items: a painted crucifix, dried roses and a huge Green Man of yellow stone, still attached to a piece of ridged masonry. His face was perfectly round, edged with broad leaves, all cheeks and nose and eyes taking part in a beatific smile. He had the demeanour of a laughing Buddha, or an anthropomorphised Sun. This was the Green Man of pub signs and summer-worship, the opposite of a misericord. I felt compelled to kiss him. It felt good.

FOUR

Pagan Middle England

The road to Clun, the back road, weaves to and fro across the border, so that you soon stop noticing the signs welcoming you to Herefordshire or Powys or Shropshire, and it is bounded by hills and forests on either side that seem little altered over centuries. It passes tiny, slumbering market towns and hamlets with names like New Invention. Towering pine forests cede to sunlit parkland, and back again.

We passed a black-and-white pub with a vine-draped garden and a railway siding that had slept for a hundred years. I think these things were in Knighton; the winding lanes were hypnotic, like watching a silent trailer for a fairy tale, and they washed over me without ever being properly mapped. The organisers of Clun Green Man festival were clear that festival-goers should, if at all possible, go to Clun via Knighton rather than via the real roads, the inhabited roads, the roads that go through towns with people in them. My father and children and I were early, too early, expecting traffic jams and diversions, and found instead a church with the Green Man adorning its porch in a large, child-made banner, and beside it some people in hi-vis jackets.

If there is a consistent signifier of the contemporary English festival, it is the fluorescent yellow tabard. The branding and signage and AA route signs are all interchangeable, and the weekends from May to September thick with cars pursuing them in all directions; it is only when you find the hi-vis people that you know you are near.

When the British enthusiasm for festivals first exploded ten years or so ago, when events popped up as thick and fast as roadside wildflowers in midsummer, you would have expected the hi-vis tabard to exist in counterpoint to a sun-tan and dreadlocks born of time in fields. Festival crew were festival folk, and were identifiable as such, and the tabard was merely a nod to the more bourgeois sensibilities of the police and licensing authorities, for its wearer was far more likely to be in possession of an eighth of weed than directions or knowledge of the onsite health and safety policy.

The hi-vis people I encountered were neither stoned nor pierced, and had the air of the WI about them. The car park was in the field to the left of the bridge; the town, which has 642 inhabitants, stopped there too. Clustered between the bridge and a high mound at the edge of the town were the coloured tops of tents and stalls, edged around the castle perimeter in a way that, if you peered over the top of the hedge to excise the cars from view, seemed convincingly timeless. A man, wild-bearded, drove his grandchildren past in an ancient Rover. My father, whose beard was neat and suburban and whose Skoda was new and clean, pretended not to notice, although I was sure that he was envious.

We walked into town, past the beginnings of an event: clipboards, portaloos, people drinking coffee by a soundsys-tem installed tentatively outside a cafe by the bridge where the action would happen, hoping that it would not rain. We looked for a cash machine. Wandering the streets, or street, since there was only one with things on it, we were indis-tinguishable from the other people who were too early: a Middle England family of three generations doing cultural tourism on a Bank Holiday. And yet there was something odd about this bit of Middle England. It, or some of it, was wearing garlands of artificial flowers in its hair. Its skirts were longer and more embroidered, and its beer guts projected screen-printed forest-gods into view. We walked past the Sun Inn, bathed in yellow render and with a handpainted sign depicting the sun.

There are ways of depicting natural phenomena that are respectable, a *Reader's Digest* model of the world around us in which birds and bees and sunshine are represented in accurate little sketches and etchings, like the inside of a new British passport with its swallows and swifts and meadows. There are childish ways of doing so, too, oversimplifying things into unthreatening jollity, a nature as seen in *In the Night Garden*. Then there is another way, a way that imbues it with a face or character but in a way that is not the childish way, and that has the quality of an animist god.

This image of the sun was like that of a sunflower, dominated by a round face and surrounded by rays like golden petals on a background like a dark blue summer sky. I suppose this was because it was an image of the sun elided with an image of nature and an image of a season: it was a sun that was alive. Across the road, schoolchildren had made a Green Man collage that sat in the ironmonger's window. The ordinariness of seeing these images in small-town England had an eerie quality: it was a world as we know it, but underpinned by a set of principles so radically different from our own that it felt as though we didn't know it as much as we thought we did.

We wandered back down to the bridge. A man in a bright hat and waistcoat, simultaneously medieval jester and Goa casualty, danced to his own internal beat, eyes lowered ecstatically. I thought I overhead someone nearby refer to him as the Creative Director, but there was a crowd forming, and it might have been an error. In the queue for the loos, the woman behind me summoned her partner to carry her cloak. My three-year-old daughter got restless, climbed the railings and started rapping about the fight between the Green Man and Jack Frost. The queue looked on approvingly, despite the inaccurate substitution of Jack Frost for the Frost Queen, which was my mistake, passed on in the car.

The Clun Green Man festival is England's last surviving example of what Laurence Whistler calls 'Perhaps the best pageant . . . a very ancient one: The Battle of Winter and Summer.' At Clun, summer is embodied as the Green Man, and winter as the Frost Queen, but the pageant is otherwise identical in its conception to Whistler's description of it, with a procession of the wintry entourage banging drums and playing 'rough music' intercepted by the summer crew, who are then roused by the audience to win the ensuing mock battle. The set-up is that Team Summer always wins, but it is not supposed to be a shoo-in: the winter folk are numerous and put up a good fight, and the audience needs to do some work to ensure the summer's safety.

Summer felt a way off. As the crowd coalesced along the banks of the river Clun, forming a neat two-pronged amphitheatre with the bridge as its stage and the pebble island between as a sort of Arcadian moshpit, we settled at the base of a young chestnut tree whose branches framed the top of our field of vision.

The air hung damp around us. It was too early in May to be warm, and people were dressed for rain. They had mostly done this in the usual Marches manner of sensible rainwear, but a distinct minority took a more medieval line, in green velvet cloaks and layers of heavy knitwear, and they wore their garlands defiantly, heads unhooded, as though provoking the rain to come on the day their man was there to defend them. They may not have been pagans. They may have been enthusiastic medievalists. It wasn't easy to tell at first glance. It was the men, with their Green Man T-shirts, who were the giveaway. If your thing with cloaks is primarily about dressing up fourteenth-century style, you'd make your husband wear breeches; if they were happily anachronistic priestess robes, he'd be fine in a T-shirt with a man-god on it.

I counted heads on the opposite bank in an attempt to determine a pagan:cagoule ratio, which I estimated as about 1:8. The people who had dressed up had done so in clusters, tribelets of fairy-women and boys with ivy crowns. They were the elite in this audience, the cool ones. They let their children slip down the grassy banks and across the water to the island, so that their feet got wet. The best ones went with them.

The people in cagoules did not approve of this. Their children, who were wearing wellies, begged to go to the island too, for there was still time before the pageant began. There was a moment that looked as though it might become an anarchic tipping-point, when there were enough children on the island for the ones in rainwear to sense a weakening in parental control, and they were about to exploit it, and then a man on stilts with a tree-embroidered cloak and a branch in his hand turned on a microphone.

The cagoule-people listened attentively. On the island, a woman danced with her child. She was wearing a silver brocade dress with a pattern of the sun on it and a green velvet jacket. She danced as unselfconsciously as the children.

She was pretty, raver-slim and long-haired, barefoot and unmade-up, and the semi-ceremonial dress nominated her as May Queen, but nobody seemed to notice this.

Some drums started up and a woman in a swirly red cloak began to dance on the bridge. Everyone sat and watched attentively. A boy swirled some fire poi. The Creative Director swayed and rocked, as if invoking something. The drums rolled, and a silvery procession appeared from the town. The Frost Queen arrived with a gang of fierce little girls and chanted some threats about everlasting winter. The crowd photographed this on its phones and booed tentatively, so as not to disrupt the performance. The stilt-man asked the crowd how it felt at the prospect of eternal winter, and announced the Green Man. The crowd, understanding this to be a cue to cheer, cheered. The Green Man arrived, hulk-like, horned, bearing a club. They faced off.

The Creative Director reached a point of mystic ecstasy. Beneath him, on the island, the May Queen and the children danced and jumped and cheered. The cloaked people cheered from their bank, and the cagoule-people observed the scene on the bridge, regarding the revelries beneath it as an irritation, a distraction from the main event. You could correlate the degree of joining-in-ness to tribal membership, and the way this membership was indicated by dress. You could construct a huge Venn diagram with intersecting sets of ravers and pagans and folklorists and hippies and the cagoule-people. It was not clear at this point which group dominated, but on grounds of authenticity of experience, the May Queen, the kids and the Creative Director were winning.

There were people who were being celebrants, or performing being celebrants: the dancers and the drummers and the fire poi. There were other people, the cloaked people and the garlanded people, who were wearing clothes that alluded to ritual and were at least engaged and cheering and being present, but they remained resolutely seated next to the cagoule-people. There was not much joining in here from the grown-ups.

Whistler lamented the lost art of joining in back in 1947, saying of the May celebrations that 'only the children are unselfconscious enough to dance in public'. Watching the scene on the river, I thought about this some more. Whistler mentions King James's *Book of Sports*, a document sent out to every parish in the land detailing which folk activities, as, for example, the maypole, were to be permitted, apparently in order to prevent the Church's more puritanical impulses from banning fun entirely. The *Book of Sports* also offers an interesting snapshot of the rise of organised team sports supplanting private enjoyment of free time in an ever more socialised world. Fun became leisure, serried in its own way, and the ability to do joy, or be joy, was something that got legislated away into sets of rules for proper behaviour.

And that was when Britain remained a largely agrarian culture. Even if you were a tenant-farmer, you still decided what to do with your time. You might have been dirt-poor, but you had a degree of autonomy. And even if you worked domestically for someone higher up the feudal ladder, you were instructed by one or two people, whose concern would be that things got done, not that a single task took place in a precise mode and at a precise time.

Theodore Kaczynski, better known as the Unabomber, America's notorious home-grown terrorist of the 1990s, gave up his academic career teaching mathematics at Berkeley in favour of living in the woods in Montana. He bombed airlines and universities in protest at the encroachment of technology upon individual liberty, and the ever-greater organisational structures that enabled it; he wanted people to read his manifesto on *Industrial Society and Its Future*, even if there had to be collateral damage along the way.

Kaczynski is particularly astute on the impact of industrial society on the individual capacity for autonomous action, and on the dangers of over-socialisation, seeing the individual human spirit being subjugated into the ever-increasing repression of institutional activity. His manifesto, though extreme, is not very crazy.

As industrial society sucks human existence into an ever-more organised, restricted and comfortable existence, in which the individual will-to-power has no meaningful outlet, Kaczynski designates sports and art and most forms of non-urgent work as surrogate activities which create an illusion of purpose and autonomy for those engaging in them. We are all like the emperor Hirohito, immersed in marine biology lest the ennui of existence drive us mad. We exercise pretended freedoms in our art, no longer knowing what freedom really is. We are post-instinctive and inert.

You could describe anarchic, wood-dwelling Kaczynski as taking an extreme Green Man position, one that places the individual freedom of all forms of life above all else, and that seeks to dismantle all impositions on this freedom from authority at all costs. It is a call to primitivism of necessity rather than romance. The key cost is the loss of technology, for any technology that requires large and complicated institutions to make it entails a degree of institutional repression.

Here, in our post-industrial world, we behave according to unspoken sets of institutional rules and expectations, and take our cues from what is expected of us rather than what we feel like doing. Watching the scene at Clun, which had slowly altered from being a mass participatory ritual to a small performed spectacle, I thought about the neat rows of audience, for that was what we were, sitting and observing and occasionally taking photographs. We formed ourselves naturally into orderly positions, so as best to share the space, and understood the scenario as one in which we were there to observe a performance.

Being and performance are entirely different things. Being is all about intention, engaging with whatever spirit it is that you are inhabiting and living, and taking it into your body and mind, suspending your self in the process. Performing is all about presenting a story to your audience, and without an audience there can be no performance. It requires only a superficial adoption of the story. It is semiotic rather than mindful in character. When the audience is not in the same space as you, when the audience is sitting on its arse elsewhere, your relationship is one where you provide it with the commodity of entertainment. It's hard to see how that can be a truly ritual act, one imbued with intention. It is an act being given to other humans for consumption, rather than to the gods.

The event at Clun was organised with the desire for joining-in in mind. The master of ceremonies, in his long robes, did all he could to raise cheers, and in doing so raise his audience from its slumber, to get it to become something instead. The audience sat on the riverbank, imprisoned by the assumption of performance, watching.

When the pageant finished, the gates to the castle ground opened, and an orderly queue formed to enter. The sun came out. The cagoule-people shed their outer layers like snakes emerging from dead skins. We climbed the castle mound and watched lines of people move from tent to tent, buying trinkets and ice-creams, at their ease now. The Green Man was available for photo opportunities. You could buy jute bags and garden ornaments with his face on. It was time to go home.

A few days later I called a contact, Z, hoping to negotiate a solstice tour of Avebury, where she had grown up. She was somewhere noisy, and escaped to somewhere less noisy, and I still couldn't make out much of what she was saying, except that it contained the words 'mayhem' and 'dancing' and sounded fun. She called back later, saying that she'd been in Helston, as though that were an explanation, and I looked it up and realised that I'd missed something.

The Helston Furry Dance was a whole-town affair, where the dances began first thing, and varied from orderly lines of paired-off lords and ladies in their Sunday best to wilder, more riotous affairs of people decked out in garlands of foliage, like gangs of Green Men and Women, some beneath a Green Man banner, taking to the streets. There was a programme of different dances through the day, for school-children and adults of diverging degrees of respectability. It didn't sound like an audience-oriented activity.

It also didn't call itself a festival, a word that was sounding a bit sedate these days, something you could televise and market. As soon as you have to call something a festival, you admit defeat so far as spontaneous revelry is concerned. All the words we use to describe the coming together of people, in its various structures and forms, have their own shifting colour. A festival was once a coming together of people with feasting and revelry, but now we feast daily and the feast has lost its meaning, and we no longer know how to do revelry in public. We need it brought to us instead, at a safe distance denoted by a stage, and a barrier beyond it.

A festival is now, instead, an entertainment comprised of a plurality of entertainments – one performance is a gig, three a show, ten a festival. A carnival is still able to party, even if we have to import the term from sunnier places, having lost sight of our own native word. Import the term 'parade' into the carnival, and it loses its carnivalesque quality – we're back into the safe sphere of performance again.

The Russian critic Mikhail Bakhtin describes the carnival as place of sacrilege, in which normal mores are temporarily upturned. It is a coming together of people on equal and anarchic terms, and an exercise in being. The carnival also provides a political outlet, an overthrowing, for a moment of time, of the established order of things, in the way that the Roman Saturnalia inverted the roles of masters and slaves, and in the way that our own festivals were once overseen by ephemeral Lords of Misrule. Without misrule, there is no carnival, or festival in its original sense. It is simply an entertainment, a transaction.

Perhaps I'd over-romanticised an event in a county I had never been to, and that I might well never get round to actually seeing, but I felt slightly mournful at having missed it. Z said Cornwall had stayed wild in way that other places hadn't. Maybe it was just too far from everywhere else. Z was starting to think that she wanted to be there for the solstice – she'd just got back from Africa and wanted to settle for a bit – and I said I'd be at Avebury, but would come down later in the summer.

When the time came, going to Avebury seemed like it had been divinely ordained. The sky was high and cloudless all the way, down the steep mountain pass where it was bounded by hard reddish hillsides, reflected in the Usk and the golden-green leaves along it, above the vastness of the Severn crossing, making the sea blue. It was perfect solstice weather: the forecast on the radio said so, and in *The Archers* they were planning bonfires and getting laid at a festival, which seemed authentic.

I had agreed to meet my friend M by the M4. The Swindon business park where we slept a few hours displayed signs of magical activity. There were the people at the drive-through Subway in striped breeches and crimson robes. There was the hare the size of a dog standing in an empty car park as though he owned it. Across the dual carriageway, and sliced up by it and the Holiday Inn Express and the Volkswagen dealership and the sweeping overhead power lines was an enchanting forest of oaks, lit pinkly all the way to the back as the sun fell. The brambles were in full blossom.

On *BBC Points West,* in between pieces on local sporting teenagers and traffic updates, they did a special solstice weather forecast from Glastonbury Tor, with the sunrise time and the actual solstice, which is the point at which the sun passes closest by. This information was provided without advice on reaching Stonehenge, or scare pieces about marauding New Age travellers; it was for its local demographic. Everyone was a pagan now.

We tried to sleep, in that self-defeating mode where the act of pursuit undermines the thing pursued, and watched more TV in an attempt to get bored enough to have another try at it. There was some kind of cookery show on, in which three contestants who were, theoretically, celebrities had to make dinner for a triumvirate of marginally more celebrated judges. Three chefs weighed in with a culinary meta-analysis.

If you held a spiritual-but-not-religious yen for the sacred number three, here it was in threes. The show was edited so that every action was ritualised, with the same shot used to show each of the three contestants' preparation of each of the three courses, and with each contestant flopping, exhausted-but-relieved, onto one of three sofas at the end. The judgements were presented with a snippet of dramatic music, the three candidates in their sacrificial whites and glowing teeth standing nervous, waiting to be dispatched into the blackness of un-fame.

Even the people who weren't going to stay up all night or get up at stupid times to stand in fields needed public ritual, ritual that needed to be ostentatiously structured in order to make its ritual quality apparent. If ritual is, as Ronald Hutton would have it, action with intent, the reality TV genre made a living from the appearance of it, if not the thing itself. We tired of it and slept.

A few hours later, in the sodium-lit car park, the sky was black and the air was becoming damp with morning. The moon was veiled in a haze, encouragingly mystic, probably just a visual disturbance of the sleep-deprived. I didn't feel sleep-deprived enough, in a way; the right thing, if you were being a solstice purist, would have been to stay up all the night before, but I had a job to do, and these days my hard stimulant limits were a Thermos of tea and a quarter of a Modafinil, and even that turned out to be an error that made me stupid for the whole of the next week. If I'd done the whole thing properly I would have been dead by dawn.

By the time the taxi had crossed the M4 there was light in the north, which might have been there all along. You could make out the hedgerows and the lines of the fields. There were more cars on the lane now, and people wandering along it, some drunkenly brushing the hedgerow, some head-torched and purposeful in neat lines. We reached the Red Lion, the pub at the centre of Avebury, where there were a couple of police vans and clusters of people who were hunched and blanketed and waiting for something to happen. A few event lights lit the crossroad, which seemed an odd way to mark a light-based event.

Much of Avebury's strangeness derives from this cross-road. It is an archetypally English village built along a lane that intersects a road in a neat cross in the middle of a huge stone circle. It is a tiny and rather smart village, all very National Trust, but then the National Trust is the smart face of eco-morality these days, and that is just a tiptoe away from the old earth religions. The face presented to us now, though, was not very respectable. It was made of many faces, twilit and worse for wear.

There was a big red bin full of cans that, later, turned out to be the drug amnesty bin. It was not really a drug amnesty bin, but an image of one, like those big signs you get in the druggiest clubs restating that drugs are not to be consumed on the premises. Behind it was a gate, with bleary-eyed traffic indicating that we were in the right place, or getting closer to it. There were the round black shapes of stones, blacker than the sky, which was no longer black, and lit from time to time by passing lights. Beneath the stones were human clusters, arrayed with tealights and torches, drinking and smoking and talking and dozing. Behind, somewhere, was a wall of people and noise, and we moved closer to it, and found a high ridge with a chalk path that climbed up past a tree and, everywhere, people.

They were dressed in hats and blankets, huddled around fires and each other, moving around one another in streams and eddies like oversized ants. Oversized, intoxicated ants, passing round vast bottles of cider – always cider, as though to confirm West Country stereotypes – and talking pure nonsense about now and the party and each other, cathartic speech with no purpose other than itself. I suppose they were just being.

We settled under a tree and drank tea there. The sky lightened, the stones loomed larger, the human outlines sharpened. We walked along the ridge, balancing along a shifting path through the gaps between people. Where the grass had worn away, the ground was chalk-white – you could see that now. People with bongos, people with spliffs, people in sleeping bags. A mist pooled in the circular ditch between the ridge and the stones and the people down below, and clung to the gentle rise of the hill behind, where a car's headlights blurred towards it somewhere. The shape of a quarter-circle of stones became clearer.

We found ourselves tiring of the crowd and its noise and walked along the ridge, following its circle away past other, more sober people. There was a man with a cape and a staff and leather trousers, and a woman in robes, and we followed them. There was a tree, low-branched, the lowest be-ribboned in rainbow colours and gaggled with people playing pop music around its base, where the roots had been eroded into visibility by many gatherings. We crossed a narrow lane, and found the ridge rising again beyond it, quieter now. In the flat behind it were many sheep and a couple of lonely stones and, around them, some more sober figures. They had capes and staffs. The light and the mist rose.

Hoping for some proper druids, we made our way towards them. The sky was pale all over and fire crept around its edge. There was a round stone and a tall stone, guarded by robed people: a fierce-looking middle-aged woman in purple and her gang, who were of a similar age and demeanour. A stout, bearded man in a green robe wore a T-shirt with the Green Man on it. I didn't want to disturb them. They looked like they were defending their space.

In this field, the serious field, the median age was fifty-something and the vibe meditative. People wore blankety shawls and wild beards that had seen many hilltops, and carried magnificent staffs topped with antlers. They didn't all look like druids; I had an inkling that the seventy-something woman with the neat white bob and Alice band in the powder-blue anorak and matching skirt was more in tune with the dawning than any of them. Men of a similar age who looked like my dad sat in silent thought. People in BBC lanyards hovered with cameras.

A frame stood at the field's inside edge, and at some unspoken point gongs were attached to it and then brushed to make a noise at the edge of hearing, a brush or rumble that could have been the wind or the sky, and this sound, or the many sounds that made it, rose with the light until the stern priestess hailed the sun.

Soon enough, it arrived, a brightness without shape in the trees that became a line and then a curve of sharp light. The gongs ceased. The priestess and her gang re-hailed the sun. Distant cries and cheers came from the other side. I held the palms of my hands out, to see if I could feel it, and saw that everyone was doing this, and that the stones were now lit in pink. I did the other instinctive thing that we do to salute events, and took a picture of it on my phone.

A silence fell, the silence that you get when everyone has fallen into a good meal, or after sex, or in the lull of a conversation between old friends. The priestess led a third and final hail. The robes greeted one another, and went off, content.

I started to see why the priestess was fierce when a pissed, toothless bongo player and his friend with the didgeridoo, which may have been a bit of painted guttering, rocked up and planted themselves next to us. If moments could be sacred, and obstacles to their sanctity removed without redress, I would have done away with them right there. They were in the wrong field.

It's not as though there is anything particularly authentic about dressing up in polyester robes from eBay. I remain unconvinced of the assumptions that the primary purpose of sites such as Avebury, and the enormity of human endeavour that went into making them, would necessarily have been religious – you'd need a degree of political and economic sophistication to get a site like that to happen, and trading and meeting places must have been of at least equal importance. Even if it was, the traditions espoused by the various strands of modern-day pagans date back a century or so at best. But if there are solemnities happening near you, and people using a space within another, larger space to do them in, it really is quite rude to fuck it up for them by disrupting their space.

When I was a raver – or trying to be one, because the intrinsic happy-go-luckiness common to all proper ravers was something I could achieve only with vast and problematic quantities of artificial entheogens – the grim side of the more hippyish raver factions – the psy-trancers, for example, with their neon Hindu deities and mushroom art – would dawn on me at dawn, when the drugs wore off. The greenish complexions of the faces that, sweat-slicked and UV-lit, had looked so happy and alive hours earlier displayed their chemical genesis. Peace and love and unity bickered over taxi fares.

And then there were the casualties, the ones for whom normal life was no longer an opt-in possibility, who could make sense only in this occasional and unnatural sphere where nobody else did. You get bronzed, bendy, bearded old sages on beaches in Goa and Thailand who are still raving, but they tend to integrate it into a life where production and consumption, work and play, exist in some kind of balance. It would be better for most of us to do more playtime that revolves around things beyond the status-trappings of restaurants and dinner-parties and the booze required to tolerate them, but the twitchy old ravers, the have-nots of the party scene, aren't a great advertisement for it.

There were a lot of them about. I thought again of Emboamboa, the Baka jester-spirit whose job was to be silly, and of Johnny England in Jez Butterworth's state of the new-age nation play, *Jerusalem*, who happened to have been portrayed on the original poster as a Green Man, as riotously hammered as a Jack-in-the-Green at the end of the May Day revelries, and anarchic like a woodman should be. I thought of the Happy Mondays' iconic wreckhead, Bez. Bez wasn't a one-off. He was an archetype. All cultures had one, and had done so across all time. Bez probably would have had the nous not to play bongos next to the meditating people, though.

It was the zombie hour now. The novelty of the sunrise had worn off, and so had the tea, and it was not yet warm enough to sleep. We looked for a sunny spot on the far side of the ridge and found one, and huddled there on the blanket, listening in on the end-of-night interactions and zombie conversations, the wandering people needing to talk, to anybody and about nothing. There was a man with a tattooed face which broadcast a need for attention that he now assiduously sought by means of aggressive banter at anyone who'd listen, or who wouldn't. A well-meaning creative writing student patiently held forth on the perils of misogynistic language to a black-clad lad able to respond only in grunts. We couldn't face the party field, because there would be more bongos in it.

The shouty man with the tattooed face was still trolling the people who would listen. Not many of them would now – the outer edge of the ridge was lined with sleeping bags and blankets, and bodies in them. Only the hardcore people remained, and they all had bongos.

An incident, which may or may not have been supernatural in provenance, happened as we passed them: M, whose movements are neat and accurate, and who was a talented footballer in his youth, tripped, his foot sending a bongo flying down the hill, where it rolled to a stop in the last thread of mist in the ditch. Its owner, if bongos can be owned, did not notice. M, who is a faultlessly honest person, maintains that this was an accident, a slip of the foot occurring in tiredness, but I suspected it to be a Freudian kick, or, more accurately, a subconscious enactment of the will of a greater force. I suppose that it is also possible that the grazes he sustained running down the hill to retrieve the bongo were supposed to happen, although whether they were for kicking the bongo or retrieving it remains open to interpretation. We needed tea.

The National Trust cafe had set up a breakfast stall by the bus stop. The tea was hot and the bacon dense and smoky; I experienced a strong rush of emotion, a conviction that we needed more of the National Trust, ideally as a benevolent dictatorial presence governing England and its mores. It was a very good breakfast. Z, who had been to Stonehenge and was on her way, texted to see if we were awake. We made our way along the lane that formed the village, past the Henge shop, where I got my father a handsome staff for his birthday and a leaflet about sacred energy lines, hoping for a map in it.

We wandered up towards the church, where there was a poster advertising a Celtic service at nine. I thought of L, the Church of England vicar with his Celtic-pagan bent, and realised that there were more of him than we had thought. Having a little church, a temple to the weird mystery religion of Christianity, in the middle of this other, vastly bigger religious site, was a reorientation of normal in which the Church had to set out a pagan-friendly liturgy in order to fit in. We set an alarm for five to nine, and went back to the stones, which were warm, to sleep.

We slept through the alarm, and I only woke when Z arrived. We had met once before, seven years ago, at night under a huge cypress tree at a festival in Clyro, but she was instantly recognisable. Z is small in stature and elfin-faced, and grew up in the house where J. M. Barrie wrote *Peter Pan*. You could cast her as a convincing fairy. She may well be one, and probably wouldn't be offended if you asked her.

Her family, which was aristocratic in the best way, entangled with eccentric overachievement and self-effacing about its provenance, had a house a couple of miles away that backed onto a valley that Z and her siblings grew up calling Woody Dene; she had recently discovered Woody to be a corruption of Woden, the ur-Green Man. She wanted to check in on her strawberries anyway, so we got in the car and went there, past the West Kennet Avenue of standing stones and a lane with lines of converted ambulances and ancient camper vans that the itinerant New Agers lived in.

Z ran away with New Age travellers as a teenager and spent a few years on the road with them, in the days when they got beaten up by police and their children taken away into care. On Solstice day in 1985, a phalanx of armed riot police set upon a line of camper vans known as the Peace Convoy as it approached Stonehenge, wrecking the vehicles and dragging whatever was in them out – men, women, children, dogs. The dazed travellers escaped where they could into neighbouring fields. It wasn't what they were expecting – for years previously, Stonehenge had hosted the Stonehenge Free Festival every solstice where people of hippyish orientation would rock up for a week and celebrate the summer in peace.

The rest of the eighties was underscored by the threat of more of the same, and a four-mile exclusion zone created around the fenced-off stones and patrolled by police on horseback. Hanging about at stone circles was a heresy, stuff for Satanists and an unwashed underculture. A persistent druid who called himself King Arthur Pendragon was arrested annually.

In 1989, a couple of years after the Summer of Love parties had started up around the M25, the New Age travellers found their ranks swollen with ravers. A few of them broke into Stonehenge and danced on the stones. The exact nature of the hippy-raver sympathy is something that eludes me, because I was far too young to be out in a field back then. However, the way that normal people with normal jobs and lives in normal suburban England found themselves dancing in a field at dawn, in a fashion that was no doubt similar to what the travellers had always done, moving from free party to free party, and the way that behaviour became normal for those normal people, of whom there were many, must have had something to do with it.

We think of the sixties and seventies as the time of great social change, the dawning of the Age of Aquarius or simply a softening of Victorian cultural strictures. But the changes that happened then, so far as the mainstream of British culture was concerned, were pretty trivial compared to the nineties. For people who weren't rich and educated and in the tiny, rarefied rock-star circles that swung and travelled and experimented with drugs and thinking, the sixties and seventies took place on a small dark island full of people who went to church, trusted institutions and conformed.

You could make a case for people's drug culture shaping their mindset, and say that the privileged minority of that generation who did the hippy trail and concomitant bits of psychedelic culture used their status to do good things with their newly opened minds. If that was true, the impact of Ecstasy was overwhelmingly greater on the British people at large. Those synthetic hours of joy and trust didn't just make people dance all night, but hang out with each other and talk too.

Maybe the solidarity was ephemeral, and faded as the sun rose, and maybe it was chemical, a matter of misfired serotonin that would hurt a few days later, but for a moment in time it altered the way people were with each other and the world, and forged new connections in their millions. Even if you feel like crying a few days into an E comedown, you don't forget the night of mashed conversation and empathy with the random people you met and shared backrubs with. These were mass memories, and shaped a mass understanding of what constituted a good time, and a mass trust of other people in their diverse forms.

The hippies and the travellers, with their festival-centred calendar and pagan sensibilities, formed the spaces where this all took place. The seeds of alternative culture which were sown in the sixties and scattered in remote corners of the land in the seventies flourished into a bigger, noisier and more mainstream New Age movement by the nineties. The Conservative government, in its death throes, outlawed public gatherings with music 'wholly or predominantly characterised by the emission of a succession of repetitive beats', but by then the parties were everywhere, and my class of prepubescent twelve-year-olds wore Global Hypercolor T-shirts with Smiley logos on them. The battle had been lost.

By 1999, English Heritage were issuing pre-booked tickets to Stonehenge, but vetting them to ensure the travellers didn't get in. The druids and the travellers stood outside as a trickle of acceptably normal people entered. A face-off with the police ensued. By 2000, the police didn't want the trouble any longer, and decided to let the party happen, since it was going to anyway. The Stonehenge revelries grew and grew. This year, Z said, was a year of celebration for the travellers, because it was the first time in thirty years that they had been let back in with music to the stones.

We drove through a perfect English village of thatched houses and immaculate lawns, and down a lane past a field strewn with huge stones like those at Avebury. We pulled into Z's driveway, by a picture-book cottage, and sat on a swing under a tall yew looking down Woden's Dene, a long valley of meadow bounded by woods, and in the middle of it more rocks, vast rocks, as though they had been thrown down by giants or gods in play.

She took us through the valley, her dog running off in the long meadow and popping up now and then by a rock.

Some of the rocks had straight edges down the side formed by human hands, and some had straight cracks down the middle, as though they had been cut ready for something but were too big or awkward to move.

How the rocks got there was a mystery – they are thought to be post-glacial remains and are known as Sarsen stones, a Wiltshire corruption of 'Saracen' from a time when Saracens were Muslims and Muslims, as non-Christians, were lumped together with all the other non-Christians, pagans included. It was, in an etymological meander, a way of stating a sense of a religious otherness.

Z spent her childhood playing in the stones and the trees around them. Naming the place after a Teutonic forest-god seemed to fit the context of her family quite well. Her father was named after the old Saxon outlaw smith-god Wayland, and she had described her family mindset as 'Spinozist'.

We'd talked a little about Spinoza earlier, the Enlightenment's best heretic. Spinoza held that everything in the world is an attribute of one base substance, which he called 'God, or Nature'. In the original Latin, it reads *Deus sive Natura*, and *sive* is an 'or' denoting the interchangeability of God and Nature, so that it is either one or the other, and the one might be the other. The oneness of this base substance, whatever you want to call it, sits in sharp contrast with the Cartesian notion of the split between the mechanical physical world of the body and of objects and the thinking substance of mind and of God.

For Spinoza, the God-or-Nature substance manifests in endless variations with their own distinct characteristics and identities, but there is no distinction between the mind and body as separate entities. Everything has a mind, or a consciousness, or a will; there is no distinction between plants or animals or rivers as being mechanistic, mindless things while humans are uniquely endowed with Godlike consciousness, like there is in Descartes.

The more you read of Spinoza, the more counter-intuitive Descartes's messy metaphysics becomes. Apart from one dodgy line of reasoning that seeks to prove the existence of God, which everyone probably had to do no matter what they were trying to argue in order not to be burned at the stake, everything in Spinoza makes perfect sense in that retrospectively obvious way.

I can see that Cartesianism suited the power structures of the Church and of monarchy, in creating layers of special Godlike consciousness available only to special people, but apart from that it doesn't make much sense. And yet that was the way of understanding the world and the stuff in it that dominated through the Enlightenment, and whose conception of the uniqueness of humanity still prevails.

I liked the term Spinozist. I had found myself using an analogue of it accepted in today's academic philosophy, pan-psychism, which baffled people outside of it, and vowed to use Spinozist instead. We walked past the line of oaks and hawthorns that marked some ancient border, past the big, pitted rocks, into longer and longer grass until the wood thickened and we turned back. An elder was in full bloom, heavy-scented in the midday sun. The grass brushed our shoulders and a pair of buzzards circled above.

Z dropped us at the avenue and we walked for a mile or so in the high sun, passing the male and female stones and the people camped out at the base of them. It was like a fest-ival, but better than a festival, because there was nothing in particular to see or do – we were not distracted from distrac-tion by distraction.

The oldest festivals were probably like Avebury or Stonehenge at midsummer: the music was incidental to the gathering, if people felt like making some, but it was really just about enjoying a passing moment for what it was. The moment, place and people were the thing. Glastonbury started like that too, but outside in the real world music was an industry and people came to expect it in industrial form and quantities, and so it came to pass that there was a perimeter fence like the Berlin Wall, and Metallica headlining.

I had hoped to go on the road to Stonehenge and then follow the New Age travellers to Glastonbury, but Stonehenge was heaving and unreachable, and I hadn't managed to get tickets to Glastonbury – the days of crawling through the bushes to sneak in, as my less-square student comrades used to do, were long gone. Instead I found myself back at the school gate between adventures, comparing weekend notes and apologising for not attending a number of competing local solstice advents.

There was the festival celebrating the rock 'n' roll hill farmer who died the year before, and a fortieth birthday party up on Hay Bluff, where, I had been assured, there would be sun salutations by standing stones, and all the hippies I could handle. This latter event was hosted by a vet, as staunchly rationalist in her worldview as you would hope of someone whose job is to operate on your dog, and who nonetheless professed to have found the solstice celebration delightful, even magical. Someone whose older child was at the local public school, populated by the scions of army families and rich farmers, said that they had been out climbing Pen-y-Fan all night in time for dawn.

At the point when I realised that Glastonbury was not going to happen, and that in an era when my parents watched it on telly this was probably not the end of the world, Z mentioned Mazey Day. Z lives in Cornwall, which is unsurprising, because it is the sunniest of the various bits of Celtic fringe and she was bound to be in one of them. Having missed the Helston Furry Dance, the prospect of finding something like it, which she described as riotous magic, or a magical riot, sounded good.

The train from Plymouth was small and ancient and it belted along the line, over a high bridge across the watery divide between Devon and Cornwall at Devonport, and through stations with signals that looked like they were last used as a prop in a war film and with names that seemed misspelled. It took more than two hours to cross the county, past strange earthworks that turned out to be tin mines and rivers and hillsides and stations where people, who seemed to be happier than the Welsh average, perhaps because the sun shone here, got on and off with shopping bags, talking of the weekend.

Cornwall looked very like Pembrokeshire, which if anything is more Arthurian in character with its rolling hills and rocky outcrops undisrupted by Londoners, except Cornwall was full of people and they were all deeply suntanned. In the Welsh borders we start to disrobe when it gets warmer than the eighteen degrees of the summer mean; that doesn't happen very often, and even the smallest town will have a beautician whose main income stream comes from spraying people orange because it will never happen naturally.

Here, the sun prevailed. The sea was dark blue and clear, even by the dry dock, where heads of swimmers edged out under the bridge and past the boats into the sea. I was envious of them: I'd been swimming only once so far this year, in the river behind the woods behind my house, and found it murky and uncomfortably forceful.

I bought a swimsuit in a charity shop and went in. The water was heart-stoppingly cold, grasping every pore and muscle so that you had to thrash about like a mad thing to survive the first few minutes. Then the peculiar mental peace that comes from frenetic physical exertion came upon me, and there was sea and sky and St Michael's Mount and the rocks, like a film set spray-painted all around, and by the time I got out I was ferociously hungry and the sun no longer felt warm enough, and I went to bed to get some warmth and fell into a deep sleep.

I woke up to the sound of gunshot, and listened to it, half-sleeping and confused. It exploded in great bangs and then trailed off, and the sounds of different guns rang out, and I realised that it was the sound of fireworks, and that they were nearby. I got up and went outside.

You can feel a crowd of people before you see it, the weird crowd-energy it gives off. The fairground had changed character, and in place of the kids in their candy-coloured tops were older, darker folk, drunk and chaotic and moving in human tides from one place to another, although there was no obvious pattern to them. Some were dressed as pirates; some were dressed in black with white crosses, in Cornish allegiance, but the overall effect was pleasingly like the Antichrist. Someone emerged from the fortune-teller's caravan. Somewhere there were drums, which were not the same as the noisy poppy techno coming from the fairground rides. These drums were being played by human hands, and many of them, and the drums and the hands were coming closer from wherever it was they were.

Torches flickered along a narrow alleyway behind a pub.

I left the fairground and made my way towards it, at odds with the rush of people moving downhill. I moved back with them and we pooled at the bottom by the quayside, waiting. You could hear other sounds now, pipes or flutes or something like them, weaving in and out of the drumbeat. A large, unwieldy figure made its way along, attended by eddies of riotous dancers, and as it drew closer it took on the shape of an animal whose head was the skull of a large beast, decked with garlands, and with a body of black rags which shimmied about as it moved.

The torches bobbed about in the black sky. More rain fell, and they burned. The procession moved along, meandering through the crowd, and bits of the crowd followed it. I tried to follow too, but a sober incomer in a sea of drunken orgiasts doesn't stand a chance.

The Cornish Obby Oss ritual is probably one of the oldest surviving British folk rituals. The Obby Oss is most closely associated with May Day, where, in Padstow, the black Oss takes to the streets and snaps up any passing maiden of its fancy. There is a particular style of what we might otherwise call morris dancing that is associated with the Oss: it is called teazing, or guising, and is a sort of moving act of flirtation in which the Oss is kept in a state of high party arousal, and so is the crowd.

People who have run successful clubs and bars speak of 'building a room' or 'building a vibe' as an art, one that requires constant and focused attention. There are things and people that raise the energy, and there are those that sap it. Turning a street full of observers into a swirling mass of revelry is not something that happens spontaneously, even if they are drunk enough for this to seem to be the case.

If, like the inert cagoule-people of Clun, you don't hold

much truck with the idea that big and involved ritual acts derive their power from some sort of collective will, or energy, or whatever you want to call it, revelries become exercises of chemically induced delusion and events become things performed by the few for the many.

Unticketed street parties can still sometimes do things the old way, where everyone present, or most of them, get inveigled into the dance, so that the party subsumes them into a messy whole. It was happening, in a fashion, here, and I wished I'd been more prepared for it, so that I could have been in more vigorous spirits.

The Obby Oss procession wasn't exactly advertised. Mazey Day is the endpoint of the week-long Golowan festival, which derived from the Tansys Golowan, or midsummer fires, which were lit from beacon to beacon to celebrate the solstice, and this became a fire-lit street party before somehow transforming into the other, respectable sort of festival. The fires couched their heritage in the Christianised date range of St John's Eve to St Peter's Eve, and the name derives from the Cornish for St John, but they existed long before the Church got hold of them. The fires were revived during the folkloric renaissance of the early twentieth century, a time when you might say that folkloric became a tacit substitute-term for pagan in its original Roman sense of *paganus*, being of the county. There is nothing more pagan than lighting up the sky as far as you can see with bonfires at midsummer.

The official Golowan programme, replete with advertisements for B&Bs with sea views and sponsored by the local college, was good on listing sedate things: the daytime parades of twin town banners, the schools and their floats, the international marching bands. I asked a man in an official

T-Shirt about the Oss, hoping to see it again, on better form, on Mazey Day, and he looked blank. A woman next to him said it was a Mazey Eve thing, to celebrate the mock mayor of the quay. I think I caught a glimpse of him, and that he was a pirate, but this didn't really narrow it down; a lot of people were dressed as pirates.

There was a distinct town/quay divide, in which the advertised activities took place in the disarmingly named Market Jew Street and the real stuff happened on the quayside. A controversy broke out a few years ago when the founder of the Penglaz Co-operative, the group who revived the Obby Oss tradition to protect the ritual character of Golowan, was ousted by the festival committee's new director. It happened to be that the founder had recently married her partner, who was also female, and also a Wisewoman, or witch, and that the handfasting ceremony had been front-page news in the local paper, whose motivations were unclear. The director announced that Golowan needed to maintain its secular character and that her involvement, which made the festival a pagan-religious exercise, was inappropriate.

In one of the side streets, the Methodist chapel was doing a roaring trade. It boasted a running order of musical events that were very much on-programme as far as Golowan was concerned: Celtic fiddle bands, Christian folk acts, dancing, the works. It wasn't so much that Golowan needed to be a secular activity, more that it needed not to be pagan.

The pagan controversy story, which would have passed me by if I hadn't nearly missed the dockside procession the night before, and hadn't been irritated about it, offers an interesting little snapshot of a common story I'd heard from many occultists: ancient spiritual acts and traditions excised from public space.

The ridiculous thing about it all is that even if it was witchcraft – and in a way you could say it is, it all is, for harnessing the magic of crowds is a pretty magical thing to do – nobody would notice or care now. The Methodist church hosting all those acceptable music events took care to brand them as Celtic, in that vein of churchy pagan semiotics that I'd seen at Avebury and with S.

But no entity in the world is less aware of the rise and fall of cultural waves than local officialdom, and so the old, famous, deeply Cornish pagan ritual of Penzance persisted in billing itself as a secular and international festival. They can call it what they like – I stood behind middle-aged women with deep-tan décolletages and garlands in their hair, holding their granddaughters aloft in Disney Princess dresses and floral facepaints, all of them watching the parades.

I remember watching an Easter parade as a child on holiday in Spain where a dead Jesus was carried through the streets. We're over crucifixes and saints here now, thank goodness, and most children in primary schools don't have to look up at a dying man looking painfully down at them, like I did during a brief stint at school in France. Here, instead, they build vast floats shaped like dragons and serpents and butterflies, and wave bright sequinned flowers in the air. Forms of life, real and mythological, are being celebrated, which is how it should be.

The little girls in their princess robes cheered on their older siblings as they went past. Even in the sanitised form that sits comfortably with primary schools, the secular bugs and plants on the floats were vast enough to be used for ritual purposes and looked a little like nature worship. If you checked their websites, I bet they all had Forest School and

Eco School status. Middle England is going pagan. We may be secular, but we still like a bit of ritual, and plants and animals are nicer than tortured dead people.

I dozed in a park full of strange imported plants that all seemed out of scale, like in Wonderland, and I watched the comings and goings of pirates and babies and more little girls in princess dresses. Maybe the princess-dress thing was actually pagan-medieval in allure, like the robes were for grown-ups. I reconsidered the Disney Princess genre. You had to acknowledge, at the very least, that the Tinkerbell movies were explicitly pagan in character; maybe the dresses were about being in a place where magic still happened. The little boys who weren't pirates were dressed as Native Americans, with headdresses and facepaint, some trailing dreamcatchers; there were no cowboys. The unofficial dress code here was either anarchic or earth-spiritual. I felt as though I should have made more of an effort.

The Serpent Dance was the last dance of the day, and did not go down the main street, but turned towards the quay. As we followed it, hurrying through the crowd to catch up, I wondered whether the old dances with their ritual qualities were dispatched to the quay, down the unrespectable end of town where the pirates hung out and away from the respectable normality of the main street. I'd heard it said that there were often rituals and celebrations at these sorts of affairs that, if not secret, were left unprogrammed, or kept for an inner circle of people to attend.

It was not clear how much of this permission came from above or below, whether heavy-handed festival organisers like the Penzance pagan-basher actively sought to distance the strangeness from the tourists, or whether, as Z said was the case in other, angrier Cornish towns, the people just wanted a bit of space from gawping, uninvolved emmets, which seemed fair enough.

The Serpent Dance became more serpentine, pooling in a crossroad and looping around and back on itself in concentric circles. Z spotted R, a witch she knew whom she'd met at Stonehenge at solstice, and someone from her tango class. The serpent grew longer, acquiring people along the way. Apparently, dances like these once lasted for days, with chains of people dancing across the country from village to village, so that the dance grew and grew and its constitution shifted as people came and went from it. Now the whole street was in the dance, young and old, led by the morrismen playing their looping tune, and the tune was distant and secondary to the laughing and the beat of feet along the lane.

The dance ended at the quay, and we met R, who was dressed in green from head to toe with skirts that swirled in the dance. She had performed a new moon ritual on a hilltop that morning, and was reluctantly heading back to London after a wild swim somewhere to the north, where the sun would set.

R and her partner had been on a ten-day solstice road trip to the West, starting at Stonehenge. Along the way they had met some kids, just seventeen years old, who were army recruits. After six weeks of training they were off to Iraq – they'd just been told. They had the weekend to get themselves together and pack. R and her partner asked if they would like to come to Stonehenge with them. They asked what it was. R explained that it was an ancient sacred site, that the stones had magic qualities, and that in a few hours it would be full of people celebrating the solstice. The kids wanted protection in Iraq. R said she'd see what she could do.

They were some of the first to arrive at the stones.

Together with the other people there they made a circle and R asked for protection for the soldiers, and, tacitly, that they should bring protection to others. If they were going to Iraq, she wanted them going as peacekeepers. As the ritual took place, the stones filled up: people were arriving now in hundreds and then thousands ready for the big party. The recruits saw the circle grow and thicken and were impressed. They thanked R and went off to party with the others, dropping by at intervals during the night to thank her and express delighted disbelief at the whole scene.

Whatever your position on magic, those kids came out of Stonehenge with a sense of safety and a trust in the benefi-cence of other people that would do them good, and might lead them to do good too. You could describe the mech-anism by which this outcome might happen as the flow of unseen energies, or as a spell, or simply as an exchange of trust with others and the world. I liked R; she seemed sane and good and happy. She went off to swim.

We went off to the pub with L, a friend of Z's who lived in Penzance. The Admiral Benbow was one of the most ec-centric pubs I'd ever been in. Even by Penzance standards, where everything is piratical in character, it was heavy on the naval references. Behind the bar was a long shelf of Toby jugs, like a row of grotesque corbels, and figureheads the size of giants popped up here and there around snugs and behind tables, and a huge ship's wheel nearly touched the low ceil-ing of the bar. You didn't need more than half a pint of cider to find it a disorienting experience.

Z and L talked about their shamanic training group, with whom they were still close, and about the dynamics with-in it, and their teacher, who they liked a great deal. They went into the woods on vision quests, where they sat alone, fasting and meditating, and learned techniques from various indigenous cultures: Native Americans, Siberian shamans, whatever worked. There was no particular dogma to the right way to approach things, and they did not see what they did as having a particular heritage either. It was about getting better at being.

The root of the things that we commonly call pagan lies in the same sort of thing – it is just that some people refine their practices into a certain technique that they then feel to be correct, and they teach it to others, and it becomes a thing with a name that some people adhere to, distinguishable from the other things with names. The term 'pagan', Z and L agreed, was problematic, because it gave a label to too many different things and made images of witches and purple, when really it was, or should, be all about being.

Even the pagans, insofar as we can call them that, as though they are a single entity, or even an entity, made their own, smaller, institutions and policed them. Z was down on this. Stonehenge had been left strewn with bottles and rubbish, as you'd expect when thirty-six thousand people have a party in a confined space. Some of the serious spiritual people complained about that – they didn't like a sacred monument defiled by litter, and, perhaps, unseriousness. It was as though the frivolity, rather than its trace, troubled them. Z didn't have much time for people who were into authenticity, or attached to ritual – she described the robes and ritual as a twentieth-century invention, and was unimpressed by the need to legislate for one's beliefs, because that's where you get into the same territory as organised religion, and it no longer had much spirit left in it.

Z and L wanted to go out dancing. L went home to sort out babysitting with his wife, and Z went to put her dog to bed. I walked down the bright lane to the sea. The town centre was empty now, and the distant vibration of many voices on the quayside rang up again. That was where the action was now. A hotel on the seafront had set up a stage, and already the dancefloor was full, and spilling out onto the pavement and the road, which the police were starting to block off with cones. A party was brewing.

The sun caught St Michael's Mount so that it stood out gold in the sea, which was calm and glassy. A tide of people came, slowly at first, and then in dense streams from the town and the quay, filling up the whole road with cidery laughter. I walked through the town, going nowhere in particular, going down side streets that fed back to where I had come from, going round in circles. The top of the town was cold and still, and the sky darkened.

At some point I ended up back at the seafront. The whole road was a moving mass of people. Somewhere within it, on the wall by the stage, were Z and L and his wife and their friends, beaming and shaking like proper ravers, the type whose only drug is the moment.

'If you have to call something pagan,' said L, 'this, right here, with the sea and the sky and the people celebrating it all: this is pagan.'

And so they danced.

FIVE

The Shaman

Our ancestors were tree-centric: the Celts had their Tree of Life, which symbolised the interconnectedness and harmony of the world, and which you can see, only slightly transformed, above the doorways of Archenfield churches. The Anglo-Saxons brought their German gods with them, and even the gods who weren't tree-gods existed in a universe structured around a vast, invisible tree called Yggdrasil.

These grand unified tree theories could be borne out by spiritual endeavour, ideally in the form of going alone into the trees and getting into a place, the Wyrd, in which talking to them was possible. The trees, as well as issuing advice and guidance, worked as portals into other worlds, or other parts of the universe-tree. The trees were a place of both shelter and magic.

It felt like due diligence to give this magic a try. I quite liked the idea of a sacred grove. It seemed relaxing, and a good soft-marketing technique for a tree-based cult. And maybe, within the woody rhythms of a tree, I would find an essence or a message or some inspiration, pointing me in the direction of the Green Man.

A couple of months previously, earlier on than I had planned, I had decided to go and see a shaman. I like to think that this was a shamanically instinctive decision, although it was at least partly timetable-related, and timetables do not possess shamanic attributes.

It was also partly a thought-experiment: I wanted to learn some tricks for engaging with nature and, specifically, trees. I liked trees; I thought of them as a good thing. It's just that I never really noticed them, only whether or not they were there, and whether or not I liked them, and sometimes not even that.

Now, finding myself forced to think a bit harder about trees, since one of the few things anyone could agree on about the Green Man was that he had something to do with trees, I needed to learn to notice them a bit more.

There are ways of writing about trees. It hadn't escaped my notice that tree-writing was a modish thing, and that people seemed to find themselves enriched by a mention of the double-serrate margin of a hazel leaf, or some other graphic arboreal detail. None of this, however, told me much about the religious quality of a tree, just as the phrenological detail of a human skull failed to say much of the mind within it.

I needed to notice trees in a way that was not dependent on taking photos of them as a visual notepad. I needed to notice them in a being way. It occurred to me that a lesson from a professional tree-communicator might be just the thing.

I found myself shopping for shamans online, which seemed a little perverse, and was therefore enjoyable for it. There was a man called Michael Harner, the Colonel Sanders of the shamanic training scene, who seemed to have a number of affiliated organisations who trademarked their courses. I don't know how trademarking shamanic techniques went down with their spirit guides. Maybe the Upper Realm is more like our own than we think.

The people I had heard from who were into shamanism,

and who had an uncanny ability to transmit good vibes electronically, which seemed auspicious, recommended the Scandinavian School of Shamanic Practice. I exchanged emails with one of their chief shamans and got stuck on the idea of going to Sweden for a week at midsummer before realising that I couldn't afford to. Shamanic training is an expensive business: doing it properly costs thousands of pounds.

I learned that people who do shamanism often do healing too. Some people who do healing are the maddest and most broken around, or at least that was my dad's formative instruction to me, based on working in mediation in Lewisham; maybe Lewisham lacked the ley lines and earth energies necessary for these things to work. I soon learned to read the semiotic energies of web design, where overformatting and bright colours red-flagged crazies and where dreamcatchers and ethno-folksy images waymarked a truer path. One morning, feeling a bit panicked about it all, I looked for shamans in Wales and found one close to home. Synchronicity. I called her.

The shaman had a calm voice and didn't think my request, to connect shamanically with trees, was weird. If anything, a microscopic pause indicated that she seemed a bit put out at the assertion that it might be. We talked about trees and intuition and shamanic journeying. Her house was in a village bounded by rivers and hills. She wore purple, which was how you would expect it to be, and had shrines to various creatures and deities dotted about the place: Pegasus, Shiva, Buddha, gods and goddesses of all origins and hues.

She described herself as an animist, a believer in the spirits in things, and did not legislate for the validity or purity of any single tradition – it was as though all these various godheads were attributes of cosmic forces that were identified in effective ways at certain points in time and space, and worth importing and keeping for their efficacy. She saw animism as a common-sense position, far more credible than materialism, which had always seemed a bit silly to her. She had always found the otherworlds open to her, and had never taken consensus reality to heart. She described the material world as a delusion.

The deal was that we would do some initial shamanic journeying before going out to apply it to trees. As a profoundly unspiritual person, or at least someone profoundly irritated by 'spiritual' as a term, the prospect of engaging in what is essentially a guided meditation into a pre-structured cosmography, with drums and another person present, was always going to be a thorny task.

The shamanic cosmos has been shared in some way over time by most indigenous cultures, including those of the ancient Britons and the Norse forefathers of subsequent Anglo-Saxon and Viking invaders. It is constructed of a Middle World, an Upper World and a Lower World. Many versions of it are connected or underpinned by a large tree like the Tree of Life or Yggdrasil. We exist, day to day, in the Middle World, where material things materialise. The Upper World is a place of ethereal spirit guides, and the Lower World is a grounding, nourishing earthy space of sleep and regeneration. You find your power animal, which leads and looks after you, in the Lower World.

When the Christians took over religious headspace they demonised the Lower World and reframed it as Hell, the Underworld. The only place to do transcendence was up above, with their God on their terms. The Lower World was never supposed to be demonic in character, but a place where refuge and growth could be sought in nature.

I can imagine that if your waking life is bounded by earth, trees and sky, your metaphysical worldview will look a bit like that too. I struggled with it. S beat a drum; the sound was indeed hypnotic, and I lay on the floor trying to disappear down the rabbit hole, trying a little too hard. Just as the Anglo-Saxon and Norse wyrd-worlds were shaped by their waking thoughts, my attempt at shamanising, taking place immediately after a year spent writing a PhD thesis about Lewis Carroll, looked suspiciously Carrollian in character. When the time came to find an animal – and I pursued a wolf, who didn't care, a sneery hare or perhaps White Rabbit, and a fox that ran away – the one that rejected me least was a stag. I had pulled over outside the White Hart in the village earlier, to check directions, and was self-consciously aware of this throughout, trying to bat the thought away but never quite succeeding, so that the best strategy to combat it was to run, run, run after the running stag, and to keep running, away from thought and mind.

The shaman was satisfied with this, and we talked about it a bit. Feeling a little uncomfortable at my lack of immersion in the Lower World, I gazed out of the window at a fine, tall tree that dominated the hill opposite. It was bigger and greener than the others – the sum of my tree engagement.

We went for a walk to look at it, climbing a path out of the village: a huge beech, maybe fifty metres tall, with that uncanny luminosity that the first beech leaves have. Having identified it, I was happy. We moved on. We went to a small park on the hillside above the village. S greeted a young maple in the way that you might greet the child of someone you know a little but not well, pausing for a moment to acknowledge it before reaching over and stroking a frond, in a hair-patting sort of way. She asked me if I would like to greet it too. I did. She asked me what I thought about the tree, what I was getting from it. I found it child-like, I suppose, but that's where the function of metaphor gets involved – I'd already attributed child-words to it, and so the child-quality could be made from those verbal frames as much as any description deriving from the character of the tree. Getting rid of all of that would take more than an afternoon.

We moved on. I learned that there is a shamanic way of walking, and, by extension, a non-shamanic way of walking. If you walk with purpose, looking at individual things beneath your feet or nearby, you are fixing things into discrete objects on the ground and in your head. You are not being present in the space, or opening yourself up to the spirits of the things in it.

Shamanic walking involves looking into middle distance, at the horizon, so that you engage your peripheral vision rather than focusing on any one thing at the exclusion of others. It softens your vision, so that the blades of grass in a meadow merge a little, and it also alters your colour perception in a similar way to the beginning or end of an acid trip, when colours intensify as though a digital photo filter has been switched on. That last analogy is mine; nothing irritates people who access those headspaces without drugs more than a lazy acid comparison. People who practise something dismissed as a bit 'woo' by mainstream society exist in a conflicted relationship with the practitioners of other sorts of woo.

There are rivalries and alliances. Some are critical of all drugs as delusory agents, or see them as dangerously easy ways in to accessing things better encountered gradually with mental preparation. Finding certain sorts of woo through drugs, as any lengthy conversation with a lifelong stoner can tell you, is a pretty common thing, and the ranks of the non-normal world would be significantly thinned without them. It is then the done thing, though, to renounce them rather than to continue to extol the virtues of drugs as a way in. I suppose everyone wants to maintain the validity of their own woo, and if a bad association invalidates it in the minds of others they distance themselves from it fast.

It was, however, precisely this sort of internal digression from the task at hand, in this case the task of immediate being, that I was supposed to overcome. I paced up and down the little park, switching from mode to mode. At some point it seemed to start working: rather than looking at things in order to taxonomise them I was getting a sense of how they were. Words are an ineffectual medium to describe this; if writing about music is like dancing about architecture, walking about trees might not be such a crazy thing to do if the aim is to access their nature. Getting into this vision-space was, apparently, the first step to getting to know the trees. S asked me if I would like to choose a tree to meet. I chose the hawthorn that I had noticed on the way, thick with blossom.

I stared at its leaves until my vision blurred them and entered a reverie which veered, again, rapidly off-topic into the semantic ambiguities of *Sinn* (meaning 'sense') and *Geist* (meaning 'spirit'): in the otherwise unambiguous German language, which is not loaded with synonyms like English is, and in which you are more likely to be told off for being wrong than validated for exercising poetic licence, *Sinn* and *Geist* overlap slightly in meaning.

It occurred to me that we are fine, in unspiritual society, with the idea of sense. It is OK to acknowledge that the sense of a thing is something that cannot always be broken up effectively into words, and that sometimes it must, simply, be sensed. If you start on about the spirits of things, you are dismissed into the woo realm. Spirits are deeply unfashionable, and the word 'spirit' is OK only where it is used interchangeably with 'sense' – as it can be in German, or in 'the spirit of the law' or whatever. Isn't the spirit of something the same as the sense of something, though, viewed through a slightly different metaphor?

The spirit of a thing implies that it must have a psychic quality – I suppose you could say that the law, or any other institution, has a psychic quality imposed on it by the people who make it. Where you get into difficulty saying things have spirits is if they are things generally considered to be inanimate, or unconscious. Even if a tree is alive, saying it is conscious stumbles out of our normal understanding of consciousness. Saying a stone has a spirit is even trickier. Describing the sense of a stone, even if the description contains exactly the same stuff – a calm, serene stone that had seen many things come and go, like the one we found later – is less weird, because sense is assumed to be the sense of the perceiver, rather than the perceived.

Anyway, I was supposed to be engaging with the hawthorn. I had always been a bit dismissive of hawthorn, which is unlovely in the winter, and the winters are long round here. I suppose I would have characterised it, if we're being anthropomorphic, as a scrubby urchin-ratboy, male and small and scrawny, and now in full May its leaves were green, plump and perfect, and its blossom flirtatious like a girl after a couple of glasses of wine. It looked as though it was having fun, as if every little pearl of blossom, the little virgin balls and the full-bloom flowers with their dark stamen and pink-flecked petals, were all out partying at the Hawthorn May Ball. S asked me how I was doing and I communicated this to her; she approved. We moved on to the witch elm, which was smaller and different from the dead, big elms we used to have. Its leaves were slightly furry. I was unmoved by it.

The river, which was not the Usk but a tributary of it, was so clear that you could see the stony bed and individual bubbles of water as they came up from it. We made our way along it to a huge old oak, reddish leaves emerging. We approached the field of the tree, which is something like its aura or perhaps its sphere of influence, palms outstretched in an inverted sun salutation, which was the courteous way in. It seemed as though the tree was OK with this.

Dozing beneath an oak tree in the month of May had always been fast-track to fairyland in what little I recollected from Middle English. I was close to dozing now, and in danger of not waking up, and so found only generic things to think about it: things like its solidity and heft and age. Perhaps I should have slept, and magic would have happened. I did not feel familiar with this tree, although it was benevolent.

There is only one tree with which I could claim to have much of a relationship, a vast and ancient oak up on H's hillside, where I lived for several years. It has been estimated to be nearly a thousand years old, a millennium in which a house and then a hamlet were built beneath it, and through which generations of a sprawling family were born, and loved, and died; it saw a school open and close and fall into ruin, and the place rebuilt by successive new owners who were not from there. When we rebuilt the barn beneath it and had to dig close to its roots I had felt fiercely protective over it as I am on occasion with my children, although it could hardly be said to be like a child. It is still there. It seems happy enough – since I have known it, for about twelve years, it has had one old branch that is black and leafless and one that is younger and new and doing just fine.

I would hug this tree spontaneously, as would my son, but he was a shaman anyway in the way that all children are, with the fanciful possibility of things still untrampled by adult sensibilities. The old oak tree will outlive his children's children. I thought I would repeat the exercise alone, with the old oak and the unimposed intimacy that comes from having been around something for a while.

Down by the river was a great flat rock, a few metres long and half as wide. S asked me, now with the pleasing gnomic tone of a Taoist riddler, to describe its surface, and how it came to be; I said that it looked indented, as though it had been chiselled out by hand. She told me to look again, and said that it was old red sandstone with ripples that had come from being on the bed of a sea or a lake. She mused on the passing of time, that a rock on a grassy bank by a stream in our world, now, had once been undersea, and before that a desert. Someone had formed neat piles of rounded river stones in top of it, in a way that could, variously, be viewed as Zen-like or henge-like, or like the artistry of Makka Pakka, the beneficent stone-obsessed troglodyte from *In the Night Garden*. The children's TV programme moves between worlds in a deeply trippy way too, but nobody ever seems to acknowledge this.

I hung out with another lovely hawthorn and admired it

133

and tried, as instructed, to connect with it by chanting. This involves singing a note and moving around a little to find the right frequency, and then when it feels like it is resonating with the tree you can use it to open a channel of communication. I suppose this is like the use of Om when meditating, except you are meditating, or mediating, with another being rather than doing so alone. I began this exercise by repeating the piano riff from the camp house anthem that I had on in the car on the way over, not expecting much from it, and was surprised to find it striking a chord with the tree. There was a point at which it felt right; the sound continued, as though it had its own volition to do so, and the hawthorn was down with it. I became quite certain that this hawthorn was a raver like its sister, perhaps all part of the magic of May.

Buoyed by this, I hugged the tree carefully to avoid getting spiked by its thorns, disengaged with it, and tried the same thing with the river, which had its own shifting, riffy quality.

Maybe if we modulate our voices to the frequencies around us, the frequencies that we do not notice when we are getting on with getting things done in the way adult life demands of us, we become aware of them, of the multitude of sounds that exist, layered over one another, always shifting, and usually dismissed into the single lumpy entity of background noise. I became aware of the invisible rave going on all around me, a thousand distant rhythms of diverse bits of life, and could now hear it without trying. This was different, an altered mode of being, one that was unusual if not unique.

I once got lost on my bike at dawn in Berlin, at the end of a long night, after following the faint strains of techno I heard in the distance. I cycled through empty streets, turn-ing left and right to wherever the music seemed to come from. Any sense of time had long since faded, and it may have been minutes or hours later, just as the light crept back into the sky, that I found myself at the Hasenheide, a heath to the south of the city centre, where no party was visible: just long grass and, like the name had promised, some hares, jumping about in the dawn before the people took over their space. That was in May, too, although it came from a less sober baseline state than now.

I'd always assumed that those sounds were an illusion. What if they weren't? Maybe they were all there, then and now, and I was simply in a state where I could, and would, hear them. The untapped energy made me fanciful. All of the trees were in their party clothes, and they were all at the party, and I was at the party too, and the party was now. It was a May party, a Beltane party.

This mindset, which I came to label as magical in the ab-sence of a better term, came back to me from time to time afterwards. I slipped into it in Hereford Cathedral and all the way down to Dore Abbey a couple of weeks later, and found it watching bats dance about chasing flies beneath a full moon at home, and sometimes in the woods on a warm day. I'm not sure I'd call it much more than being, in a way that bypasses the self-consciousness that usually eats being up, but having a way into it was a good thing.

We went back to S's house and attempted another sha-manic journey to the Upper World. I was supposed to find a spirit guide there but if I did it was defined only in its elu-siveness. I nearly fell asleep again. This spirit business was tiring. We stopped for tea and talked about life.

I lived and worked for a while in a Scottish therapeutic

community which practised a form of Tibetan Buddhist therapy that could be summed up as kindness with a bit of mysticism. It was a friendly place, run by psychotherapists of hippyish demeanour rather than anti-psychiatric anarchists, and it was good for people, largely because kindness is good for people. People sometimes came there from a spell in hospital, which from their accounts often seemed – with its routine of disrupted sleep and incarceration in front of day-time TV, with unhappiness, coffee and cigarettes as diversion – to have more of an adverse impact on people's well-being than whatever brought them there in the first place.

S had been a psychiatric nurse before, and had also had the strange experience of being hired, subsequently, as a shaman by the NHS to take care of the spiritual needs of a patient, with whom she was still in contact. We talked for a while about one of the people I used to live with in the community in Scotland, and the voices he heard and communicated with.

Her account of what was happening for him was pretty much the same as his was: he had had a trauma, or psychic crisis, and dealt with it by doing too many drugs. This had hastened his access to a space in which he perceived gods, and heard their voices, and needed to placate them. He sometimes used hand gestures to communicate with them, perhaps because it was less socially disruptive than talking back at them, or perhaps because that was their preferred form of communication; I don't recall asking about it at the time. It was as though he had got stuck in this shamanic headspace and couldn't switch off from it, in what the shamans would describe as the Middle World, the spirits behind the things we see in the material world.

His psychiatrists didn't see it like this. They knocked him

out with major tranquillisers and locked him in a ward. He had put too many of the wrong chemicals into his brain and they had knocked its chemistry out of sync. He was simply making too much dopamine, which was creating hallucinations of things that weren't there, and delusions about gods. He needed to lose the dopamine.

The psychiatrist's hallucination, as opposed to the shaman's vision, is a term predicated on the assumption that there is such a thing as a real and accurate way to perceive the world. It is an odd situation in which interventions are basically determined by the practitioner's metaphysics.

There is a stark contrast between the materialist underpinnings of neuroscience and biological psychiatry, in which the world is made out of bits of interacting stuff, or what you might broadly call the transcendental idealism of shamanism or the Eastern religions. It is either a matter of chemistry gone awry, which then needs fixing chemically, or something is happening to the mediation of the metaphysical realm, where other entirely valid worlds are being accessed.

I wondered, fleetingly, at the fact that the two people I have known reasonably well who have been diagnosed with psychotic disorders were, variously, raised by academic metaphysicians or philosophy students at the time of diagnosis. Perhaps overthinking makes you mad. Perhaps mad people are merely thinkers.

Having seen the outcomes of the neurobiological approach to people's heads, I would send someone in a similar mode to S instead. I would rather they found their god or gods or spirits in the manner they chose than be locked up and drugged. I would rather someone listened to them, believed them and worked through the troublesome bits with them so they felt better placed to cope with their experiences. To be fair to the NHS, cognitive behavioural therapy does this to an extent, and, like its less respectable cousin, neurolinguistic programming, it is founded on a tacitly non-materialist concept of the mind's ability to mediate and alter what is out there. Human time costs more than drugs, however, and we do not care much about the cost of the bad times to the dispossessed, or the possessed.

This inclination is less out there than it sounds. In the 1970s, the Harvard psychologist Julian Jaynes published *The Origin of Consciousness in the Breakdown of the Bicameral Mind*. It was controversial, and therefore cultish in its popularity: Jaynes's central thesis was that prehistoric human consciousness was dominated by the right brain, which manifested as a godlike guiding voice.

The brain is walnut-shaped, and, like a walnut, divided into two main hemispheres which are joined in the middle. The term 'bicameralism' refers to these two hemispheres, or chambers, and to the idea in psychology and neuroscience that each hemisphere has its own distinct function and character in the working of the mind.

If the right brain perceives the world and transmits a stream of its experiences of it in the form of an ongoing auditory hallucination, the left brain's job is to enact the right brain's will, to make things happen. Jaynes describes the determining role of the gods in Homeric epic verse, and how they dictate the actions of men, who seem to have no reflective capacity or will of their own, and also in the early parts of the Old Testament, where men blindly enact the will of God. It is an account strikingly similar to the set of experiences we now call psychotic, an account of hearing voices and acting on them. Yesterday's prophets are today's madmen.

Jaynes's line on bicameralism seemed so far-fetched to the mainstream of academic psychology that the term soon became deeply unfashionable. More recently, however, the English critic and psychiatrist Iain McGilchrist revived the idea of the divided brain with a renewed cultural and neuro-logical slant, in *The Master and His Emissary*. McGilchrist describes the left brain as the locus of fixity, of rational thought, where things are conceived of and manipulated. Without the systematising qualities of the left brain, and its ability to separate things out and put them in order, we would not be able to make a cup of coffee or drive a car.

But McGilchrist laments the increasing over-dominance of the rational and systematic sphere in human behaviour at the expense of being. The right brain, where feeling and experience take place, is increasingly disempowered at the expense of the left. The right brain sees things in their great-er context in the world at large, and makes broader and deeper connections. The right brain deals with the world as an interconnected whole, rather than a series of disconnec-ted tasks.

McGilchrist's brain perceives the world in a way that looks a bit Spinozist to me. The right brain has a monistic conception of the universe, in which everything is con-nected, and in which everything stems from one universal entity. The left brain, by contrast, takes an atomised view of the world as made of material bits that need to be pinned down and labelled in language. It imposes a concreteness on things, and makes those things into things, and in doing so enables things to happen in the world.

McGilchrist's hemispheres are engaged in an ongoing and unspoken philosophical debate between the left and right. The left brain is concerned with the objects right in front of it and how to make them work. The right brain is concerned with the whole, the big picture, and how to harmonise everything within it. The left brain is doing; the right is being. These sorts of oversimplifications are themselves left-brained affairs, and yet without them we have no way of communicating anything – without summarising things as words, there could be no language.

For Jaynes, language drove much of the transformation into human self-consciousness. The need for language, or a more complex and fixed form of it, arose out of crisis and the need to organise human endeavour more effectively. The second millennium BC was thought to have been characterised by environmental catastrophe: a series of severe earthquakes and the mass migration of people fleeing from them. You can't plan for, or in, contingency without having an effective means of communication, and effective ways of grouping people. The human brain, over time, adapted to this necessity.

What got lost in the process was the hotline to the gods. The relatively few people who could still access the god-voice became oracles and shamans. The process of prayer, or meditation, was used in an attempt to get back there.

If you want to look at the intervening millennia as an ongoing left-brained success story, society, with the occasional exception, became more and more organised, and with it came the need for language and rules and public discourse. If the god-voice had once been a right-brained phenomenon, a left-brained lust for legislation had altered the nature of religion, too.

The early English pragmatist philosopher and professional controversialist Ferdinand Schiller wrote a lengthy screed denouncing formal logic, that most left-brained of activities, as being responsible for much of the evil in the modern world. For Schiller, the drive for fixity and control that Jaynes and McGilchrist might call left-brained was the source not only of bureaucratic pedantry and delusional scientific conservatism, but also of social intolerance and political tyranny. As for its effects on religion, Schiller puts it so eloquently that it would be a shame not to quote him at length:

> No religions originally show themselves so obsessed with the idea of fixity; at their first appearance they do not conceive themselves as final, but all look forward to Messiahs, Second Comings, Mahdis and other forms of future consummation. Their formulation into rigid Creeds which must be believed in every syllable and on no account be revised, is a phenomenon which comes later, when logically trained theologians have got the religious movement under control.
>
> How profoundly irreligious this change is, appears from the negation of the notion of the revelation which it involves. For is not progressiveness implied in the very notion of a revelation? Can the divine revealing of a new truth be conceived to leave a mind that imbibes it unaltered and unfortified, and in no better posture for religious growth? A revelation that carries with it no spiritual enlightenment, that forms no stimulus to spiritual progress, but merely fixes a status quo, is a futility and in no credible sense a revelation at all.

It might not be as simple as a relentless march of left-brained fixity at the expense of freedom, being and whatever other idyllic attributes we deem to be right-brained. The development of organised religion over the ages shifted from a world in which the trees possessed spirits which spoke to men, because that was the nature of human experience, to one that had to be mediated by a vast institution in the absence of any personal engagement.

This story of the mind also has a particular elegance when you look at shamanic accounts of the world, with their spirit guides and worlds accessible only through an altered mindset. Jaynes, describing the voices of the gods in the *Iliad*, might be describing the later stages of a shamanic vision quest: 'Sometimes they come in mists or out of the gray sea or a river, or from the sky, suggesting visual auras preceding them. But at other times, they simply occur.'

I drew a few conclusions from all of this. Firstly, the descriptions of the headspace that shamans seek to inhabit is like the right-brained headspace described by Jaynes. The need for oracles, hierophants and shamanic techniques came about only when left-brain dominance took over.

Secondly, the trance-process by which this headspace is approached in shamanic practice is something that happens in most transcendental belief-systems. Christian monks got there through hours of chanting and prayer, and from fasting and sleep-deprivation, getting up at various points in the night to pray. Buddhist ascetics do much the same thing; so do Hindu yogis, albeit with more focus on the body and the breath as a meditation tactic. The animist belief-systems that are thought of as being somehow primitive might add drumming, dancing or the endurance of physical pain into the mix, but the basic methods of altering consciousness are otherwise the same. The spiritually minded like this trance-state. It doesn't matter much which label they give it, which brand of transcendence they espouse – it is all the same thing.

Thirdly, the monistic, big-picture qualities of McGilchrist's right brain lend themselves to the immanent, interconnected view of the world shared by shamans and Buddhists and Sufis and yogis and, it seems, the old Celtic Church. It is God as Logos, the ancient Greek understanding of the life force underpinning all things, and, perhaps, the voice underpinning all consciousness.

If you eradicate God or Nature or the Logos entirely from your cultural understanding of the world, any experience of it is heretical. Madness is the word we use to describe psychological heresy, of dancing to the tune others don't hear.

It had never seemed sensible to tell people what they are perceiving, or to write it off as a brain error. It is impractical if the aim is for them to feel well; cultivating mistrust of one's perceptions is dangerous and builds paranoia. It seemed far more desirable for people hearing voices in crisis to consult S, and to understand these voices in a shamanic context and in doing so find strategies for dealing with them in life, than for them to be drugged into silence for the comfort of others. There are some areas of medicine that respond well to chemical cures – I'd rather take the antibiotics for an infection than be chanted at – and there are some that don't. When it comes to fixing broken minds, shamanism looked less crazy than the bad science of psychiatry to me.

Our final trip was to a sacred grove, up a long lane a mile or so out of a village, a circle of very ancient yews, several thousand years old, into which someone had thrown a square grey church that looked even more of a silly interloper now that nobody went there any more. The yew trees got older as you moved clockwise around the church. S went off to look for a yew seedling to grow in her garden. She was really into yews. She wouldn't tell me why – I suppose because she wanted me to work it out for myself, which I failed to do before I went home to Google. I entered the church, which was unremarkable and surprisingly large inside, and wondered how big the congregation it inherited was.

The oldest of the yews was a male and female couple, who stood together at the north-east of the church, branches touching so seamlessly that their canopy was one. They were about five thousand years old. Yews are harder to date than other trees, because they can lose their core and grow elsewhere and thrive, and they grow more slowly as they age, so that when they get into millennia the growth is imperceptible and requires micro-measurements. This slowing, however, is a predictable enough process: you can determine the age from the slowness of growth, from how close together those imperceptible rings are.

I climbed up into the crook of the female yew's branches, and leaned against some of the others in the correct way with one foot on the root, and must confess that I did not succeed in knowing the yews, any of them. They all eluded me. I found them tall, dark and handsome trees. I felt entirely clichéd things about them that were all bound up in vernacular language: my brain said words like grave and brooding. It is all very well to say that one should simply be more intuitive, but when your mind is formed from words the process of de-wording will, I wager, need a fair amount of time and wilderness to happen satisfactorily. S politely and obviously knew I didn't get it.

When I got home I looked up the yews, engaging with the virtual information of Wikipedia and ancient tree sites rather than my own raw intuition, of which there was little. There was a man standing by the yew we'd just seen with a measuring tape around its girth. It looked vaguely pornographic. I found myself outraged on behalf of S, and of the yew. He did not ask its permission. A sacred grove cannot be diminished into a set of measurements. But maybe, if you were a yew of several thousand years, and had seen men come and go in the grove, you would no longer be outraged by anything. Maybe you would just find these little moving creatures funny as they scuttled about in states of agitation over one passing thing or another. Maybe you would find the idea that it is possible to know things by quantifying them funny.

I let the shamanism thing rest for a while, because life got busy, too busy to be with trees. As time passed I felt a little guilty that I hadn't put much into developing my relationship with trees, and tree spirits, and whatever it was the trees would say of the Green Man. In the pub in Cornwall, I had eavesdropped on Z and L talking about their three-year training and vision quests, and felt a bit mournful.

I promised myself that I would do my own vision quest, on my own terms, at some point in the near future when the time felt right. I had no intention of doing it properly, with months of meditative preparation and a proper wilderness up a mountain. I was simply going to hang out in my woods. I could accept that fasting would help me stay awake longer, so that was fine: I needed all the help I could get. I was taking creature comforts: a sleeping bag, a mat and a torch, and my phone, which I would attempt to hide away for the duration.

My wood is not ancient. It is a few hundred metres of disused railway line. The trees on it grew, or were planted –

I do not know which – sometime after Beeching closed it in the early 1960s. The railway line was not a holiday line, shipping tourists from idyll to idyll, but there to keep the sparse bits of industry that stopped poor rural areas from being destitute ticking over, and to make those areas habitable. My house, which was built by the industrial petit bourgeoisie rather than wild hill farmers, belonged to the man who ran the chemical works next to it, making naphthalene from coal tar. One of Wales's few trunk roads runs between the house and the wood, bringing a steady rumble of huge, fast lorries.

The old railway line runs at a slight angle away from the road, so that as you go further into the wood, which is really just a track lined on both sides with trees for as far as you can see, the thunder of the road becomes more distant. At the end of it is a lean-to that once stored wood and an ancient tractor which departed with its owners, and in the lean-to is space for a campfire.

Behind the lean-to is a fence, and beyond the fence, on the neighbouring strip of ex-railway land, is an enormous climbing frame with a fifty-foot climbing wall, all manner of high ropes, a zipwire and various other metal loops and racks that look a bit like an oversized children's playground or, on a bad day, torture gear for exhibitionists. It is a Multi-Activity Centre, and every now and then the relative quiet of the wood is disrupted by the motivational cheering of grown-ups enlaced with karabiners.

I am very fond of the unromanticness of my wood. There is no way of mythologising a deep druidic history upon it – it is a bit of industrial society that lost, over time, to nature. Finding myself ever more critical of claims to authenticity, in trees as in religion, and finding a beauty in the unlikeliness of the giant climbing frame and the rumbling trunk road and the path of the old railway track which, encroached by trees, was no longer straight, I could get on with the wood aesthetically.

Aesthetics are a value judgement on things, even if you don't adhere to the notion that beauty implies some externally fixed moral good. When we see something and find it beautiful, it is a perceptual acknowledgement of its desirability. We all have our own divergences within this, some socially influenced and some more personally motivated. We read the detail of the things around us without always having a vocabulary to describe it, some of it visual and some of it aural and some of it kinaesthetic in quality, felt viscerally.

I tried to get my head around the basics of Anglo-Saxon paganism, and around the shamanic Upper and Lower Worlds, and just couldn't do it. Part of it was that the idea of the Lower World does nothing at all for me. I can access meditation states just fine but do not see elves. I have no desire to see elves. Elves and fairies and all those other humanoid weird creatures are bits of *deus ex machina* from times when people failed to conceive of better stories about the world, and could think only of themselves and the brown earth and things like it. The tree-world cosmography is dendromorphic, dendrocentric. I'm not sure it's any healthier than anthropomorphism. Give me shapeless Zen nothingness any day.

If god-voices once appeared as elves, I'm sure there's an interesting study to be done of today's psychotic voices, and what shapes them, although it would be hard to separate their intrinsic character from the grim contexts that forced the listener into that headspace, and they would probably mostly be about the NSA and imperceptible tracking devices in phones. They would be about superhuman institutions and their power, rather than the superhuman qualities of elves.

In fact, the more I thought about it – and I had thought about it rather too extensively after so much time on my own – the more I saw similarities in the psychic ecosystems of cities and woods, the neoliberal struggle for plant existence, the attempts by the nettles at forcing monopoly on their patch, the discarded human exoskeleton of abandoned buildings in the shitty bits of cities, the lichen-shaped sprawl of Greater London seen from space, so that no granular detail could reveal the processes of it, although they were there, and what made it.

The lichen is a symbiosis of a fungus and a photosynthetic partner organism, an alga or bacterium, in which the algal or bacterial photobiont fuels the fungal structure. The photobiont – the alga or bacterium capable of photosynthesis – can live independently of the fungus: you sometimes see patches of orange *Trentepolia* algae on damp tree stumps in the woods, and this is how they manifest left to their own devices. The biologists call this existence 'living free', which throws the cuddly association of symbiosis into relief.

Symbiosis is one of those biological terms adopted by management consultants, and in the case of lichen it is misconstrued in a way similar to a managerial spin on capitalism. When the *Graphis* fungus gets its hands, or whatever the correct non-anthropomorphic metaphor is, on the *Trentepolia*, it forms an entirely different structure. The most striking example is the *Graphis scripta* lichen, which, as the name suggests, looks like runes carved into a stony surface. It is impressively entrepreneurial: the fungus would not exist at all without this system in place, and the alga would just be doing its own orange thing on a tree somewhere, yet in part-nership something far more complex is created.

The fungus, which manufactures long, strong strands called hyphae, traps the photobiont within them. A layer of hyphae seals the top of its cage, and a layer forms an an-chor at the bottom; in the medulla in-between, the hyphae form organic bars to keep it in its place. Each photobiont cell then gets to work photosynthesising, creating energy for the fungus to keep growing. This system is so effective for the fungus that lichen can create elaborate reproductive and sexual structures to propagate new colonies. It may indeed be true that the photobiont would struggle to exist outside its fungal cage, but a cage is what it is. The fungus controls the means of production.

The photobiont photosynthesises atmospheric carbon di-oxide into sugars, which feed both elements of the lichen. While the fungus might provide a more effective catchment for minerals and other nutrients, most commonly lichenised cyanobacteria grow faster in their unlichenised form. Lichen fungi can generally operate in symbiosis with a number of different photobionts, and the structure and characteristics of the lichen are determined by the species of fungus. The photobionts are interchangeable, disposable. They are alive but they are units of industrial production, the fruits of their labour exported to other purposes than their own.

This entirely inequitable set-up is responsible for some amazing structures, tiny megacities on the surfaces of trees and walls, and the beardlike *Usnea,* the old folk antibiotic that still works, and may be our last line of defence against infections resistant to our own technologies. Whatever the cost to the poor, simple bacteria and algae entrapped in its hegemonic fungoid tentacles, the lichen is a marvel of technological progress. And, like those early Green Men whose heads disgorged tentacles of foliage, everything is subsumed by something eventually, large or small.

A couple of weeks later, on a Friday evening, I sat with M in a graveyard next to the tiny deconsecrated chapel where X puts on gigs. We drank cider before the music started, admiring the array of lichen on the gravestones as children ran about playing zombies.

Inside, a disparate bunch of people sat around contentedly, gazing at the stage, which was decked with lights and ivy, waiting for something to happen. There were children and people in their eighties and everything in-between, black-clad people who once lived in cities and people who parked their white work vans on the street outside, and when the music started they all clapped and cheered as one. Everyone was having a great time; there is no better balm than a roomful of happiness. I can't imagine there was as much of it when the room was a Baptist chapel, although the demographic might have been the same; but there was a sort of holiness about the applause at the end, even if X laughed unholily when someone called him Rev.

It was still light when we left. I ran through my feelings about religion, ranting at M like a half-cut nomadic preacher on the street in a looping rejection of the whole idea of cults and beliefs and whatever it was I was supposed to be doing with the Green Man story, which, the more I read of it, was steeped in boring bits of religion from boring times for which I had never held much interest anyway. M said I should get out more, that being inside was making me grumpy. He was usually right.

It was still warm when I got home, the room was too hot to sleep in, and I couldn't open the window at this time of night because the bats would come in and roost in the airing cupboard, and that was the point where I exercised human privilege regarding home ownership. Rather than face a sleepless night indoors, I went out to the shed and grabbed a sleeping bag and a yoga mat that had seen little yoga, and shoved as much newspaper and card as I could fit under my jumper for kindling a fire, for my hands were full, and crossed the road into the wood.

At the end of it I dropped my things on the ground and sat on one of the logs around the fireplace. The air was heavy, carrying the hot damp smell of summer rain. There was a roof; maybe it would be fine. A gentle gust of wind made the foliage above swoosh gently, and then more loudly, and then the wind stopped and the rain started. I sat and watched the rain for a bit, falling in heavy sheets across the field to the right and up towards the road.

In the wood, the trees caught it all along the edges, and it was only the long green line along the track's centre where it fell, so that all the nettles sprung up there when they could. The ground wasn't wet, considering how much water surrounded it – but then it was an embankment, and might have been built out of loose rock or gravel beneath the topsoil.

It was strange, really, that the trees were so happy there, that you could see a birch, which I'd thought of as a delicate tree prone to sickness and short life-expectancy, thriving so well on it. This birch was huge, like the ones you see in the mountains in Austria, not small and feeble like the ones I knew here. Maybe the dry embankment suited it, for it was one of the tallest trees in the wood, thick-trunked, a long silver pillar to the sky, or what you could see of it in the low wet cloud. All the trees were tall like this, as though in competition to get to the sky first and grab most of it. If they had only grown, or grown up tall, after the railway went, they had grown impressively fast.

The damp in the air was starting to make me cold, and it was time for a fire. There is something absorbing about setting a fire, about getting it right first time in rapidity and shape, making the perfect kindling by degree of paper, card and sticks, and above it bigger sticks and then the proper wood, just enough of it to get properly hot, and not too much to dampen the heat and the air that feeds it. Beneath the lean-to, where the ground was dry, I laid out the fire's constituent parts and set to work with the zeal of an amateur mechanic, concocting the correct quantity and density of substance for each part. The paper into fist-sized balls, the cardboard into strips, the sticks snapped into two-foot lengths and set into tipi formation, and then the larger sticks.

It caught, the flames working their way in and up, the early rush of the kindling going up and dying back, and then the longer fire setting in on the proper wood, old trimmed branches of birch which were rotting slightly but that caught beautifully and burned hot. I watched the concentric layers of fire around the end of a stick, white powdery ash and then a ring of hot pink flame within it, moving its way into the core. The stash of logs at the base of the tall birch depleted.

I unrolled the mat and the sleeping bag at the other end of the lean-to and lay down on my back, watching the light of the flames move gently across the corrugated iron, more lava lamp than disco ball. It would be fun to have a disco ball there. The people who owned the house before were convivial sorts who had lots of parties and probably had lots of parties in the woods, too.

They had been quite attached to the wood, and to keeping the trees in good order. They had turned the old concrete bases of the railway sleepers into a sort of roller-coaster sculpture shaped like an infinity sign. They had a terracotta Green Man in the garden that they took with them to their off-grid cottage in the forest, so it must have been important. Maybe if you lived in an off-grid cottage in the forest you needed the Green Man on your side.

I wondered if they'd left some residual Green Man spirit there. I hoped so. I tried to perceive what this might consist of, gazing at the iron stripes as their ends flickered. Maybe this had been their sacred grove.

Maybe it should be a sacred grove. Maybe it should be a sacred grove, sacred but not sacred, so that it was a place kept with good intention, a place for the trees to be loved and used and for people to be away from houses and the habits and technologies of them. Maybe it should have a disco ball so that the celebrants could celebrate by dancing and avoid the annoyances of purity and ritual. It would need music too, then, and this music would not happen on lutes or bongos – there were honourable technologies out there, and the portable PA system with internal rechargeable batteries and iPod dock was one of them.

I liked this idea. It seemed manageable. It also made it possible to invite people down for the weekend and sell the whole thing to them in a way that felt innocuous and fun, an adventure with purpose. I turned to my side and watched the fire die away, and saw the moon rise behind the birch, and heard rain begin to fall, magnified on the metal roof like a thousand tiny drums, and slept.

The sleep you have outside is weird sleep, in the etymological sense of weird as *wyrd*, the old Anglo-Saxon attunement into the otherworlds, and in the contemporary sense of freaky dreams and confusions. Somehow you are on your guard more, querying each passing noise.

I am not sure what these noises were. The structure of the embankment meant that there were no foxholes or badger setts, presumably because whatever was under the topsoil was hard and sharp rather than earthy. There were rustles and cracks and shuffles, perhaps of tinier creatures, and I noted each one and returned to sleep, which came with ease and which was redisturbed with ease. I was aware of the strange make-up of the ground beneath me, which was not really ground, or hadn't been, and the strangeness of its becoming a wood which looked, on the surface of it, like an ordinary wood, but that had been man-made. If people planted trees were the trees still trees? Did they have the nature of trees without the random befalling of their seed? Wasn't it a bit perverse to celebrate a fake wood, if it were a fake wood? Wasn't it more perverse still to own one, or to believe that you did?

It was a different form of sleep, and when I woke, which was early because it was light, and there was no shortage of birds high up in the trees, I felt more awake than I did in my bed in the house, perhaps because it was less comfortable here, and the decision to slumber carried few advantages. Today would be a day of action. I would build the sacred grove.

I had entertained the unrealistic notion of rejecting all technologies in order to validate the Unabomber conception of anti-institutional anarchy, but it seemed a bit dull and joyless, and also unattainable. If shopping is, as a wise friend once pointed out, our modern-day response to an innate urge to forage, then foraging for un-woodlike things outside of the wood seemed a perfectly reasonable thing to do.

At the recycling centre, set in an un-signposted location at the edge of an industrial estate off the A470 that seemed intended to maintain its secrecy, I found a collection of discarded mirrors. I knew where the disco balls were kept for the festival, and stole one. There was a ball of bright green ribbon set aside for birthday presents in the house, and scraps in other colours too, and a couple of old sheep skulls, and I put the lot in a wheelbarrow and made my way back down the track into the wood.

It was only nine-thirty; I had been up for hours. There was something to be said for the sheer productivity born of slight discomfort, the way that having no recourse to synthetic comforts made you occupy yourself in constructive purpose. A light rain fell. I attached the disco ball to the central beam of the lean-to roof. I hung the larger mirrors in the corners of the lean-to by the fence, and the smaller ones from the nearest trees, which was difficult because their trunks went straight up and the lowest branches were high, and needed a rope thrown over them. I wound the ribbon round the birch.

The rain came down harder. I rekindled the scraps of last night's fire and brought in more wood before it got too wet to do so. I lay down on the mat and dozed, the effort and the strange night's sleep catching up with the day. I lay there for some time, sank beneath the beating rain, and woke only when I heard human voices, louder than the rain, nearby.

In half-sleep I wondered if this was how the Wyrd began for people. It wasn't wyrd, not in its original sense, at least, though. Something was going on over the fence. It sounded like it was happening up high, up the giant climbing frame. There were shrieks and groans, the creak and clank of chains. Perhaps there was something in the way its apparatus resembled torture gear – these sounds were not the cheery hoots of children in a playground but of angry, tired adults in pain. I tried to separate out the threads of voices, to hear some discrete words, but the roar of people, who sounded like they were many, and the noise of the rain, made the sound into a thunderous mass.

Over time, the sound-mass fluctuated in pitch and tone but did not alter significantly in character. It had male and female attributes. I could hear the slosh of mud and the occasional explosive interjection with it, as though someone fell. Then two voices came closer. I sat up.

A man and a woman, in their early forties and both wearing cagoules emblazoned with the name of a well-known retailer and the word CHALLENGE spelled out in an arc along the top, slipped around the fence, talking anxiously to one another. They were immersed in their conversation and continued it, leaning against the fence and peering round it now and again, and did not see me for some time.

It sounded as though the people, who I'll call D and E, worked in the HR department of the large retailer. They had been sent to the Multi-Activity Centre on a team-building weekend. The company was about to renew its Investors in People status and hoped that taking a particular percentage of its employees on a weekend-long event would have a big impact on its Continuing Professional Development score.

The weekend was not going well. The weather had been bad and morale was low. The workforce's expertise lay in the management of customer services provision, from which you might suppose that they sat at desks with headsets on all day and were not outdoor types. Their feedback sessions indicated that they valued effective air-conditioning and the Friday cake round. The night before, on arrival, they had all got drunk and were now hungover and underslept. They had just completed an exercise on the giant climbing frame and were muddy and exhausted. Their hatred of D and E was becoming palpable. D and E had slipped behind the fence, out of sight, to converse on what to do about the situation. It was feeling a bit mutinous.

D and E looked edgy. I greeted them, trying to make up for the weird environment and my dishevelled state with an upbeat front. They looked bemused, and then smiled politely and asked if they were on my land. I said that they were, and that it was fine. They explained their predicament, and their fears of the angry mud-people, and asked if they could sit it out on the safe side of the fence for a bit.

'You could bring them here,' I said.

'That's very kind of you. They'd probably find the decorations on the trees a bit weird. They're not – not into trees. It might freak them out.'

'What is it that would freak them out?'

'The – well, it's not a normal thing to do, is it? The disco ball and the sheep skulls and the ribbons on the trees.'

'Maybe it would make the trees more friendly for them.'

'Yeah. They're just not tree people, I think.'

'But everyone basically likes trees, surely?'

D paused. 'In the right setting, like in a park, on a sunny day, yeah.'

E interjected. 'In a strange environment, in the rain, when they're really tired and pissed off, I think they've probably had enough of all the things that remind them of being here. Like trees. But we like your trees. They're lovely.'

They looked at each other, as if trying to telepathise what to do next. D asked E if they should go back and end the day early. E looked over to the fence.

'Thing is, G's coming down at five, and it won't look great. The idea was to sign off fifteen hours. If we stop them now, they won't come back later. That'll be it. We probably need them to see it through, really.'

'What are we going to do then? I can't face going back there. They'll keep on about how miserable they are.'

'Maybe we should just avoid them. Can we stay here for a bit until they've finished the Challenge?'

'I've got my performance review on Friday. I'm just thinking that if G gets bad feedback this weekend it's not going to be good for it, that's all.'

'Is being there going to help?'

'No. Yeah, you're right, it won't. And actually, if they hated it, G might think it was more worth doing than if they didn't.'

I'd lost the thread a bit now. 'Can I just clarify something here? Are you worried about your boss coming down and what you'll have to say if everybody is either really angry or disappears early?'

'Yes.'

'Can I tell you a little about what I'm doing here?' I wondered how it felt to be a Jehovah's Witness doorknocking for the first time.

'Yes, sure.'

'This place, here, I'm turning it into a sacred grove. Do you know anything about sacred groves?'

D looked over the fence at the giant climbing frame. 'No.'

'Once upon a time, before we were a Christian country, ancient Britons worshipped trees. They worshipped loads of things, actually, but one part of that was tree-worship, because they were so dependent on trees for shelter and on plants more generally for food.'

'Are you a druid?' asked E.

'The druids did worship trees. Well – maybe. I don't actually know. But I am not a druid. I am advocating, or rather re-advocating, a cult of the Green Man, who, these days at least, is a composite figure of tree-worship, fertility ritual and anarchism.'

They didn't say anything. E nodded. I had a sense that silence would be problematic, and that it must be filled with words.

'Basically, I think we'd be better off if we acknowledged that the trees are conscious too, and so is all life, and so are all things. So that we stop thinking of humans as being better than everything else. And also that it would be better for us to exist in a sense of being connected with all other life, and that it would be better for us not to be oppressed into human institutions so that our inner life and autonomy is sapped away from us. What would be great is if you could bring your people over here to help me bless this birch tree. All they'd have to do is dance. No chanting, nothing like that. What do you reckon?'

D shook his head and half-laughed in a way that tipped towards hostility.

'In terms of personal development, I think it could be really significant for them. They'd be able to develop their capacity for intuition and communicating in non-usual ways. There are studies indicating the beneficial qualities to mental health and perceived well-being that come of contact with nature. I'd be happy to explain it to your boss if you like. He might really go for it.'

D looked at E. She acquiesced to his look, and they turned away.

'We should probably just go and deal with the situation

over there, actually. Thank you for your time, though, it was really interesting meeting you.'

They edged round the fence back to the giant climbing frame and the angry muddy hungover workers who dangled from it and their giant all-subsuming company with its technological entrapment of the human spirit in which, I now realised, they were more complicit than most.

'You are trapped in materialism. You are trapped in late capitalism. You are trapped in industrial society. You are slaves. You are worse than slaves – you are complicit in the slavery of the spirit.'

I'd like to say that I cried this fiercely across the fence as they retreated, but in truth I said it quietly, leaning my hand supportively on the birch, as a lorry rumbled faintly past. I liked my sacred grove, though. Even in the rain, the sacred grove looked good.

SIX

Fairy Tales and Witches

There is no shortage of literary movements inspired by the philosophies of their time. By contrast, philosophical movements with a literary heritage are rare.

Goethe's forays into German hills and forests soon escaped the literary confines of the late eighteenth century into a wider intellectual domain. Here was the vastness of the natural world, a world in which the human sphere felt small rather than dominant, a world driven by its own pulsating will.

Central to the Romantic idea was a rush of awe, the speechlessness at a glimpse of a world that was unsayable in words. Goethe was explicit about the metaphysical endpoint of it, an out-and-proud pantheist, for whom God was Nature and Nature, God. Art may not articulate an idea with the mapped-out veneer of what we call philosophy, but it can work as a call to arms. And perhaps you could call Goethe a philosopher anyway, for he described, in letters at the end of his life, that time when the limits of reality are most starkly revealed, a detailed account of the driving desires of matter.

A living, conscious Nature, a Spinozist God-or-Nature, caught the minds of Goethe's contemporaries. He exchanged letters with his friends Herder and Haeckel, and threads of their ideas can be seen interwoven into Schelling's *Naturphilosophie*, and again into Schopenhauer's *Will in Nature*, and again, more radically still, in Nietzsche's *Will to*

Power. It was a way of thinking that dominated not only nineteenth-century Germany but England too, a time of German cultural and intellectual import. Although Hegel's wake of absolute idealism, which shaped much Victorian thought, was less explicitly concerned with the will of Nature, it too rested on the assumption of a great immanent being that lay beneath the surface of experience, to be glimpsed, godlike, at rare and awe-inspiring moments.

It wasn't just Goethe responsible for all of this, of course; there was a whole public mood involved. The bits of it that we remember now are the most moving or noisy: the poetry and *Bildungsromane* of Schiller and Goethe; the folk-loric thunder of Wagner; Caspar David Friedrich's *Wanderer* atop misty forested hills. And the old tales of those hills and forests, the ones that still persisted in far-flung valleys, were ripe for collection again, harvested by the Brothers Grimm, so that a sense of an ancient Germanic conscious-ness, of a human sphere bounded by trees and the life within them, was intertwined with the grand metaphysical vista of an underlying God or Nature.

On the way to the Black Forest, where I sought this elusive soul of fairy tales and transcendental Romanticism, there was a sign that, in the spirit of magical thinking, seemed to be a Sign, for it was both neon and portentous. The queue in the ticket hall at King's Cross was inert. Non-Londoners, disgorged from long trains, stood waiting, staring, while the ones at the front swiped their hands across screens whose meaning evaded them. I needed to get to Heathrow, and might have done so sooner if I'd switched queues, but my attention had wavered.

BLACK FOREST, it glowed pinkly, and I would have taken it as fate or a promise of something, but it was advertising cupcakes, and I had already been informed by my mother that I would find little more than cake there. Perhaps a little more than cake: cake, and people who consumed too much of it on rest cures and cuckoo clocks and casinos – those sorts of things. Coach-tour things for coach-tour people, and certainly, she said with the concrete certainty that only a German can muster, no pagans.

I was relaxed about these assertions. I had read the lengthy tracts on a website called *The Great Learning* about the many Green Men of Germany, more even than in England, proof of some deeply rooted, firmly wrought connection that would lead me into a greater understanding, one that would transcend the illusion of national boundaries. It had been written in enthusiastically formatted German by a Dutchman who identified himself simultaneously as Green Man and Laughing Buddha, evidently seeing in them two complementary sides of the same archetypal coin.

I had hoped to find him, but he was on a worldwide healing trip with his psychic therapist wife, so I made do with his list of German Green Men, organised regionally. This list was extensive. It was significantly longer than the list of Green Men on the British part of the website, where, I noted approvingly, much attention had been paid to Kilpeck, which he regarded as an undoubtedly pagan site with magical qualities. The strange thing was that there was no modern-day folk myth affiliated with the Green Man in Germany as there is here.

Maybe that wasn't how German folk myth worked, though. I was looking for the dark forests of the Grimm fairy tales, thick with possibility and danger. As the plane descended, it passed the edge of a thick forest that stretched away into cloud, and I was tantalised, for then the cloud took us, and the Germany beneath it was neither romantic nor forested.

It was a place that I had been through before as an adolescent – all beige pointy houses, circumspect and oppressively orderly – on the way to a summer-long linguistic incarceration that consisted of 70 thirteen- and fourteen-year-olds of various nationalities being locked up in a castle on the edge of the forest to learn German.

I learned little German, and much about the cultural inferiority of the Anglo-Saxon world, stuck in a room with the Francophones and able only to look on in awed mute silence as they smoked out of the window, talked about blowjobs and, on one occasion, pinned down their Italian ally, who had the flu, and inserted a suppository between her impossibly golden buttocks in a sisterly manner. The crude Darwinian game of high-school politics revealed certain inescapable ethnic superiorities. The French were the coolest, the Italians the hottest. Everyone loved the Spanish and the Mexicans, who were warm and nice. Being an Anglo was rubbish: we were pallid, unsexy and culturally deficient, but at least we weren't German.

Coming back there now, treading the path out of the airport and onto the train, I was seeking to prove, somehow, that we were German, that we were all German, that getting to the bottom of the German mythical relationship with the forest would reveal English truths. Our language is corrupted Low German, our ethnicity as German as not, and our royal family almost entirely German. I anticipated friendly strangers telling me folk tales in sun-dappled forests that had crossed the sea into Kentish or Mercian analogues, hidden phalanxes of Green Man geeks, overly earnest aspiring druids: the same thing in a different accent.

The woman opposite me on the train looked cross when I sat down and tutted as people got on and off it, as though this act of disorder contradicted the true purpose of the train, which was as a place of stillness. Sheets of rain fell as I left Stuttgart on the next train, the fast train, which reached a speed of two hundred and ninety kilometres per hour. Perhaps the old clichés about charmlessness and engineering still held true. I wasn't too concerned either way: Germany was full of forests and there had to be something to find inside them.

And Germany really was full of forests: a third of the country's surface is covered by them. I was going to the Black Forest because it was the famous one, the iconic one, and it was also vastly larger than any forest in England, stretching eighty miles from north to south, and twenty miles across. I stayed at its edge, up above a town falling away into the valley and the sound of crickets and birds and water from earlier storms beckoning uphill. I wove among tall beeches, wet-footed, unsure exactly where I was apart from uphill, past a clearing with a hornbeam heavy with sunlit dewy keys, and something that ran away as I approached.

As the light faded, I made my way back down. There would be plenty more of this: I caught a glimpse of the other forested hills, stretching interchangeably in ever-diminishing shades of pastel green to the horizon. I would go deep into the forest, away from all human life, only occasionally reminded of the towns and villages nestled in the valleys with handsome churches painted the colour of egg yolk, and perhaps a castle on a rocky outcrop.

I got up at dawn and set off into the forest, admiring its peace, for nothing soaks up the sound of human things like a thick bank of trees. I made rapid progress from hut to hut to designated panorama point. The paths were broad and maintained by the steady beat of human footfall. It did not seem wise to go off-piste onto these hillsides, which were steep, and although the sun dappled the forest floor early in the day when it reached beneath the canopy, which was high, it did not throw light onto anything that drew me in. There were only tall pines, with wildflowers at their edge, and I could not find a way back to the oaks and beeches of the night before, so I kept on walking, through the sun, past the people and their sticks and boots and children.

It was no Grimm fairy tale, for fairy tales have jeopardy and here was none. It was too safe and sanitised for that. I would have needed bears and wolves, and definitely witches, and the only animals in this forest were the many stolid humans in walking gear that the gravel track, which was practically a road, did not necessitate. Perhaps that is not entirely true – I spotted the odd hide in the trees, which, from what my mother told me when we walked through forests such as these in childhood holidays, were used for hunting rather than birdwatching. There may have been some deer out there, but if there were they kept themselves well hidden. If there was danger in the forest it was more likely to be wearing lederhosen than fur, although even lederhosen were lacking. Today's woodsmen and women were uniformly beige and grey, breathable and waterproofed. As the day drew on my hopes subsided. I would have been happy with a stag, a fox, a felt hat – anything, really. I needed to move on.

The forest waned into the upper reaches of Baden-Baden. The average age of its visitors was indicated by the discreet signs advertising *Klinikum* after *Klinikum* on the way down the hill, which eventually segued into cosmetic surgeons' offices and then a shopping avenue whose sedate luxury goods signified the presence of the international gerontocracy: Hermes scarves and sensible shoes, made in Italy.

England had her thing for spa towns, which sprung up around the time that cities got big, and the water in them bad. The spa waters were imbued with magical powers in urban myth, but in reality their powers stemmed more from not holding the same pathogenic load as wells and rivers shared with the urban poor. Taking the waters soon became a displacement activity for the wealthy, and while Tunbridge Wells and Bath and all those Spa-suffixed places are now just towns, they retain a slight grandiosity. The Germans never really gave up on this whole exercise. Until quite recently companies were expected to budget for rest cures, the *Kur*, for their workforce, which involved going to a spa town *Pension* for a week and sitting in tepid waters, being vigorously massaged and eating lots of cake. Even if its health benefits were not straightforwardly quantifiable, the *Kur* was good for labour relations. The *Kur*-town needed waters and proximity to nature, as though this would infuse life force by osmosis, a not entirely crazy thing to think if you were in Romantic mode. Beyond this, all that the recipient need do was sit there.

I suppose Baden-Baden was like any other genteel German spa town would be when subjected to steroidal quantities of international money: all expensively renovated imperial architecture and luxury goods stores. Winding to and fro between these was a vehicle like the covered children's trains you get in parks that are not really trains for the people who were too old and insensible to walk. The

Kurgarten's name implied that there was, somewhere, a park, although all that you could see was a shopping arcade with some small trees in it. It had a sign at its entrance depicting people doing things that you might do for enjoyment in a garden or a park, like sitting down, playing ball games and walking a dog – with big red crosses over them. Picking flowers, listening to music and having a picnic were also forbidden – everything, it seemed, other than shopping. The bottom of the sign reassured its citizens that they were being watched for their own safety and convenience.

Up above somewhere was the scattergun noise of a helicopter, possibly in comforting observational capacity, possibly carrying octogenarian steel magnates to hookers in the casino. Three Chinese tourists wearing face masks walked down a pedestrianised cobbled street past Louis Vuitton. They needn't have bothered – the place was as sterile as if it had been boiled and frozen a million times. I went to the station, ordered an abominable coffee, watched it cool, and got on a series of very fast trains to Trier.

Kathleen Basford's authoritative guide to the Green Man states that Trier Cathedral was once adorned with the earliest foliate heads in Europe, and I strode, mapless and somewhat lost, through the hot, pretty town in the hope of understanding more of how they might have turned into the Green Men of English churches. I also had a bit of a family connection with the place: my maternal grandfather's family were Trier folk, and one of his ancestors had baptised the town's most famous son, Karl Marx, who was a cousin.

I caught sight of a sign with Marx on it while looking for my hotel, and saw as I drew closer to it that it was for Marx-Mode, a shop selling blousy floral clothes for middle-aged women. I wondered whether its proprietor was another

Trier Marx or if it was a bit of intentionally perverse branding. There was a Karl Marx Strasse too, which honoured its namesake by being the red light zone, with strip joints along one side and sex shops along the other. All West German cities have their smart Willy Brandt Platz commemorating the postwar economic miracle, and I wondered fleetingly what I'd find if I tracked down every Marx-related street name in them.

Apart from the shops and strip joints, every other building in Trier seemed to be some Catholic organisation or other. The German Liturgical Institute, the Catholic Women's Guild, the Union of Catholic Youth, comprising another twelve Catholic sub-organisations – it was like a bigger Vatican. The old town, which was pretty and full of coloured stucco buildings laden with Catholic kitsch – Jesus, Mary and an embarrassment of cherubs dangling from their sides – was teeming with tourists, who may have been enthusiasts for late antiquity, but were more likely engaged in unchallenging pilgrimage.

I drank coffee in an ice-cream parlour called Christi's by the cathedral; across the square was a blingy jewellery shop called Christ, which I imagine might have elicited a similar response from its namesake to that which the blouses and dildos would from Marx. The sense that Trier was essentially a Catholic theme park was further substantiated when a little red-and-gold train emblazoned with Römer-Express along its side – exactly the same as the one in Baden-Baden except for its more patriotic colourway – materialised before me and slipped away under a baroque archway decorated with a picturesque dying Jesus.

Trier sang its heritage loudly. The Rheinisches Landesmuseum had a huge Ozymandian foot in front of it, the

169

remains of a statue of the emperor Constantine, after whom much of the city is named. I stayed at the Hotel Constantin, which was full of well-behaved religious folk and therefore quiet, although confusingly situated at the end of Karl Marx Strasse, so that to walk to town was to run the kerb-crawl gauntlet, a moment of rare entertainment on a hot day. There were various Constantin-prefixed cafes and streets, and bits of memorabilia in museum shops.

Constantine oversaw the Edict of Milan, which put into law the favourable treatment of Christians, ending waves of persecution that lasted for three hundred years, and that ebbed and flowed with the shifts and rifts of the powers of the time. The process by which Christianity became the dominant religion of the Empire is known as the Constantinian Shift, although Constantine presided over relatively little of it, for it took up most of the fourth century, and if you had to choose its key player, in terms of altering the political status of Catholic Christianity over the old religions, it would probably be St Ambrose.

Born into a Roman Catholic family in Trier in the early fourth century, Ambrose, one of the less loveable of the saints, is pictured in a fresco at San Giuseppe alla Lungara in Rome with a bible and a whip. A gifted orator from his youth, Ambrose started out with a liberal interpretation of Catholicism, allying himself with the rival Arian sect, before taking the bishopric of Milan and dedicating much of his life to establishing a Catholic orthodoxy, which excluded Arianism. Wiping out the Arians was only a partial success, though, and in the meantime there were Jews and pagans who needed to be dealt with too.

Roman paganism, which was polytheistic and able to tolerate the presence of other faiths, did not die out as soon as the singular Christian Truth grew from one of many cranky mystery religions to something that respectable Romans could believe in. We are somehow sold the story that once the Bible got out, that was that; there could be no response to it other than rapid and consistent wholesale conversion to the Book, but Roman culture was cosmopolitan in character, and all manner of odd beliefs rubbed alongside each other without too much trouble for centuries. The many varieties of Roman paganism were still being practised, and the Jews still living in relative peace, when Ambrose determined to put a stop to it all.

When a gang of Christian zealots, led by the local bishop, attacked and burned the synagogue at Callinicum in Mesopotamia, the Eastern emperor Theodosius decreed that it must be rebuilt at the bishop's expense. Ambrose wrote a sternly worded letter informing Theodosius that the issue was a matter of the Glory of God and that to condone the blasphemy of Christ by building a temple to it was an unconscionable matter. It is one of those moments where you can't help but wish that the Christians had been thrown to the lions sooner and more efficiently: just decades earlier, Ambrose's institutional forefathers were consolidating their religion's position by invoking religious tolerance, and now that it was safe they were out to obliterate any deviation from it.

Not content with his increasingly muscular Christianity having taken its place as the religion of the Emperor and Empire, Ambrose fought to remove all reminders of prior beliefs. Of these, the most significant was the Altar of Victory at Rome, a statue erected by Augustus after the battle of Actium, and a symbol of the old Empire and old polytheistic pagan religion.

Although occasional sacrifices of incense were burned there, the site was not of particular religious significance in itself. The issue was its location in front of the Senate House, and that senators, before entering, took their oath there. The Christian senators didn't like this: to do so was idolatry. The altar was taken down.

The prefect Symmachus, an old-guard pagan whose image can be seen in the British Museum, lifted up to the Sun-god by angelic genii against a background of zodiac signs, wrote to the emperor Gratian requesting the reinstatement of the Altar in the wake of a catastrophic famine, and as an act of religious tolerance and pluralism:

> We ask, then, for peace for the gods of our fathers and of our country. It is just that all worship should be considered as one. We look on the same stars, the sky is common, the same world surrounds us. What difference does it make by what pains each seeks the truth? We cannot attain to so great a secret by one road; but this discussion is rather for persons at ease, we offer now prayers, not conflict.

This plea for many paths to the same sky marked the end of Rome's pagan era. Ambrose, in a technically brilliant piece of rhetoric, refuted Symmachus' account of the famine as factless superstition, and attacked the vested interests and excessive luxuries of the old Empire. He turned Symmachus' invocation of nature against him, speaking poetically of the bounties of the moon and overflowing harvests, undermining the notion that the pagans owned the image of the Earth.

Accompanying his request for the altar, Symmachus urged that the Vestal Virgins, who cultivated the sacred fire to

Vesta, goddess of the hearth, needed a new set of purple robes and an increase in their retinue budget. Ambrose, an ascetic, was in a strong position to mock the Virgins' urgent need of finery, and did so, arguing that their virginity should not need material glorification when chastity and austerity were virtues that everyone should live by anyway.

It is a moment of institutional shift, of the Christian Church moving from a principled cult for the poor towards the power and wealth that dominated Europe for the next two thousand years. Ambrose aligned his virtues, and by extension their opposing vices, so that sexual incontinence was linked to obscene surfeits of wealth, making the personal political in a new morality that left the likes of Symmachus mystified and concerned for the health of a society forced into public chastity.

And the Roman polytheistic system had hardly been a fair or ethical place, at least by Judaeo-Christian standards. The old religions were embedded in feudal and economic hierarchies, and were complicit in maintaining them. The practice of slavery, and beyond that the vast disparity of wealth, had helped steel the many have-nots against any moral claims by the old order.

The Altar of Victory is one small episode of the changing of these orders, one in which moral high ground is taken, occupied and ceded. British neo-pagans today may pride themselves on the non-hierarchical quality of their belief, on its emphasis on the individual relationship with the Earth and cosmos, but you only need to look at pagan Rome, or the extent to which the Hindu caste system remains embedded in contemporary India, to see how polytheisms can fall prey to corruption and power like any other cemented belief-system.

And yet, for all that, Ambrose scares me more than Symmachus. It is the absolutism of his faith, the sense that in Christ a finite religious instruction, a word to end all words, is given. His call to orthodoxy set out a new dogma and a new set of powerful institutions of the same exacting character as those that Christ sought to overturn among the Jews. Ambrose's response to Symmachus' plea for pluralism is a thunderous account of a single, fixed truth, against which any other is a heresy:

By one road, says he, one cannot attain to so great a secret. What you know not, that we know by the voice of God. And what you seek by fancies, we have found out from the very Wisdom and Truth of God. Your ways, therefore, do not agree with ours.

Ambrose took great care to praise Gratian's piety, and to drop in ominous rhetorical questions about what might happen if too many Christian senators and bishops became displeased. Gratian took his advice. By the end of the fourth century, Ambrose had both Gratian and Theodosius entirely under his thumb, forcing Theodosius into penance for earlier massacres and outlawing all pagan practices.

Trier, like its first fundamentalist, is an artefact of the end of pagan Rome and the birth of Roman Catholicism as we know it. By the Middle Ages, the Archbishopric of Trier was one of the most powerful in the Holy Roman Empire. The Green Man motif, which is everywhere in the city once you know to look for it, is a consistent image throughout, from the height of imperial Roman rule through the Dark and Middle Ages to the baroque era. Its use straddles pagan and Christian, public and private, religious and civic spheres.

In the tombstone gallery of the Rheinisches Landesmuseum, all marble and expensive calm, was a first-century Roman tombstone with the Green Man at its centre. His position echoed that of Triton in many of the nautically themed tombs, as though one's spirit is consumed either by forest or sea, earth or water, after death. I had read something about the Green Man as Sylvanus, the Roman forest-god, and saw another tombstone with Pan, his analogue, beside Jupiter and some kind of big cat. There was a second-century sandstone head of Attis, the ancient fertility god of the Near East who died and was reborn at the vernal equinox: the argument in *The Golden Bough* that all these figures are slightly varied manifestations of a single mythic archetype made good sense here.

The same images were in the medieval cloister of the cathedral, as small stone capitals bearing foliate heads of varying mood: some have a sylvan peace about them, and some take on a more grotesque quality. Although the cathedral inside was teeming with hot tourists and worshippers lighting expensive, pious candles, the cloister was cool and empty, symmetrical and light, with a small Green Man peering down every couple of metres from the roof, as though mystified by its emptiness.

In the museum archive are casts of earlier Green Men that adorned the cathedral itself in the sixth century – the image never went away. The earlier foliate heads – the faces of Sylvanus, Pan and Attis – are generally jollier, more beneficent in character; the later medieval versions either comic-grotesque or monstrous.

Maybe the Catholic Church, in its early catholic mode, in an analogue of Ambrose's earliest and more conciliatory times, adopted the sylvan image for its popularity and attractiveness, before its developing dogmatic rigidity demanded that the image be altered into less appealing and more admonitory forms. That was what seemed to happen in England too, the earliest images either abstract or friendly, with the tongue-tied gruesome versions coming later.

Trier was the best indication yet that the image of the Green Man was, just as all the old hippies had said in their tone of paternal exasperation, a kind of pagan archetype that the Church, and the tree-dependent peasants that it served, never quite managed to shake. The consistency of its appearance in one place over the centuries, without significant pause, but with a gradual darkening of the mood away from jollity to demonic mischief and then misery, marks time alongside the growing power of the Church and its sedimenting layers of dogma.

And all of Trier's Green Men were radically nicer to be near than the more modern decorative stonework in Trier Cathedral. Its exterior was a fortress-like wall of high brick, somewhat like London's Victorian prisons, and its inside breathtakingly ugly. Huge carved tableaux, ten metres or so high and nearly as wide, hung from the towering exposed walls, featuring complex seething huddles of saints and sinners carved from marble in weird colours, orange and purple and green, resembling cathedrals in their complexity. They seemed to have been tacked on at the random whim of whoever commissioned them, so that the basic symmetry of the space was knocked out by their bulk.

I have always held that the most effective psychogeographic test is whether something would make a child laugh or cry, and I was pretty confident that this would be the stuff of nightmares, like the purple and black organ that hung from halfway up the wall, somehow resembling more a weapon of mass destruction than anything musical in character. There was more, though, far more than I could bring myself to look at, and the morning service was about to start. It was time to go.

I drank coffee in the town square and tried to make sense of the place. Someone designed those images. Someone, perhaps many people, spent much of their working lives carving them. I could only imagine the shade of their internal life, and assume that it was a dark place, bedevilled with demons straight out of Hieronymus Bosch. What if we judged the souls of religious people by the images their religion created? What if we judged religion by the aesthetic quality it imposes on its adherents? I was not sure that you could quantify the ugliness and beauty conferred by the Christian Church – it has generated plenty of each in its time. If I were to choose between going back in time, though, between one millennium or two, I'd choose imperial Rome any day, for all its dangers and intrigues. At least there was some dynamism, some learning and some laughter, and the voices and viewpoints of many people and their worlds. The darkness of early Catholicism's religious thought-police made that part of our past seem as appealing as rural Afghanistan did now.

I left Trier on a train that went through thick forest, nothing to see but trees and rivers, broken only by tiny one-horse towns. I considered leaving this reverie of passing beeches and chocolate-box houses to get off at Koblenz and revisit Maria Laach, which I remembered from shady lakeside walks as a child. Maria Laach is an ancient abbey, still going, whose points of interest for my current purpose were some Green Men and historical Nazi sympathies. I remembered it like I remembered running around the gardens of stately homes as a child, uncritical and slightly bored, and the indifference somehow prevailed. The view from the window was too pretty and too comfortable.

It was perfect, picture-book country, sleepy pastel houses and clear water, and even the thunderstorm held off until we got to the outskirts of Cologne, where a dramatic sheet of rain attacked the side of the carriage and great purple bolts of lightning streaked to the ground, as if to declare their displeasure at the inferior landscape. I changed trains at Cologne, and again at Hagen, where the interior of the station hall was falling away from the ceiling and armed police patrolled the platforms to keep the drunks and crazies out.

Past forests and rivers and steelworks, and a face-off between the ticket inspector and the only non-white person on the train, I waited for a fictional bus and then a taxi in a town that looked as though it had been nuked. It did not make me hopeful for Bilstein, and nor did my reason for visiting, which was that one of my ancestors had been burned there as a witch.

But as the taxi took me up a steep hill above the little black-and-white town, and as we rose above the low cloud in the valley and I realised that the youth hostel I was staying in was actually a medieval castle built upon a high rock, the place looked somewhat better. The castle hung from the hillside, jutting out across the sleepy town below, where the mist from the rain was starting to lift, and the evening sun hit the castle wall and lit the beech forest behind it. Excess water fell in heavy drops from the trees and lit the path brightly. Someone had put a little statue of a frog prince in the well, and children ran around, delighted. I found my room, which looked out across the valley, and from where I could have done all sorts of damage with a cauldron full of pitch, and went for a walk in the wood before the light went.

A frog leapt in front of me on the path. It did not flinch or jump away when I bent low to get a better look, and I wondered if it was a tame frog, given to teasing people chasing witches in these parts. I didn't kiss it, or use it for a spell; nor did I make a concoction from the vast orange slugs that were everywhere, like a curse or biblical plague. All I did was walk, and watch the hares that emerged in the clearing, shaking the water from the long grass, and the mist ascending further until it tickled the tops of the forested hills, which turned pink as the sun dipped behind them.

I didn't expect a fairyland here. Maybe the element of darkness made it, the knowledge that this idyll sat upon acts of great cruelty, that you don't get castles without fighting for them. My ancestor – her name is not known – was one of several women from the village tried as witches at the end of the sixteenth century. It was a time when the Holy Roman Empire was starting to fall into disarray leaving rivalrous prince-bishops, who held absolute political and religious power over their diocese, struggling for order at a time when warfare and bad harvests had left the peasants hungry and restless.

I had, at first, thought that the witch-burning had happened in the Rhineland, which is where my family is mostly from and where witches were burned in pogroms in their tens of thousands, so that in many villages no women over forty remained alive, but it was a practice common throughout Germany for the duration of the Holy Roman Empire. Some of the witch-hunt stories have the effect of making Germany's more famous genocide look moderate, for their scale of annihilation of communities and the unrelenting waves of persecution over centuries.

My intention is not to diminish the more recent German

holocaust. My Jewish great-grandmother was killed by the Nazis in transit between concentration camps, and my grandmother married into a brave Catholic family, worked quietly in admin for the Luftwaffe, kept her head down, and just about survived. It is a family tree that seems impressively grim to Brits, but it is not particularly unusual if you delve back far enough into German history. Maybe my mother's ancestors did badly out of German bloodlust; maybe, in existing, they had a lucky ride.

I did wonder if my ancestor got accused of witchcraft for being a Jew, making the perhaps understandable error of eliding the two misfortunes, but there was no reason to think that this would have anything to do with it, and she probably would have simply had her assets seized or been run out of town if that had been the case: the prince-bishops had a talent for those sorts of community endeavours.

I also wondered, somewhat wishfully, if she had been a witch, hoping that there lurked within the bloodline some hitherto buried gift that would return to me, magically, when I came to find it. My aunt, who teaches history in Bavaria, set me straight on that. She was simply a middle-aged woman: the witch-hunters' classificatory standards were not exacting.

The witch-hunters worked from the *Malleus Maleficarum*, an extraordinary document written by Heinrich Kramer, a German Catholic priest. I once had a vocal men's-rights activist for a neighbour, a situation that I cannot recommend for various reasons, although at least he didn't get round to posting me roadkill like he did with someone he dated around that time, and from whom he now has a restraining order. In his more lucid moments, though, you could have a colourful conversation with the guy, and I can imagine him one day sharing a pint or three with Kramer in the great old man pub in the sky, agreeing heartily on matters such as the undoubted causalities of witch-related impotence, and the scandalous phenomenon of stolen penises stashed away in birds' nests, where they bounce about pecking at oats and waiting to return to their masters. I will desist from psycho-analysis here.

Kramer had a passion for witch-hunting, and got sacked from the priesthood for setting himself up as a witch-hunter and attempting prosecution in Innsbruck. He did not let this setback deter him from his quest and wrote the *Malleus Maleficarum* to share his expertise with the world in the absence of a working practice. Although the Church distanced itself from the book within a few years of its publication in the late fifteen century, it soon gained popularity and proved the key authoritative text in the spate of witch-hunts that tore across Germany like firestorms in the sixteenth century.

The people were getting angry, and the anger needed a channel, an enemy. There needed to be a reason for poverty and hunger, and it needed to be a better reason than a greedy and incompetent ruling class. An enemy was needed: one hiding in plain sight, one that seemed to be entirely normal but that harboured malign supernatural powers, one that endangered prince and serf alike, and united them in its menace. Witchcraft was a threat that, additionally, had the virtue of consolidating social and religious orthodoxy: deviate too far from normal behaviour, and anyone might be accused of it.

Witches were the original folk devils, a term coined by British sociologists in the seventies and eighties to describe other behavioural heretics, but with explicit reference to the way in which the ruling institutions of medieval Europe used religious scapegoating to create mass moral panics that shifted public attention away from other, more structural reasons to be angry. It was a situation that worked for the princes, that worked for the Church, and that worked for the angry – at least until the point where the witch-hunter himself got out of control.

In Bilstein, the town bailiff, Kaspar von Furstenberg, got into witch-hunting after the death of his wife, which was blamed on the malign influence of her friend, the wife of a judge. Being rich or powerful – or rather being married to someone rich or powerful – seemed, if anything, to be more rather than less likely to invoke accusations of witch-craft. Perhaps to accuse someone of witchcraft was to accuse her of possessing some individual power that had not been entirely suppressed by her marriage, the Church or the State – it was a heresy in a broader sense than undermining the Bible with newt eyes.

If witches were able to ruin a harvest or impose illness, there must have been some residual belief in their powers to promote fertility and health. You either have power or you don't. It seemed as though the big institutional powers wanted to demonise what was left of the small powers, the small people to whom people came when they needed to get something done.

Heresy needs oppression. A heresy can exist only if there is an institution proscribing it; otherwise it is merely a thought, a behaviour. No doubt there were still some folk myths about things you needed to do to maintain a good harvest that we might call pagan, but these were retained in communal superstitions that were not deemed to be heretic-al, because they did not compete with the absolute power of the Church and its prince-bishops over the people.

The process of the absolute power of the Church that began with Ambrose and his ever-tightening grip on the religious lives of the people, with its proscription first of symbols of other beliefs and then of the practice of them, found a logical conclusion in the witch-trials. If you take recourse to your interpretation of your single truth, and see anything that does not align to it as a blasphemy – a heresy – there are no limits to the violence you can justify. And so the witch-hunts ate up all the women who were no longer useful for breeding, and ate up the rest of society in suspicion and anger, and they kept on coming in waves for several generations after my ancestor, whatever she was called, met her end.

Many of the Westphalian witch-trials took place at Arnsberg, the ancient judicial capital of the province, in a stone circle that, but for prior knowledge of its history, might hold the romance of a miniature Avebury or Stonehenge. It sits in a hollow edged with trees, a ring of neat square rocks with what looks like an altar at its centre. This was the Judge's Table, where the judge would hear out the cases, sword in hand. If you recreated it in England everyone would leap to the assumption that it was a druidic religious site.

It offers an interesting counter-story for the functions of some of our old, and structurally similar, stone circles. In some sense, all justice was and is divine in character anyway, for it always entails recourse to some external legitimating morality, whatever it may be called. The medieval Catholic church used the Judge's Table as an expedient slaughter-slab, just as we imagine bearded druids sacrificing virgins at their altars. What if the German historians were being bluntly honest about the function of their stone circles, in that very German way, while we distanced ours from their more banal and brutal function?

I left Arnsberg and attempted to leave Westphalia, which took hours because it is so big, and because the German trains were no longer running on time. The Germany I remembered as a child, all slick homogeneity and safeness, had turned into a more normal and disorderly place. The police were still there when I changed trains at Hagen again, and the train was running late. There was nothing much to see from the window, just flatness and heavy industry, and I dozed until Hanover. The ground only rose hours later, at the edge of the Harz where the weather altered too, becoming damp with mist.

The Harz is a mountain range in the exact middle of Germany, thickly forested and notoriously cold and wet. The average annual temperature is about five degrees Celsius, and this is not because the mountains are very high – they are moderate, Welsh-sized mountains – but from a combination of the extreme winter cold of the Central European plateau, which stretches from here, in middle Germany, all the way to the Urals, which are the next elevation along, and the orographic lift effect, which cools the dampness in the air as it forces it up over the hills, and creates a year-round island of cloud and fog. This fogginess is probably responsible for the big dark shadowy figures that seemed to dance atop the mountains at dusk and dawn and, the villagers therefore reckoned, all night inbetween, figures whose tenebrous qualities must stem from some occult source. When the sun rose and fell through the mist on the clearing at the top, just above the treeline, it extended any human figure into these long and ghastly silhouettes, and the place soon earned its mystic reputation as the place where Faust's witches partied.

I was meeting up with W, a friend from Berlin who professed astonishment at how cold it was. A hundred miles away, when he left two hours ago, it was thirty-six degrees. On the railway platform at Wernigerode, rain splashed down the gap between roof and train, and people pulled waterproofs out of their bags. We ran across to the steam railway, which operates on old narrow-gauge lines across the Harz, and found it empty of people, so that as it chugged away out of town, past pretty *Mitteleuropäisch* houses and into the misty woods, it felt like a ghost train, and we hung across the damp cage behind the engine catching tiny glowing orange flecks of ash, watching trees intersect trees as they passed.

We were headed to Schierke, a village at the foot of the Brocken, which is the highest mountain in the Harz and considered to have magical qualities in German folklore. As well as the witches who notoriously congregated there, the vast boulders strewn across it were hiding places for demons and other eerie creatures. As a nod to the horror-movie part of Faust set there, in the empty train carriage were posters advertising *Faust I & II: The Rock Opera*, with a steam-train ride thrown into the ticket price, a white face with doomy panda eyes leering out, Mephistopheles via Black Sabbath.

At Schierke, we got out and made our way down through the forest into the village. The forest floor was alive with water, which rang out and trickled and babbled in many voices with invisible springs rising here and there beneath rocks and strange holes in the path. The rocks were vast and everywhere. Even in late July, it was an emerald carpet of moss, and when we reached for sticks to steady ourselves they crumbled damply in our hands. It looked promising. We walked through the village, still as death on a Friday night in high season, shrouded in cloud, past hotels and pubs and a shop selling witch merchandise.

The witches were ancient, haglike, astride rickety broomsticks, with giant hook noses drawn with no concession to subtlety. In England, the proprietors would have been accosted by upset pagans years ago; the Brocken would have been appropriated by Wiccans and druids, and you would have been able to buy amethysts and dreamcatchers and maps of ley lines there. The gift shop here was all about biblical good and evil, Halloween hate-figures and an invocation of Faust as distant from Goethe's pantheistic awe as a rock musical.

We walked past the information stand, with the town symbol of a black ibex skull carved along its top, and had *Pfifferlinge* and cocktails until it started to get dark. We wandered down to the river, and crossed it, where, beyond a new road, the forest began. The moss sank beneath our feet; we took off our shoes and walked barefoot between the trees, looking for a path, looking for some kind of pattern in it to make more sense than tree after tree after tree. Somewhere, deeper in the forest, came the hoot of a distant train making its last journey back down the mountain for the night. Dotted between clusters of tiny, delicate white mushrooms was a giant Fly Agaric, the size of my outstretched hand, overripe so that its edges curled upwards, and a couple of metres away a Death Cap. We thought it best to put our shoes back on, as the fog ate up what little light was left, and make our way home.

I slept in a room straddling the river, my head upstream from my feet, listening to the water rush away, and slept more soundly than I had in weeks. We got up early to climb the mountain, and found the place altered in the sun. The mist had lifted away, apart from in the trees where the sun's rays cast diagonal stripes into it, and the dewdrops in the grass at the path's edge were lit into prismatic rainbow colours. Water rose from springs along the way, as it had the night before, but you could see it rising now, in little bubbling jets beneath the rocks.

The rocks were probably the most spectacular thing about it. They were huge – rough and speckled with crystal, the size of cars – and lay across the entirety of the mountainside. If they had been moved there by a glacier, it was a glacier whose vastness I could not get my head around. Down in the village was the most famous of them, the totemic Schierke Feuerstein, a towering edifice with deep horizontal notches carved into it by time. It looked unlikely, as though it might topple over at any moment. We passed a rock the shape and size of an upturned van that lay atop another, smaller rock and a spruce tree whose trunk had stretched and warped to accommodate it. The tree was downhill from the rock, and its trunk, bulging like an overworked biceps, must have been taking ten tons or so in weight.

The trees further along weren't made of such stern stuff. A stand of them stood stripped of bark and foliage, and beneath their corpses the forest floor sprung back into life, with clover and elder filling out the gaps, in the sudden large-scale dieback that you seem to find with monoculture. In the end, there was very little of the natural left on the Brocken, if what you see as natural is whatever is untampered with by human hands. The Harz was mined extensively from the eighteenth century onwards; the fast-growing Norwegian spruce covering those scars made a useful source of quick fuel in times of war, and soon created a canopy beneath which nothing much beyond those thick mosses could survive for long. It was fenced off militarily for years, first by the Nazis and then by the East German State, to avoid it being used as a crossing point into the West. On the top of the mountain, where we expected to find grassy clearings above the treeline, was a big red-and-white striped thing like a moon-landing site, an old TV mast, and a monolithic building housing a hotel and museum.

The first steam train of the morning arrived, laden with people, who massed around competing sausage stalls. The mist lifted a little. I had heard that Walpurgisnacht was still a thing that happened there, on the eve of May morning, but unlike the pagan-favoured sites in England, where you would catch sight of the odd person in a robe, or bearing flowers, on their way past at other times of year, here there were none. The Harz witch myths were steeped in Christian binarisms of good-and-bad, God-and-devil, steeped in the green-faced age- and woman-hate, invoking a supernatural defined only by its blackness in being un-Christian in character.

My mother was right: *Heidentum*, which translates exactly as heathenism, being of the heath, clearly wasn't a thing in Germany. And yet in Carinthia, where she had taken the children to stay for the week, the springs on the hillside forest by the next village now had a ribboned bower and a shrine where people left pebbles and flowers, and someone had put up an altar bedecked with ivy where red tealights burned as they arrived. No mountain-top or tump visible from the valley escaped round there without a cross erected on it, so there were good grounds to think that the altar was not for Christian purposes. At the far edge of the German-speaking lands, something was stirring in the forest.

And, besides, I was in Saxony, ur-home of our tree-worshipping ancestors, and a short train ride from the

Hannoverian palaces of our monarchy, which brought us Prince Albert and our contemporary Christmas-tree-worship rituals, and I couldn't help but notice the inspirational tree posters in the youth hostel, with spiritual quotes about nature and the wilderness written beneath them. The Germans obviously still liked nature, in some sense; it was just that they didn't articulate this into much beyond a sense of trees possessing some external moral good.

Along the way I had lost count of places named after oaks, and of the beers and wholefood shops and restaurants bearing oak leaves on them that I saw down cobbled streets and beneath railway platforms. They were all used to connote wholesomeness in a very National Trust sort of way; I'd thought of the oak, or perhaps the image of it, as a conservative English emblem, as owned by establishment Englishness as Jerusalem – but the Germans owned it too.

I had hoped to be able, for it to be theoretically possible, to write about Germany without getting the Nazis involved, but they kept on creeping in. There was the Order of Oak Leaves, which was awarded to exceptional military officers. I also started to think that the peculiarly German need to order the forest might be born either of an inheritance of the conflicting Nazi obsessions with the forest and the need for control, or from an acknowledgement that the last time Germans were encouraged to wholeheartedly get into the wilderness it didn't end well.

Unpicking credibility from the sensational nonsense written about Nazi history is a thorny task. Too many people to be ignored, and who were not otherwise mad, had urged me to read about Nazi paganism, Nazi occult practices and Nazi tree-worship.

Much of Nazi ideology about racial purity stems from

a sense of place, of soil as well as blood. It is a deeply romanticised ideal of the forests of the North, and the strongmen within them, a set of ideas that share their roots with some of our contemporary neo-paganism. There are two kneejerk responses that would usually crop up here: the first to be furious at any Nazi association, to treat it as a blasphemous error; the second to dismiss anything the Nazis did, said, or liked as inherently corrupt; both represent the sort of thinking that gets you into the jackboot headspace in the first place.

A popular trolling technique from neocons wishing to aggrieve the ecologically minded is to remind them that the Nazis were the first European Green Party. It hurts because it's true. The Nazis were ecologists, ecologists over humanists, which is probably where it started to go wrong: the Nazi ecology extended beyond field and forest into the human sphere, so that some sorts of humans were ecologically desirable and native, and some were non-native and problematic, and needed weeding out.

The northern Europeans came from the northern European landscape, and were of it, and were at one with it. The Jews, forced into perpetual diasporic exile, were not of the land. They were the rootless cosmopolitans, making their living in, or on the back of, industrial bourgeois society, which was not of the land. The land became the external morality that dictated which bits of its ecology were good, and which were bad.

This was interpreted in a way that sought moral fixity from Nature, and a conception of the natural, supernatural, state of Nature, and that, in contradiction, sought to tamper with it, by weeding out all undesirability and encouraging selective breeding. In this way, Nature was imbued with the same strange contradictions as the God of the Christian Church, both open and closed, beneficent and wrathful, contradictions that could be mediated and exploited by a hierarchy for its own purposes.

A life that was of the land was idealised, and a philosophical idealism prospered, the transcendental idealism in which the ineffable spirit of God-or-Nature could be glimpsed from high mountains and deep forests. It was a way of thinking more suited to paganism than the Church, and while both Catholic and Protestant Churches were tolerated, for it was too difficult not to, many of the Nazi ideologues held pagan sympathies.

There is Alfred Rosenberg's *Myth of the Twentieth Century*, a peculiar mix of racist pseudoscience, anti-religious critique and feudalism. Rosenberg, who edited the Nazi paper *Völkischer Beobachter*, was one of the inner circle of early Nazi ideologues and proposed a new religion to fit the awakened Aryan race-soul, something primal and animistic to fit the Romantic wildness of the Teutonic spirit. The popular Victorian theosophist Madame Blavatsky, whose bizarre and wildly popular worldview took in selective bits of Hinduism and the notion that white people stem originally from Atlantis, advocated a type of racist neo-paganism ripe for Nazi adoption into Ariosophy, a peculiar mix of bad garden science and spirituality.

Rosenberg probably would have gone crazy for the Green Man. I found, to my relief, no references to it. The Green Man has a sound Germanic heritage, ticks all the nature boxes, is somewhat chauvinistic – I seemed to have inadvertently adopted an ideal Nazi icon. At least I could take solace in being a Jew. It was darkly fascinating, though, how close you can veer to the bad bits of history by taking a line on something, anything, every stance a deviance in one way or another.

There was much talk in Nazi mythology of the organic nature of human society, which lives by the same organic rules as all other life, and is thus in a state of perpetual violent flux and subjected to, and made of, inequality. Although the Nazis were, in a fashion, anticapitalist, they were also feudal, regarding some races as intrinsically better suited to rule than others, and some types of people as better ruling stock. Nature didn't do equality of outcome, so why should mankind? And mankind was, and should be, interlaced with Nature. All manner of lengthy compound nouns abstracting this ideal prospered: *Erdgebundenkeit*, the binding or oneness with the earth; *Volksboden*, the connection of the people with the soil; *Bodenständigkeit*, or the nature by which life was shaped by earthly forces.

There is nothing intrinsically problematic about any of these three terms. Their adoption to make the argument that one race of people should be superior to others, because it stemmed from those values and that soil, was where it all went wrong – and, of course, the inherent dodginess of the whole idea of race, that such things as racial distinction can be said to exist in any concrete form.

But ditch the feudalism, which is nonsensical even by eugenic standards, for as we see with our own German royalty, all that inbreeding between *Übermensch* and *Übermensch* soon delivers Prince Andrew and Prince Edward, and ditch the silliness about races, as though anyone could be a pure-blooded anything without, again, swiftly turning into a sickly and incontinent analogue of one of those poor malfunctioning dogs you see on the telly at Crufts, and I had fallen for much of the same stuff as the Nazis.

So did many others. The same threads of Romanticism birthed the work of Rudolf Steiner and Kurt Hahn, the founder of the Outward Bound movement and our most Establishment of schools, Gordonstoun, both of whom were persecuted by the Nazis for suspected Jewishness. The Germans were into organic and biodynamic farming – the latter carried out, paganically, to the cycles of the moon – long before they became fashionable here. A gentler political Greenness prospered in the seventies and eighties, one aligned to sharing and non-violence in a distinctly un-Darwinian way. And the world is not short of German hippies, although I have never found many of them actually living in their homeland: there are loads of them out there, in yurts in Scotland and on beaches in India, doing Nature away from home turf.

The Germans I saw on my travels were cross about the trains running late. It took an impressive thirty minutes to complete the paperwork required to stay in a German youth hostel. The woods in the Harz were no-go, *Naturschutzgebiet*: no communing with anything metaphysical here. There were, generally, a lot of signs about detailing things that you weren't allowed to do.

Despite the impossibility of defining a race, there is something identifiable in the practice of German culture, something fixed and formal, which seems to lead to a black-and-whiteness about the world. I wondered whether this was what could end up getting dangerous, the illusory grammatical certainty about things, and by extension about things deemed to be wrong, and bad. It felt a bit like the Apollonian imposition of order upon meaning that Nietzsche railed against, invoking the wild open Dionysian spirit in its place.

Some of Goethe's Weimar contemporaries held that

language formed our *Weltanschauung*, or conception of the world. What other language craves such fixity of meaning that it needs both inflection and sentence order to attain it correctly? What other language has such a strong sense of discrete denotation that it creates new conglomerate monster-nouns in order to avoid any confusion or overlap from existing words? How can this not shape the thinking of the minds embedded in it?

Not all of the stereotypes held true. I stayed in W's gloriously chaotic flat in Berlin that belonged to a Bavarian obsessed with all forms of kitsch, and lay on her bed in her room, which overflowed with all manner of stuff: candy-coloured rucksacks, Chinese calendars, an oil painting of cherubs in a forest, books and ancient laptops beneath a towering pile of empty Turkish sausage crates.

Through the door to the balcony and the window, which were both wide open because it was thirty-two degrees outside, plants exploded into the courtyard. There were pots of pink geraniums hanging on the inside and outside of the railings, in four rows, and a huge palm tree in a pot, and climbing red-flowered beans with leaves like huge green hearts falling away from the window.

We had both moved to Berlin a decade previously, in an earlier wave of underemployed graduates seeking salvation in the cheap rent and parties that still characterise the city to this day. I shared a flat near the Volkspark Friedrichshain with three earnest students from the West and too many pot-plants that spilled over the mezzanine balcony and shed leaves on the floor and blocked out the daylight.

The Westphalian students liked to go out into the park in the evening, where they took a spliff and some bongos and would start drumming, taking it in turns to go off to get beers from the shop. I quickly got a sense of the social rules of Berlin parks: it was fine to take drugs or have sex in them, as long as you were pale-skinned and middle-class.

If white working-class people congregated there, the police got twitchy, in case they were neo-Nazis, and if large Turkish families gathered there, everyone appeared to get cross. They couldn't quite articulate why, but it seemed to involve the term *Schutz* – protection, as though the grass were at risk. The importance of preserving plant life was emphasised in weekend tabloid horror stories about Turks holding family barbecues there, scorching the earth in their wake. White irreligious Germans were, however, allowed to go cottaging in parks, which must have caused no end of damage to the poor bushes, and the police, who by day chased off Turkish kids with unsettling ferocity, patrolled the park at night to protect the right to cottage, so that at 4 a.m. you would frequently see wild-eyed men emerging from the undergrowth wearing only boots and thongs, mounting their bikes and pedalling home to bed.

I soon fell out with the Westphalian students over the chore rota, which they had taken literally, designing it as a rotating device composed of two segmented circles fixed together with a central pivot, and moved to another, cheaper flat in Neukölln, which was occupied by hippies with no chore rota and even more pot-plants. We walked that way now, through the hot evening, over the Warschauer Strasse railway bridge towards the river.

Neukölln, considered the ghetto a decade previously because it was where the Turks and Arabs lived and somebody once got shot there, had now been whitewashed into hipster blandness by the millions of international twentysomethings who thronged the city, and who thronged the bridge too, hanging out drinking beers and waiting for something desirable to happen. There must have been several thousand of them on the bridge, like an advanced metastasis of the phenomenon that starts with fifteen-year-old kids drinking cider at a village bus stop on an internationally mobile scale. In a moment of Nazi thinking, I critiqued the out-of-balance human ecology, and, by the time we got to the edge of Neukölln, found the whole swathe of the city we had passed through in a state of unsustainable and parasitic monoculture.

It was a giant urban theme park dedicated to the entertainment of a more giant travelling class of wealthy and mostly Anglo-Saxon kids, who alighted there for days, weeks or months at a time to party. It was Las Vegas, with an edge of history. I'd been one of them once, one of the worst sort, pretending to be creative like all the other fake creative people who weren't actually writing, making or photographing anything at all, merely indulging borderline drug and alcohol problems, and had done it at a time when the scale was small enough for it to feel like there was a city and a life to feed upon.

The length of the intervening decade was further made apparent when I suggested getting up early and going to Berghain, a club in a former power station that we used to go to all the time when it first opened. W was appalled, because it was full of tourists, all those kids we saw on the bridge, and nobody went there any more. In a semi-conciliatory gesture, aimed in part at establishing his superior knowledge of late-scenedom, he mentioned a party by a lake out near the airport, and suggested we go there instead.

By the time I had packed my bag and we were on the right train it was the last one out of town. Beyond the colonial blandness of international nightlife, about to peak in a uniform haze of cheap beer, out past the endless allotments with their huts and German flags fading in the dark, out past the places where people slept at night and rose at dawn.

At the second-to-last station, I balanced unsteadily on the back of W's bike, knees pulled up, leaning forward so my bag didn't knock the whole thing out. We wove through dark, silent streets and down a road out of the village, and stopped to row about directions. We paused and listened and followed a faint sound like a kid playing music on a tinny phone far away, and went into the woods on a broad path, and stopped when the path diverted into a smaller one, hearing the cue again, somewhat louder, and then saw the shifting mass of bodies in the dark and the red ends of cigarettes and, beyond the bodies, a pale light that swam on the broken surface of the lake.

W went off to find people and I wandered through the crowd and the clearing to the little beach where water lapped at the feet of the party. The moon was not up. Perhaps it was a new moon, for it was certainly close to it, and the sky was unlit by streetlights. There was very little to see: no lighting apart from a couple of small lamps at the bar and the decks, no fires, for it was still hot, just the shadows of faces that came and went, forming and dissociating from groups, a sort of restless peace.

I didn't want to leave my bag near the water, so found a quiet spot beneath a tree where the cool forest floor replaced the sand and curled up there for a while, dozing. My usual panic about sleeplessness had departed: there was nothing much to do apart from sit and wait at airports and on planes and trains, and there could be no advantage to doing so in full consciousness. The edge of the crowd came and went and sounded like the sea, and for some time I lay there hearing it, indistinguishable from the occasional rustle of a breeze at the top of the birches, until the light crept in.

The clearing thinned out and the thicket of people re-formed into small rings. Some were in the water, swimming out into the silvery lake, cleaving smooth black wakes from it. They laughed, the sound bouncing supernaturally across the water, and turned back.

I had been to a party like this before, a party whose existence was texted to me by my party buddy U, a bike courier with the insatiable appetite for raves that bike couriers seemed to have. Now, in the dim early dawn, I could have sworn I recognised him, grinning with cold as he left the water. It seemed unlikely, ten years on, unlikely as a rural mother-of-two finding herself on a lakeside beach at 4 a.m., a thousand miles from home – unlikely enough to be grounds to say hello.

I headed over to the group, and saw U, who saw me, and gave me a cold, wet hug, welcome and as physically inconvenient as the embrace of a wet dog.

'Hey! W's here too. It's a reunion, man!'

He found a towel and sat down near a gaggle of other people W had found, and we combed our way through mutual acquaintances, reeling off lists of who left town and when, who got married and disappeared into the provinces with children, who, most shockingly of all, ended up employable, workaholic, successful. U asked me what I was doing, and what I was doing there.

'Something ridiculous,' W said, 'some English thing. Stuff about trees and starting a cult based on these gargoyle things in English churches.'

I had long suspected that he felt at home in Germany for the normativity of rudeness there.

'That's cool,' said U. 'What is it?'

I groaned. I had no drive to explain it now. It felt ridiculous and embarrassing. The overwhelming urge to sleep crept over me.

I told him about how the Brits had this new pagan folk-religion about old images from churches whose meaning no one knew, only guessed, and how they were everywhere in Germany too, only no one knew about them here, and how the more I thought about it the less I had to say, for it all collapsed into supposition, but I did think the Germans could use some softness and get over their obsession with organising nature because their forests were disappointingly tame. It was the sort of rambling soliloquy that could only make sense to someone who had eroded his critical faculties over a long night, and U nodded sagely.

'I think you should start a cult of it here,' I said. 'Having a Bioladen on every street is not a demonstration of oneness with the earth. The Germans need to get over people. They probably need to relinquish their language in order to do so, too, although I can't remember exactly why this is.'

'This is great,' said U. 'I never knew you were so deep.'

'You can do this for me,' I said: 'be my agent fomenting shifts in the forest-discourse. Will you do it for me?'

'Yes, of course,' said U. 'That would be awesome.'

'You won't need to do very much different from now,' I said. 'You should probably go to lots of parties by lakes like this, but then you do that anyway. Do not idolise Nature as something that abides by different rules than human life; do not see humans as in any way distinct from the processes of Nature. Actually, do not think of any of that. Do not think too much. Go and be in the lake again.'

U lay looking up through the diamond-patterned hands

of leaves to the pink-blue sky. He didn't respond verbally but seemed content. I didn't want to undermine any sense of the holiness of what I had related to him, so I sat in a silence that, I hoped, seemed meditative, and waited for his eyes to close before I called a taxi and crept out of the forest to go to the airport.

SEVEN

The Green Chapel

I did not have a map, although a map might not have been particularly useful, for cloud furred the high rocky ridge, and the path, such as it was, was visible only for a few metres. It was also cold for an August morning: two jumpers and a coat held it off if I walked fast, and I could see my breath as it became one with the cloud.

The crest of rocks, like the long spiky spine of a dozing mountain-sized lizard, was a godsend. At least, in one respect, I knew where I was. The rocks went on for miles, or so it seemed, for without visibility distance was a matter of internal speculation rather than anything measured against actual things in the world. I had an inkling that I should drop down towards a river when the rocks ended, although there was no way of knowing where the river might be: downhill, probably, but that was as far as the guessing went.

I didn't want to know what time it was. In these sorts of circumstances, information can only feed fear. It was early, certainly: I'd left soon after dawn, wanting to get home in time to see the children off to bed, and now the first flickers of anxiety kicked in. But it was only August, so the likelihood of my corpse – perfectly preserved at refrigeration temperature, waxen-skinned, peaceful in rest – being retrieved weeks later at the grand altitude of three hundred and fifty metres above sea level seemed a little far-fetched. Soon the sun would burn away the cloud, and it would lift, and the land would be revealed, all new in the light. It was time to toughen up.

I stopped in the cleft between two rocks and leafed through the only source of information I had, which was written in verse. At least it was in translation rather than fourteenth-century Middle English, although there was then the additional worry that poetic licence might have been exercised, blurring the exactitude of any instructive passages. At the hilltop stage they were not exact, confirming, alliteratively, the existence of mist and moor. Next time, if there was a next time, I would buy a map. This was ridiculous. I ate my last Eccles cake and peered into the mist.

I was looking for the Green Chapel, the place where Sir Gawain meets his fate with the Green Knight in the eponymous medieval tale. Gawain, a minor member of Arthur's retinue, is impelled into a mutual beheading pact with a giant Green Man out of chivalric duty, and unknowingly spends a merry party season wrestling with sexual intrigue at the Green Knight's castle before going to the Green Chapel to take the promised fatal blow.

The location of the Green Chapel is commonly speculated to be Lud's Church, a rocky chasm in the woods above the River Dane at the edge of the Peak District. You can, apparently, park a mile or so away in the village by it, but that seemed like a cop-out. I wanted an adventure, and now I had one, complete with sense of doom.

By the time the stegosaur's neck thinned out and inclined down, the mist had lifted, the second jumper was no longer necessary, and any remaining sense of danger concerned the probability of lunch happening later than intended. You could see the curve of the land now, the wooded snake of the river and the place where the wood extended up the hill beyond it, which was where I needed to get to. And there was the village too, and the road to it, revealing itself at the place and time where the 3G reception materialised, so that it was all too easy.

In the sun, the moor was brightly lit with purple heather, the last of the rocks red, and the path broad and clear. I scrambled down in no particular direction, unworried now. The best mornings often start dimly, and this one was a beauty. Along the lane by the river, beyond the village, were wild raspberries, tiny, tart and fragrant, and then, where the wood began, bilberries and brambles.

A grand old beech tree marked the place where paths crossed, a sprawling spaghetti junction of roots encircling human tracks, and above it was a signpost confirming the way. This path was well-trodden, a strange thing for a place whose character was supposedly determined by its hidden-ness. The giveaway at the entrance to the caves was the erosion barrier, put into place to prevent the curiosity of ramblers from dispatching them into deep ravines. Beyond it loomed a rocky outcrop, the open chimney of a cave, entirely covered in green.

The green was made of many different things, all of which grew on the damp, vertical surface of the rock. There was a green algal slime in the darkest and wettest places, all manner of green mosses – some squat and moist, some soft and furry, some long and dry and star-shaped – and patches of bright clover, ferns hanging from high cracks, grasses growing where grass could grow, sometimes forming overhanging curtains a metre long. Each patch of green assumed new forms at its edge, across all hierarchies of complexity, from the star-shaped sphagnum moss to the tall trees that towered in the high distance.

Lud's Church, as well as posing a hiding-place for giant Green Men, was used for centuries as a sort of church, a chapel in the woods for religious minorities who had no man-made options. At the time of Gawain, the Lollards congregated there. Opposed to the ritual and formality of the Catholic Church, and seeing its riches and ornamentation as corrupt when sickness and poverty abounded, the Lollard theology advocated lay preachers and a clergy who lived ordinary lives and enjoyed no special treatment in status or law. They rejected the doctrines of blessings, pilgrimage and exorcism, and the ritual worship of icons, seeing these as the worship of the Church itself rather than of God. They were anti-celibacy and capital punishment; some of them saw the Pope as Antichrist; they were clearly likeable.

Down the steps, which were concrete and more likely poured by the National Park Authority than by giants or Lollards, the chasm continued, formidable as a fine cathedral, twenty metres deep into the ground and perhaps a hundred long, with narrow rocky offshoots into which you could lose substantial numbers of heretics and elves. You could clamber up these other crevices as they crept into gaps in bilberry-bushes and brambles, so that you would never know they were there.

Because *Gawain* is contemporaneous with the Lollards, and Lud's Church is commonly agreed as its final location, it might be tempting to read a theology into it. The instructions for reaching the Green Chapel certainly do work if you want to find Lud's Church from the top of Gradbach Hill on a sunny morning, but, at two lines long, I'd wager there are other caves on this island matching the description, and I'm sure I could have found one closer to home.

In order for the pilgrimage to the Green Chapel to have

meaning, I had needed to read *Gawain* properly, which I had previously avoided on the assumption that it would be boring. Medievalism is, if anything, fashionable now, in its altered *Game of Thrones* state. I never had much time for it, although I accepted that medievalists existed. I had observed, with little comprehension, the too-large gaggle of people, in too much knitwear, who got too much public funding for studies of dead monks' handwriting. How did they maintain sanity in their dark lives, dwelling in the cave of the past? I tried to enthuse them with Zen interpretations of a Deleuzean logic of sense in Lewis Carroll and they looked discernibly bored.

Despite this, I did understand what people saw in *Gawain*: it is surprisingly clever and, I think, funny, for how can it not be a satire on those bizarre social constructs that medievalists are all so hot for? I had vague recollections of the medieval notion of chivalry, in which hospitality and generosity were codified to the extent that if somebody offered you something, like the opportunity to chop their head off, you were honour-bound to agree to do so and to invite them to do the same to you. This extended to the arts of courtly love, too, so that ladies were to be honoured in a hierarchy of honouring with one's wife at the top and other ladies beneath her.

It was not always clear what this meant in practice. Gawain is in a Catch-22-style triple-bind in which the competing demands of chivalry, courtly love and the Church are in seemingly perpetual conflict, leading to the least ever credible rejection of a sex scene, at the Green Knight's supernatural swingers' lodge. Gawain's lust for his host, Bercilak, is barely less than that aroused by his wife, who turns out to be Morgan le Fay in honeytrap mode. The seeming reality of Bercilak's castle and the various waking and sleeping dreams that manifest there are exposed as a delusion, for Bercilak is the Green Knight and the whole thing is illusory, with the side effect of Camelot looking pretty chimeric too, and not as much fun.

Conversations, and the poem itself, sign off with bits of Church speak, but it often feels as though the Christian bookends are tagged on as a formality, a formality as absurd as those that make it mandatory to engage in beheading games and simultaneously, paradoxically, bed and not-bed your host's wife.

I concluded, late at night in a small room above a pub on a moor, that *Gawain* was an act of anarchy against medieval poetry, and that it was therefore acceptable to like it. Perhaps it was an act of anarchy against medievalism too, and its earnest attempts to rationalise the poem. Attempts in which it was somehow held that the supernatural sphere of Bercilak, his Otherworld, was grim or scary. The Wirral is depicted as grim and scary, which is perhaps better than the dull suburban vista that manifested on the way to Liverpool a week later; Bercilak's house is divine, beautiful, a place of unreasonable comforts. The Green Knight is the obvious hero, merciful and fair despite his limitless superpowers. His territory is a heaven, a place of pure pleasure and becoming, eerie only in its perfection.

Camelot, on the other hand, seems a bland place described in bland superlative, a place where everyone washes their hands obediently for supper, a place peopled by obsequious fools who blindly adopt green sashes for themselves as a fashion accessory when Gawain turns up with one that simultaneously saved and could have killed him. It brought to mind the inane and superficial groupthink of the Idiots satirised in

Chris Morris and Charlie Brooker's sitcom *Nathan Barley*. It is in the nature of archetypes to last a long time.

In fact, you could say that the Camelot court's mindless response to Gawain's story and the ensuing sash-wearing is an illustration of the nature of institutions and of unfelt religiosity, where nothing of the original sense remains in a surface reproduction aimed only at cementing uniformity and status. I don't think Camelot comes out particularly well from the poem. I don't see much that is compelling in it about the Christian Church. I emerged convinced that Gawain would have been better off hanging out in an ongoing fairyland ménage à trois with Bercilak and Morgan le Fay, both of whom are eroticised in a way that transcends politeness.

And, if Bercilak's world is the Otherworld, the world of unlimited desire and possibility against which Camelot feels both restrictive and a little crass, it does not present Bercilak and Le Fay as particularly threatening characters in themselves: they are threatening only insofar as they threaten the limitations of the material world: the idea that Camelot is interesting, the idea that sin is in any way banal. If they are Satanic, it is the charismatic sexy Satan of *Paradise Lost* whom they resemble.

And if the Green Knight is, as people claim, the original animated Green Man, he has a superhero quality about him that far supersedes that of any mortal knight, a playful godliness in which he can manufacture any possible outcome in any possible world, and elects to do so in entertaining ways.

All of this made a lot of sense on the Green Man front, at least in our contemporary sense of Green Man: the Green Knight was a medieval supernatural hero just as today's Green Man was – at least I hoped – a superhero of nature.

The medieval sense of Faerie and the way it seemed to be inherited from the old Teutonic and shamanic otherworlds made it possible to suspend ordinary reality and its natural laws into new modes of possibility. It would be nice if the Green Man could do those things too.

Maybe you needed to access Faerie in order to make it all work, though. Maybe the Green Man was the acceptable way into it now, a way of attuning to the beat of other-worldly drums. Green was always the colour of attunement to the non-human sphere: the divine and desirous and eerie world of Gawain's Knight is unremittingly green.

You lose count of the mentions of greenness quite rapidly, because it is everywhere, just as the Green Chapel of Lud's Church is comprehensively green in all its detail. At no point is green described in negative terms. It is a heavily aesthetic poem, laden with rich description, and the response to greenness is good awe. You marvel at its hue. The greenness of the Green Knight is uncanny, but that's as far as you can take its unsettling quality. It is as though uncanny is a good thing, much in the same way that the uncanny desirability of Bercilak's Otherworld is a good thing.

The greenness in *Gawain* works in much the same way as Goethe describes the greenness of the forest as the magic sets in his fairy tale *The Green Snake and the Beautiful Lily*. It is a similar exercise in the layered repetition of green, done with intentional excess, pointing at a realm beyond the material where anything is possible; however, for all its allegory about the nature of illumination, it is no Christian fairy tale, and was taken as a parable of spiritual endeavour by Rudolf Steiner, for whom delving into the strange green powers of Nature became a life's work.

The uncanny of green is the uncanny of faerie, the uncanny of the shamanic otherworlds, the uncanny of a meta-physical realm other than the atomised material reality that appears before us. I can't help but see any value judgement placed on it by *Gawain* as positive, as, perhaps more predict-ably, is Goethe's.

However, by the Victorian era, greenness had encountered darker times. Steve Roud's late twentieth-century *Penguin Guide to the Superstitions of Britain and Ireland* is a diligently researched tome which tracks all documented historical su-perstition, and that takes a dim line on the notion of Green-Man-as-Archetype. The entry for *green* reads as follows: 'Apart from black, with its funeral associations, green is the only colour to be consistently regarded as unlucky across the British Isles.'

This was a recent development, with the first intimations of green-as-bad coming in the late eighteenth century and reaching near-universal folk belief by the time the early folk-lorists were out assiduously collecting stories.

By the early twentieth century, green had come to mean deathly, which is a strange association for a colour that sig-nifies growth in the natural world, unless you are trying to paint the natural world as a bad thing. Roud, wondering 'why such a pleasing colour, associated with nature and liv-ing growth, has acquired this reputation' concludes that the most likely folkloric explanation is its connection with fair-ies, and thus the Otherworld.

It is as though the same uncanny quality of green was turned against it, so that the colour was demonised along with the otherworlds it represented. Perhaps a people who, in the new industrial age, were no longer tied to the land for their living were more receptive to the rather counterintuitive notion of green-as-bad, and were more uniform in their acceptance of what the Church told them about the supernatural competition.

The grisly foliate heads of the later Middle Ages and beyond were saying the same thing: don't seek recourse in nature; don't seek recourse in the fleshly material world, for it is all transitory and treacherous. They tried to claim that the only otherworld was the one invented by the Church, and that anything that looked like an alternative was a vision made by demons. It is probably a credit to the British people that they had to be separated from their land in order to fall for it.

At some point in the post-industrial age, green's fortunes turned again. Perhaps the scarcity of it in nature led it to acquire a rarity value that began to feel desirable. If green had started out as Good and Fearsome, and then been banished into Bad and Fearsome, now it was the opposite of Bad and Fearsome: Good and Tame. As the industrial landscapes of postwar Europe matured, and a period of peace and material prosperity settled, human concern about the non-human sphere, if not an intrinsic concern for it, opened up.

There was definitely a bit of a generational stripiness with notions of green. My grandmother, steeped in frugality from a wartime youth, recycled everything, although she would never have used that word: tinfoil was washed and folded neatly in a drawer, plastic bags kept beneath the sink for re-use, food bought modestly and never wasted. She was generous to those around her, but a sense of caution, a deep existential worry about the impact of overconsumption, pervaded her lifestyle. It was apolitical common sense. It did not have a colour.

My parents, whose early childhoods were overshadowed by postwar austerity with its chemical honey and dyed margarine, couldn't wait to be rid of frugality. By the time they finally made some decent money at the end of the 1970s, they had earned their big house and Volvo and M&S ready meals. Shopping was an earned pleasure, too: a pleasurable Saturday strolling through the West End, taking part in a system of enterprise that looked a great deal better than its alternative on the other side of Europe. The house was always warm and so clean it gleamed. The garden was neat and well-tended. The car was fast and shiny. We were capitalism's winners, enjoying its benefits daily in our material lives.

I now had friends here who grew up on organic farms around that same time, when organic farming was a weird, unfashionable thing to do unless you were a hippy or a Quaker. People found it retrogressive, just as my parents found frugality and recycling retrogressive. Life was getting better, and had moved on; it was only in the last decade or so that the organic movement seemed like the prophets rather than heretics.

Green politics and green ideology had started to become mainstream around the time I started school in the 1980s, and all of the problems we were worried about were mostly unconnected to our own habits in eating and shopping and driving. There was, of course, the issue of the hole in the ozone layer, which seemed to be caused by hairspray, proving that aesthetic judgements – on, for example, the horror of eighties hair – can have a moral basis. Lead stopped being added to petrol.

But the environment, or Nature, tended to involve other, distant places. The Amazon was being deforested by people in Brazil. The hole in the ozone layer, even if it stemmed largely from our fridges and obscene hair practices, was on the other side of the world. The famines were in far-off places unconnected to our overwhelmingly white middle-class suburb. The fate of the giant panda seemed to be in the hands of China, about whom we knew nothing. There was a sense that it was morally right to experience sadness about these things when they formed class topics in assembly, but it was a sadness unconnected to our day-to-day lives and any sense of their impact in the whole affair.

At primary school, socialised into chasing moral superiority by raising awareness of the perils of hairspray, I set up an activist group with a friend. The Young Environmentalists Society was short-lived: we bought some felt-tip pens to make posters with and spent a wet afternoon affixing small sticky labels to them bearing the acronym YES, and then the weather turned and we forgot all about it. To her credit, my comrade did at some point get round to performing a rap about being green which remains regrettably seared into my memory, but she must have got over it eventually because, when I last checked, she edited the luxury lifestyle supplement of a well-known right-wing magazine not known for its ecological campaigning.

I wasn't sure we'd moved on much now, either. On the surface, things looked promising: there was a Transition Towns group and any number of cyclists; I knew at least one person with an electric car; and education was still doing its bit, with my children's school accredited with both Eco School and Forest School status. I asked my older child what he did at Forest School. 'We basically just play,' he said, but then round here spending an afternoon in the woods was a bit of a busman's holiday. It was notable that the school's Eco

Club was largely populated by the children whose families had recently moved into the area from London and Bristol. There were also lots of children whose parents earned a living from life or land, but the farmers had the least time for green stuff out of everyone. They were trying to earn a living.

And, to be fair, the ethos of the Forest Schools movement wasn't originally about greenness or nature or anything particularly ecological anyway, but about the very human practice of self-actualisation. It was supposed to help build creativity. The word 'inspiration' was used. Trees existed to make humans better at being human. Humans who were better at being human and more creative in finding solutions to extend human self-actualisation would be better for other humans.

It was a world in which nature existed to facilitate humans – nothing radical there, just the standard assumption of humans as divinely imbued with human wisdom with a sense of stewardship tacked onto it. Humans might have been guardians of the non-human sphere, but even this was limited to the applications of the non-human sphere to human happiness.

Nature was now becoming a word used for the pedagogical applications of the non-human sphere, something we should cling onto for the sake of the children and for their children. It contained pandas and dolphins. This new pale-green idea of nature was defanged. It was as wild and dangerous as a soft-play centre. It was a toy for babies.

At the end of *Sir Gawain and the Green Knight*, when Bercilak goes hunting, the deal is that he will share his hunting

213

spoils with Gawain if Gawain will share his erotic adventures with Bercilak. The implication is that if Gawain cedes to the charms of Bercilak's wife, he is bound to do the same with Bercilak: no hardship given Bercilak's hotness.

The extensive and graphic hunting scenes, all movement and thrilling violence, revel in the chase and its danger. Bercilak and his men are going out into the wild. You could say that they are doing so in hunter-gatherer mode, to catch things that will be good to feast upon, but agriculture worked perfectly well in the fourteenth century. Bercilak hunts the biggest boar, the wiliest fox, wipes out a hillside of stags and deers. His ingenuity at hunting is presented as evidence of his superhumanness. He is fearless going out onto bleak moors at night. He is unafraid of nature.

These long stretches of hunting porn could only have held their value at a time when they were somehow re-markable, and they would have been six hundred years ago, when going out onto the moors and into the woods for kicks would have been a wild and reckless thing to do, a foolish and dangerous thing for any mortal. The wild con-tained fearsome beasts and a vast black unknown a little like the night. The hunting scenes, and the idea that they are ex-citing, and the idea that hunting could be scary, were what dated Sir Gawain for me.

Nature, in its wild form, was plentiful and terrible. Only the supernatural could exist in it unafraid because the super-natural wasn't subject to the same natural laws and forces, but transcendent, illusory. Bercilak could lead the wild hunt precisely because he was not really human. Now, human in-genuity has made hunting so unscary that City traders go out shooting at weekends, no doubt feeling a sense of godli-ness as they handle their shotguns, but without any jeopardy apart from the risk of someone else misfiring. Fox-hunting, depending on your politics, is an abomination for its gratuitous cruelty and one-sided life chances, or merely quaint. We get venison from farms. Wild boar barely exist. People who really need that hunting kick can fly out to Africa where lions are bred in captivity to be stalked and shot at with big guns.

Humans were the Green Knight now. We invented technology that made us into him, that turned hunting into a game and that turned farming into a commodity business. But, unlike the Green Knight, we were running out of wild moors to hunt upon: we had harnessed so much of the wild into mines and factories and farms that there wasn't much of it left.

Nature, bringer of discomfort with its winds and rains and thorns and sharp-toothed beasts, had been tamed, and the bits that were not tamed were banished away to other, smaller places where they did not present a threat. Those bits shrank back, eaten up by the material needs of human comfort, with its love of food and fuel and stuff.

There is an alternative account of all of this, an account in which the apparent human dominance over the non-human sphere is, viewed from a larger scale, a fluctuation in which the impact of human activity will self-correct into human non-existence before too long.

James Lovelock's Gaia theory describes the Earth as a giant organism with interlocking feedback systems capable of maintaining stable conditions for life. Lovelock posits that fluctuations in some parts of earthly life lead to alterations in climatic conditions that, in time, encourage a correction back to the norm: too many trees, for example, would lead to an increase in environmental oxygen, which, when it exceeds 25 per cent, encourages forest fires, killing off some of the trees which caused the problem. There is evidence to suggest that this did indeed happen in the Carboniferous era – the clue is in the name. This ongoing interaction between life and environment led to an evolution of both, so that photosynthetic bacteria gradually altered the atmosphere by generating oxygen, making possible more-complex forms of life that depended upon it for respiration.

Lovelock's is a description of ever-growing complexity emerging from simplicity, contradicting the assumption that entropy must always prevail. It is the degree of emergent complexity, the idea that some of it must be taking direction from above, rather than existing in an atomised, mechanistic frenzy, that, in part, ejected Lovelock from the scientific consensus.

The other aspect of this way of understanding the Earth that goes against the tide of the humanity narrative is that the humans are only one of countless organisms, as prone to spikes and collapses in population as any other.

We don't like this story. It disempowers us. It makes our endless ingenuity look a bit rubbish. The past few months alone had seen storms that were better at breaking human habitats than humans were at protecting them, new viral plagues and new wars fed by the destructive belief-memes that promoted them. It was perpetually tempting to see the ingenuity of Gaia rather than humanity at work. Here we were, close to peak population, exhausting our resources with a rapidity that made war more likely than ever before, getting sick and seeing swathes of land obliterated by climatic intervention. And, where resources were most squeezed and populations most desperate, the human population was most prone to adopting violent religious fantasies with a talent for destroying other humans.

I fantasised about destroying other humans too, listening to misery updates on Radio 4 while trapped between endless lorries overtaking lorries overtaking lorries on the drive home, entering that distaste for one's fellow men that grows as you find yourself in their overcrowded midst. Here, on this furred artery, where the transport of largely un-needed stuff from poor to rich helped hasten the whole humanity project's demise, for a couple of sclerotic hours you could have signed me up without much resistance for various terrorist organisations – at least until I got back into Herefordshire and the sky opened out and things looked brighter again.

I arrived home with time to spare, time to climb the mountain before picking the children up, which seemed like a good idea because it was there. The long drive had made me sleepy, and I needed rousing, and now the sun was low in the sky and the day's rain was starting to clear in the way that it always seems to around sundown.

For all that, my feet ached. A rainbow stood on the mountainside before me, and a small group of people walked through it, relieved to be on their way back down. I zipped my coat and forced myself grimly up the hill, telling myself it was good for me, unsure why I was there when I could be sitting down to eat with the others, seeing the children I hadn't seen much of, being social. The walk was a battle of internal wills, one of those episodes when it is clearer than ever that the self is really a senate of elves, a chamber of conflicting voices and desires, all with their own chaotic agenda. Somehow, the uphill project happened, but not without being derailed along the way by ingenious counter-arguments and rest-breaks, and by the time I reached the top, where the Wye Valley poured across the surface of the earth in its man-made glory of piecemeal fields and roads and houses, I was exhausted and cold.

Another band of rain blurred the sky above Lord Hereford's Knob, and Pen-y-Fan, behind it, was blacked out with cloud. It was August; it was hopeless. It was almost like a regressive reference to the season's old meaning. At Lammastide, the Green Man of Oak dies back and the Green Man of Holly takes his place, bearing the Green Knight's holly-club. Lammastide was considered the beginning of the harvest time and of autumn, and this year it felt true, autumnal, the cold approaching just as it passed. Rain sucked the warmth from the air and night came more suddenly. The flowers in the garden faded. Brown crept in around the edges of the bracken at the foot of the mountain.

We take for granted the two- or three-month timelag of our maritime climate, so that the residual heat of the ocean all around sees temperatures climb and fall more slowly; it seemed as though an autumn with an August start might once have been a thing, and perhaps it would come around again sooner than we thought.

Whether the gloom was meteorological or of other causes, I felt as though I was running out of steam. I couldn't shake the ridiculousness of the whole thing, the idea that you could miraculously fix the world's fragility, or even an anxiety of it, by halfheartedly convincing people that bits of old medieval church art could be reframed into some kind of anti-dogmatic neo-pagan religion that was not religion. It was a hopeless notion. My brief and monomaniacal interest in it ebbed away. I picked up the children and took them to the seaside, where they sat digging trenches with their cousins while an aerobatic display of military planes took place overhead and naval vessels moved to and fro across the seafront. I dreamed of new things. It was a dead end.

Two exchanges happened soon after. The first was an email conversation with a writer, P, around the time his book that had compelled that conversation was longlisted for the Booker. It had been published a month after the storms and the manifestation of the Green Man idea, and, in perfect synchronicity, it bore a foliate head on its cover. He had his own artistic doom-cult and the book was brilliant and bleak and I wanted to know more. His Green Man was a dispossessed outlaw doing asymmetric warfare in the woods against the invading Normans and their authoritarian Church. It is a story about the death of autonomy and the death of the old religion, or perhaps their wake, for it follows the last embers of an uprising. Its protagonist resembles a pagan Ted Kaczynski, seeking refuge in a natural world that is as fearsome and dangerous as the new order outside it, choosing freedom over technologically assured submission.

Like Kaczynski, P had little time for the progress narrative. For most of Western history, he said, we were afraid of nature, our fairy tales soaked in this fear. For a brief period, fuelled by oil and the notion of progress, we became nature's protectors. Now nature was turning on us, the planet heating up like someone with a fever trying to burn off its pathogens, and suddenly we were on the brink of being the victims again. Returning to an animistic view of nature was probably the only thing that will save our sanity. He mentioned an anecdote about the way in which children are born as anarchists and animists, only to have both tendencies educated out of them.

It is always encouraging to find agreement where you can, and animism felt incrementally less of a fringe silliness, even if my attempts at reconstructing it were not proving fruitful. The other thing that happened was a walk that went awry.

I met a friend, G, a couple of miles from home by the side of the Wye. We went to a spot near one of its tributaries, whose name she did not know, and made our way beneath a pretty old iron bridge and up past the brook to a broad sunny clearing edged by oaks. The path was overgrown with rosebay willowherb and long grass interspersed with fat-berried brambles, and we brushed our way through it, stopping from time to time while G, a nature photographer, took pictures of rare butterflies and lichens along the way: the Small Blue, which is small enough to be missed entirely unless you know what you are looking for, one male and one, less blue, female, locked in an uneasy mating dance; trumpet-tendrilled lichen along a bank, engaged in some unknowable sexual reproduction involving the construction of microscopic satellites to propagate spores.

The place hummed with life, with bumblebees and butterflies and plants both common and strange, from the purple-pink blossom and fading fluff of the willowherb to the red fuzz of Robin's Pincushion, an uncannily fluffy and picturesque gall made by tiny asexual wasps burrowing into the stems of wild roses. It is named after Robin Goodfellow, the green sprite of woodland folklore. A buzzard swept low over the land, and we passed tiny feathered holes where wrens nested, in a reverie of sunshine and footfall and talking.

Her dog ran off into a deep forest, a pretend commercial

forest of tall pines, thickly overgrown with bracken, mosses and ferns, bright green below and dark up top and vast at the end of its lifecycle. He ran off silently, the green soaking up any sound, and we stopped and listened to the silence for a while, trying to discern the sound of water from it.

We were supposed to be finding a waterfall along a gorge. The map said we should drop down somewhere here, but aside from the forest track there was nothing resembling a path, or at least a human path – deer prints had set out their own, weaving here and there through the trees in no particular order, and at some point we abandoned the notion of a path entirely and scrambled down the steep hillside, seeing where it fell to vertical cliff and clinging to the undergrowth just before it, sunk deep into sphagnum moss and mountain ash saplings until we saw the river down below and slid down the trunk of a fallen tree into it, hoping it would hold.

Behind the fallen tree, walls of wet rock rose on both sides, improbably high for a low river in August and curving upstream around the riverbed. We tiptoed along its edge where we could and waded where we could not, envying the dog as he ploughed blithely through it all. I was supposed to be back home by now, but the gorge pulled us along in hope of greater spectacle, and eventually, around what we agreed would be the last bend, we met a magnificent waterfall feeding a large round pool and stopped to observe it, struck silent in a manner superfluous to the vast roar of the water.

The high walls of rock hung with ferns and ivy, and could have been eighty or a hundred metres high, out-chasming Lud's Church by some margin. We might have been the first humans along there in a while, for there was no sign of activity, and even the cavers' forum G found later when trying to establish the river's name said you needed a death wish to reach it. I don't know that we had a death wish; there was something awe-inspiring about the scale of it – and its hiddenness, the lack of a path and a park bench, the water that filled our boots and almost did for G's camera and my entirely redundant phone when we both, inevitably, slipped on algal rocks and fell in – that was life at its unmapped best.

We scrambled back downstream, through shallows and along the edges, or so we thought, of deep pools, no longer caring about the wet, delighting in the movement of the water and the rocks, following the dog as he nosed his way ahead, up and down banks and under fallen trees, along the moving vista of riparian life. An otter leapt up a bank in a single fluid stroke like the flick of a wet paintbrush and trout darted fast along the deeper, darker pools.

We had talked about Heraclitus before, and now we were moving too fast and concentrating too hard to hold a proper conversation, but the thought stayed with me. Heraclitus, a pre-Socratic philosopher whose work exists only in fragments and is therefore healthily prone to speculation, held that the world, like a river, is in a state of constant flux, so that nothing is ever constant apart from change. Part of this conception of change was the unity of opposites, so that everything in the world exists with, and is defined by, its opposing entity or force: darkness and light, living and dying, growth and retreat.

It is tempting to think of the world in polarities. It also sometimes seems as though there are two opposing and contradictory mood-drives: to mourn all change as loss, or to celebrate it as progress. And change is the only constant: the cyclical change of days and seasons and the life-course, and the larger changes that sweep up the world around us: the march of technology and the way in which it pulls unpredictability into ever-increasing order, and the things that it eats up and that perish in its wake, the lives that no longer have a place to be.

In a similar fashion, there seem to be two opposing and contradictory bits of life-force: entropy and emergent order, so that on a small scale, a day-to-day scale, things seems to perpetually fall apart and dissociate, so that it is all you can do to keep them ticking over, sweeping floors and mending cracks and piecing lost things back together, and yet life, on a grand scale, becomes ever more complex and ordered, and there are more rules and fewer freedoms left.

If we lived through time on a greater scale, we might see these larger changes as parts of a cycle too, with their own distinct seasons of waxing and waning, building up and falling apart. Perhaps it would be possible, in some alternative tiny dimension, to see an apple grow upon a tree and watch it ripen and fall, and then observe the swell of the lives that feed upon it, the yeasts and fungi and maggots, and watch them slowly reach their peak, the time when it is furred with spores and new civilisations before the whole thing melts away into the ground.

All these things are happening around us all the time, tiny births and deaths, the rise and fall of tiny realms, and we muster no emotion for them. It would be overwhelming if we did. Perhaps we are only inclined to perceive things that happen on our own scale, to perceive life as existing only on our own scale, in our own image. Perhaps the possibility of something like life existing on far larger and far smaller scales is too exhausting, or too unsettling, for our lives would then be lost to its vast chain of events and any sense of control might be lost.

Given the infinite prevalence of the living and dying of all things, the degree to which people chose to focus on one phase or another seemed largely an issue of mood, whether they were predisposed to optimism or pessimism, of the sanguine or melancholic aspect. Perhaps the history of protest movements, the Levellers and the Luddites, could be taxonomised by mood into progressive and conservative camps. Those terms are so lost into political and economic perversion that it is easy to lose sight of their roots: moving on versus keeping things as they are. It is generally assumed that environmentalism is the preserve of the Left, and the Left is progressive, but in technological terms deep or dark-green environmentalism has always been a conservative interest. It is teleological and retrogressive, about meeting the world's end or regressing to a bleak early human era, a darker age.

I had probably heard about the terminology of green first from G, who really lived it, when we met washing up on school lunch duty. Her five-year plan was to reframe environmental ethics from a position she described as biocentric, where the interests of all life were balanced against one another. If you take a hard line on this, it necessitates restricting the interests of humans at the very least; at its logical conclusion, human extinction is desirable. G didn't advocate killing people, and although the conversation had been curtailed a little by the need to cling on to passing branches as we scrambled down the edge of a cliff, I got the impression that to advocate the restriction of human activity was a dark sort of green, as opposed to the optimistic bright green assumption that human technology would help the situation.

And yet the interventions that she made that got the most attention in the human world were probably her photographs, the way she could pause for a few seconds on a walk and get the perfect close-up of something tiny that, magnified for that moment in time, revealed the endless complexity of small things. She got excited about it, and the excitement was infectious, so that I'd find myself on the walk eager as a child, impressed by the vastness of the tiniest bits of the world.

It is a complexity that is and should be breath-taking, awe-inspiring: the framed frenzy of wasps negotiating entry and exit from their nest, an otiose toad, watching. I didn't see those photographs live, but on her blog, and the technology that enabled all of that to happen, the camera that emerged unscathed from the river, is something that enriches our understanding of the world and the value we put on its hidden parts. I wouldn't want to ditch it in favour of returning to a dark-age utopia of dark-age understandings of the world. Maybe she was getting the balance right, doing her best to tread lightly and educate lightly, creating more than she consumed in the world.

My unfitness for propagandising about our relationship with the natural world echoed loudly across the valley as I drove my small and largely unnecessary SUV home. I did genuinely believe that morality is a social construct, an ideology embedded from the first by the association of a mother's breast and the incremental assumptions that follow, the early familial ability to be unique in its capacity for protection and all the institutions of thought that feed off it, but a deep internal conviction burned within me and it was unsettling in its ferocity. Some people and some lives were kinder and less greedy towards the world than others: you could frame it in their footprint and behaviour, you could quantify it in all sorts of ways, and it seemed inescapable.

When I got home, late and wet, the kids wanted a

bonfire. We had a shedful of cardboard left over from the move and I had not got round, as I had promised myself, to flattening it and slowly getting it collected week by week for recycling. I had held an excruciating image for a while of the Green Man peering out across recycling centres, reduced to public information icon, and felt the internalised disapproval that we call shame mount as I barrowed it across the road. I could have created a spreadsheet to determine the carbon footprint of a bonfire versus ferrying the stuff in several carloads to Brecon, but I felt wild today. Wild and nihilistic and like having a bonfire, because bonfires are fun.

I tore up the cardboard with the bigger child while the smaller one scrunched up newspaper into balls, which she laid with impressive order into a circle. We piled strips of cardboard on top and struck a match. They stood back as the fire built in height and heat, and we threw on larger pieces and then whole boxes, flames leaping metres high.

'I'm worried about the trees,' said the big one.

'About them burning down?'

'More about them getting hurt. The fire's hurting them.'

We slowed the fire down, kicking out the cardboard and the wood to separate them.

'What do you want to do about the cardboard?'

'I want to burn it. We should get rid of it. I just don't want to hurt the trees. That one's whole branch is scorched. The leaves have all gone black.'

We stood by our small fire for a long time. The big one watched it in silence, gazing at the ground and the trees; the small one wandered off, bored, looking for fairies. Eventually it was done.

The big one looked at the burnt tree, downcast. I asked him if he was still sad about the tree. He nodded and edged around the hot ashes towards it, reaching his hand to it and, checking for heat, he reached around it and embraced it. He stayed there for a while, a good few minutes, and I brushed earth over the embers, making that strange deathly smell of damp earth and fire in mutual destruction.

'We could go into the sacred grove and say sorry.'

'Yeah. Let's do that. I do think it's a silly name though – I don't understand why you call it that.'

'What do you think we should call it? We could call it the Green Chapel. What do you think of that?'

He averted his eyes to a newly fallen leaf, gold-streaked, as thought to meet my gaze would transmit pity or contempt or something, and then grabbed a stick and wove his way along the overgrown track, pushing down the nettles and the brambles that clutched at my ankles as I carried his sister on my back. She squealed and complained that the brambles were scratching her, which I knew not to be true, because they were scratching me instead, and informed me that she wanted to go inside and watch *Tinkerbell and the Lost Treasure*.

'Come on,' I said, 'come on, we're going to find some real fairies in the tree and talk to them.' She grasped my throat, which she knew not to do. 'Besides, I'm not going to carry you back to the house, so you'd better just get on with it.'

She jumped down and flashed me a grotesque face. The big one sat by the large birch.

'Tell her to be quiet,' he said. 'I'm trying to have a rest.'

Remembering the conversation with P about the resting childhood state of anarchy and animism, I moved away on the pretence of stacking some logs and watched them through a hazel thicket.

The big one was still there, the small one ambling about

227

with his stick as though to rile him, and then, when she didn't, building piles of leaves and kicking them over and singing a song in made-up words. Perhaps it was happening – perhaps he was meditating with the tree, for his position, in the crook of its base, his feet aligned with the roots, was correctly shamanic. Perhaps, in her own obstreperous way, the small one was engaged in some kind of sylvan hymnal that I could no longer understand in my adult mind.

I left them to it and went to stack the logs. When I returned they were fighting over string, trying to make aeroplanes out of sticks. So much for latent spirituality. We walked back. The fire was dead.

They bickered over the film and the small one got her way and announced at the end that we were going to have an autumn party with a moonstone. A spark of hope for the animist generation rekindled. I lay in bed with the big one later, and asked what had happened with the tree. He frowned and asked me what I meant. I asked him if he'd spoken to it.

After a long pause that ceded to a sigh, and in his most patient voice, he explained that you don't talk to trees, because we do everything in human language and trees don't, they do things in tree ways, and there's no way of talking about it like they're people because they're not, and then requested a banana and a glass of water. I didn't dare ask him what he thought of the Green Man.

I may or may not have raised a shaman, but at least he had a sensible handle on how to approach nature, and that was a good enough start. And perhaps animism, in its lightest, most commonsensical form, was simply a default assumption that everything worked in its own sphere, and humans were no exception to it. Perhaps it merely required an appreciation of how other things, like trees and rivers, were as things in themselves.

Perhaps, for that matter, the childhood form of anarchy, the rapid cycles of destruction and creation and the deviation of all structured activity into play, the relentless queries of why and how and the answering back and picking of holes in all attempts at final answers – perhaps this too was common sense, the best, lost kind of common sense. I wasn't going to succeed in making my children adherents of any cult, my own or others, and if they were unruly and often found me stupid, maybe something was going right.

EIGHT

The Wilderness

There was a storm, a new storm. It was the first of the season. In the woods, the path, which had died back flat with only a few bare skeletons left where the nettles used to line the middle, was strewn with fat catkins the size of cigars and big branches of elder and ash and maple, torn off by the wind the night before. One of the fireside mirrors in the corner of the shed had fallen and cracked, so that it reflected a fragmented picture of the leaves as they spread out into each other and the pale sun up above, a patch of birch that turned, too abruptly, into ash; an oak tree intercut with a fir.

Suddenly, the edges of the wood felt bare. You could see the height of the trees now that the undergrowth had shrunk away, and the fields on either side and the road seemed closer. You could feel how the shape of the railway embankment, those extra few metres, elevated the wood to catch light and sound in a way that had previously been dampened by foliage.

One of the things I learned living at my windy old house at the top of the hill was about how sounds, once you get used to them, form a rhythmic backdrop to your life that you barely notice until they're gone.

Now, in my new house, cars and lorries rushed by with a frequency and unpredictability that sometimes seemed as though it might drive me mad. I had to remind myself that I once felt the same way about the wind in the old house until, at some point in the second winter, it fell into place, emerging within thought only when some more basic restlessness roused it. And this new storm had actually sounded quite comforting for the way it masked the traffic, the noise of the wild roaring out the noise of human things.

When a sound like that falls into place it can even become a comfort, underscoring life with familiarity, an external heartbeat of the world at large. I definitely didn't feel this about the lorries now, and had to stop myself from fantasising with intent about felling trees across the road in the dead of night to knock one out, as a warning to the others.

But let's get back to the wind, which, in its absence, turns out to have had qualities. I got habituated to the comings and goings of it, just as you get habituated to repetitive rhythms, like when leaving a club at dawn and finding repetitive beats on the train on the way home, beats that are silent to the lines of commuters heading the other way but that are real, made of the interface of train and track and its regular irregularities as wheel meets joint. Sometimes the wind and rain stayed in my head, and could be brought out afresh with some other repetitive movement, like walking fast or running, for rediscovery.

I had also rediscovered a techno album, *Diorama*, which seemed to do something similar. It came and went in waves and layers, tunes forming and dissociating in the same way that clouds and flocks of starlings do, and I could listen to it endlessly and simply find more detail in it rather than getting bored, which was useful for long car journeys. I listened to it driving up the Golden Valley in the storms, and one of its tracks was called 'H2O', which had an obvious resonance as the car drove through a flood dissipating beneath other, wrecked cars.

It was a concept album about nature and had tracks named after plants and insects and weather. It was made by a producer and DJ, Dominik Eulberg, whose other job was being a park ranger in a forest somewhere in Germany, and who had previously made an album about birds. There was something delightfully unfashionable about the idea that one of the best bits of dance music I'd heard in ages was made by someone who got his kicks, and ideas, in the woods.

And if shamans could access trees and rivers by singing to, or with, them, catching some common rhythm, it made sense that you could do something similar musically. In the same way that Islamic art depicts godliness through intricate patterns that could be made only by godly hands, I found a depiction of Nature, or perhaps God-or-Nature, in the intricate patterns of electronic music, and it was the intricacy, the many, many layers and their own details, that made it work. You could get lost in the detail, the deep, bassy detail and the high, ethereal detail, the many winglike oscillations and the waxing and waning of various parts – in these ways it was entirely natural, or naturalistic.

Twenty years ago, someone listening to it would have called it trance, a term now permissible only as an insult. Trance had its time, and became a victim of its own success, with the detailed trippy structures that originated on Goan beaches simplified and amped up for a broader audience until they were so formulaic and bloated and bombastic that they became a bit comical. But the name reverts back to something that music is supposed to do, when it works – to create an altered state in which sounds tell new stories and allow new ways of understanding the world.

It seemed a bizarre irony that the people listening to this sort of music would generally do so in blackened clubs in gritty bits of cities, and with synthetically altered brains to take it all in. It deserved a field at least, or, at a push, a car ride somewhere in the Welsh borders with a view. When I struggled to access the headspace I needed for thinking about nature and other such magical things, I put on *Diorama* and it usually worked, reframing the internal conversation into something loftier.

I sometimes suspected this loftiness was what made people suspicious about electronic music, the fact that its complexities could do things to your mind other than overwhelming it with a big dark crash of noise.

We tend to consume word-based music, which is really words with a bit of music added to them for effect, oral-formulaic rather than intrinsically musical in character, and to pick apart song lyrics which, if they were merely seen on paper, would be mediocre poetry. We fixate on these words when we listen to them, and fixate on their narratives. When music is good and wordless, you can reach a state beyond words that we don't often find, and which takes you away from the relentlessness of the words that surround us everywhere in our over-connected human world.

The counterpoints to this were many. The lyrics, I'd be told, were mantra-like, designed solely as a site of departure, words that were somehow not words. And that might be from someone who actually quite liked wordless music, and for each of them there'd be ten black-clad men whose idea of fun was to sit around debating Bob Dylan and aimlessly strumming a guitar at parties. They were less moderate. Real music had words. Real music had a rhythm and stuck to it. Real music could be played by drunk men at 4 a.m. Electronic music was either painfully unlistenable stuff one sometimes accidentally encountered at festivals, or dance music for fluffy hippies, not so much beneath contempt as beyond consideration.

And yet these sentiments around the inauthenticity of electronic music sometimes felt as though they were starting to wane. Another album emerged, named after Wysing Forest near Cambridge, which was slower and less dancey but with a similar wordless complexity and sense of space, and everyone agreed that it was wonderful, even the people who weren't ravers. It was still made out of patterns, and patterns of patterns, in that way that wordless music is, but the patterns had an analogue content, sounds that, if not recorded from nature, felt naturalistic at heart. And something about the way it all fell together was wind-blown, loosely structured, so that it felt as though it was made of the wilderness.

Making a techno concept album about nature still felt like an audacious thing to do, given that computer-generated sounds were generally held to be the least natural of all musics. I'd never had any time for this notion: all music, if we hold music to be intentionally ordered sounds, entails some degree of technology in order to order the sounds in the first place, and the idea that old technologies must necessarily be more authentic that new ones had always struck me as ridiculous. Once upon a time – and not so long ago – the piano keyboard was considered to be both technological marvel and unnatural threat to authenticity.

And what was authenticity anyway? What reality was being captured with varying degrees of realness? The idea of authenticity depends on there being a thing that can somehow be described or reproduced. It assumes that it is possible to be naturalistic in the production of music. And in both cases, I felt that electronic music was doing a pretty good job of providing a naturalistic description of wild nature, better by far than the human voice, proffered as the gold standard of authenticity, and which can only ever naturalistically describe itself.

You could see music's re-ordering of sounds as representative of things in the world, or the sounds of things in the world, an onomatopoeia, and many musicians and composers appear to be doing this much of the time. You can capture a rhythm or tone and recreate it, but the process of imitation will always be distended somehow. Even if you record a natural sound and play it back, the equipment you use to reproduce it and the altered context in which it is heard make it a different thing again.

A friend told me about a sound-artist and musician who had recorded pondweed. The sound of pondweed photosynthesis is rhythmic and thuddy, like noisy techno heard from afar. It happens on a scale that we don't usually hear. It makes it harder to claim that there is nothing natural about the ordering of repetitive beats, like the pondweed's photosynthetic vibrations whose quick cycle makes them sound like one burst of noise to our ears. Was the pondweed music? It sounded a little like it to me. The recreated sounds of *Wysing Forest* sounded a little like the pondweed sometimes too – both the noises which were generated electronically and ended up sounding exactly like the recorded sounds of life, and the recorded sounds of life re-ordered electronically.

When I lived in a community in Scotland, peopled by a quite even split of folksy hippies and fallen ravers, we would argue over lunch about what sort of music could reasonably be considered to be music and what was not music. There was little claim to objectivity. Of course DJing was music, I'd thunder: it was a sequencing of sounds in which the editing process on the decks was the creation of a new musical text. The hippies rolled their eyes. You needed to actually be creating the sound with the human body, they said, breathing life into it with human breath or caressing life into it with human hands.

One thing we sometimes managed to agree on was that music with words wasn't really music, but words. It was miraculous, really, that anyone found time to make any music with all the policing of it going on, but the village pub, which was also the post office and someone's front room, had live music once a week and often at weekends too, and people stayed and played and danced until they fell over and had to be put into one of the caravans outside reserved for such eventualities, which were regular, and there were real ceilidhs that were not pretend ceilidhs like people who fancied themselves to be of Scottish heritage had at weddings, but where the whole village, young and old, were basically shamed into dancing. And in this remote place, where you could go for eight or ten miles without seeing a house, there were always vast house parties with more live music and dancing. I'd never seen so much dancing.

As a Londoner, it hadn't occurred to me that folk music could be like that, a living thing rather than beardy affectation, and for all our disputes over the musical validity of the decks and mixer I started to grow an affinity for it. The Galloway folk musicians came out of the wilderness, down from the hills to create a strong life that fed the whole community. They came out of a musical wilderness too, a place that lay far outside the accepted mainstream of music ghostwritten in studios and commissioned by marketing strategists. There was a culture, entirely unaffected unlike some of its metropolitan analogues, of getting involved and submerged in the

music and the dance and the craic that kept everybody together. As I fell down for the second time one evening at
the ceilidh, to much hilarity, I grudgingly realised that it was
doing the same good things as rave culture, but with fewer
drugs.

Now, seven years later, earlier factionalism calmed a bit by
time, I was sitting at a wilderness-themed wedding banquet
across from a Green Man and next to his wife, a goddess,
round-bellied with new life. I no longer had to hunt the
Green Men; they seemed to manifest around me. In the
hall were a stag and many feathered creatures, and some un-
nameable ones too. Assorted fairies and a lion came and
went.

The next day we entered a vicarless church draped with
flowers, and an ivy circle marking out the ceremonial space
where the bride and groom would embrace. The ceremony,
a non-legally binding statement of intention, was officiated
by children and had begun with spontaneous tonal chanting
and culminated in an old Scottish folksong, 'I'll Lay Ye
Doon'. The vicar didn't know about any of it, but was fine
with the church being used for a couple of hours in return for a donation for repairs to the roof or the hall or
something.

It was probably for the best. They only wanted it for the
acoustics anyway. Even in the belief edgelands of the Church
of England, where you could basically be an agnostic or pantheist or pagan and re-label it Celtic and be OK, marking
out a proudly godless and lawless union with a song that
was, essentially, about sex, would have been pushing it a bit.

It was the most honest wedding-hymn I'd heard, and probably the most sincere. The choirmaster, who had chosen it, was a well-known song collector and folksinger who I'd been to see earlier in the summer at his home up a mountain. He hadn't always been a folksinger, but had started out teaching wilderness survival skills.

I went to find him in Craswall, which might be the wildest place in England, although it is barely in England, overshadowed by Offa's Dyke, and barely even a village, a broken string of houses against a steep mountainside. You reach it by a mountain pass that is often impassable, a long straight track parallel to the high ridge of the Cat's Back to one side and desolate Cefn Hill, beyond a ruined abbey, to the other. If you cross this stretch at night, there is nothing to see but black lit up intermittently by sheep's eyes caught in the headlights, and, perhaps, a smattering of orange at the periphery of Hereford. In the day there is nothing too. You descend past a tiny church and into a steep, pitted dip and up again outside a tiny, wonderful pub that is rarely open.

The Black Mountains were called the Black Mountains by the people on the English side of them. From the sunnier side of the Golden Valley, the monolithic Hatterrall Ridge has a steepness that is rarely lit. The bit of it that forms the backdrop to Craswall is called the Black Hill, and it slopes up blackly from the farms and dwellings dotted along the road, which have no number or name. Bruce Chatwin immortalised it in his novel *On the Black Hill*, in which nothing much happens over a very long time despite intermittent episodes of brutality that never seem terribly surprising, as though the wind whips the mind into bleak places.

The choirmaster grew up in London but spent childhood weekends and summers here, at the foot of the Black Hill, which looms in half-lit crenellations over the house and garden, and makes people look small. You could see how, as a London child exposed to this very different world at the edge of mountain and civilisation, the appeal of the wilderness might win out. And to describe what he did as wilderness survival diminished it somewhat. It was more an art of living in the wilderness, and how to do it well.

He was stopping home mid-tour, arrived the night before from Scotland, and the house was full of newly risen musicians who wandered softly about in search of coffee. We went to the garden and sat beneath an old yew, where he sipped tea made from goose grass, which he called cleavers. Something between mist and rain hung in the air, and from an outbuilding came the strains of instruments tuning up in distant arpeggios. The berries of the yew, whose seed is deadly, were delicious, he said, so that you could work the brink of delicacy and death by eating the flesh and spitting out the seed.

It occurred to me, later, that human ingenuity had adapted the toxicity of the yew to prolong human survival. The things that stopped human cells from functioning could be levelled against human cells that had gone wrong. Taxanes form a key part of our arsenal of chemotherapy drugs, and their derivative, paclitaxel, which is largely derived from the bark of the Pacific Yew, is on the World Health Organisation's list of essential medicines. The wilderness is increasingly recognised as a useful medical resource: a Madagascan rainforest flower, the rosy periwinkle, was the source of two critically important chemotherapy drugs used to treat blood cancers, among many other previously rare plants.

As well as providing a source of drugs to prolong human life, the wilderness was also, according to various schools of thought, a resource for human well-being and creativity. There were wilderness gurus with their own trademarked courses and techniques, in a similar fashion to the branded shamans. There were wilderness courses for children, adolescents, men and women, all geared towards the very human-centred goal of self-actualisation. The choirmaster had a genuine love for it, though, and in him you could see the connecting thread between wilderness and music.

In the process of collecting songs, he hung out with Irish travellers. The traveller songs were largely the same as the songs of settled Britons, but they persisted longer than in settled culture. The travellers retained a wealth of old folk-songs that were passed down generations, and just about enough of their oral culture in an environment of inform-al social get-togethers – the gatherings and horse fairs – to keep some of the songs going. The movement and tight family bonds spread the songs and maintained them, and the travellers' existence on the fringes of settled society main-tained their distinctive culture.

There was a further critical factor, at least until 1974, the year that Woolworths first stocked the portable television. The travellers, until then, had not been able to consume mainstream popular culture, and although the songs died out quickly once television entered traveller homes, their memory of the songs lived on in the older generations raised before it. And the travellers had been identified by settled musicians for their rich song-culture for generations, too – Vaughan Williams acquired folksongs like the 'Leaves of Life' from a Herefordshire farm where the gypsy ballads moved through the seasons with gypsy labour.

When you looked at those songs, they were all about wandering. Even if they were love songs, like 'I'll Lay Ye

Doon', they were still interspersed with references to wandering. It was as though the process of wandering was how the songs were made. You don't wander in fixed, straight lines. You don't wander in institutions. You need some sort of wilderness to do it in, urban or rural; the folk tradition drew from the rural wilderness and still does.

A week after the wedding, my father came to stay. He brought a wood carving for the sacred grove, a man shaped from a tree trunk we had once bought up a mountain in Austria, and who, now that my brother and I were grown up and no longer there to hunt him in the bushes, had languished in my father's garden for too long. He was basically our own Green Man, my father said, and he belonged here now. The children found him good rather than sinister. My father oiled him and carried him into the woods, and the man made sense there, peeking out from a hazel thicket.

There was something going on with my father – or perhaps there had always been something going on with my father that I had failed to see. He would email me pictures of springs which, he said, would once have been sacred. He turned out to be surprisingly knowledgeable about stone circles and would point out tumps and terraces as we drove down the valley taking the children to school. He spent suspicious amounts of time in the woods, purportedly checking for the presence of mosquito larvae in the ditch, and kept wanting to visit waterfalls.

He could couch it all in an interest in ancient history, but that alone did not account for the carved figures and the lurking in the woods. You could present the interest in sacred springs as belonging to an ecological mind, but that would be improbable in someone who thought me a crank for bothering to recycle, and who loved cutting down trees.

I tried to determine whether he was jumping on my band-wagon, or I on his, and realised that he was into all this stuff long before I even noticed it, long before I was born, back when his day-to-day life involved being a beat constable in Deptford and its highlight was seeing the dawn across the river, and probably, in part at least, because of that. If an attachment to the old earth religions was primarily a romantic exercise, romanticism was an escapist exercise, and there was something retrospectively pleasing about a lone policeman on the grimmer streets of London silently hailing the dawn.

We were in the car, talking about folk music and the wilderness. He told me about a grocer in Kington where he once bought tickets for a secret gig who knew everything about folk music. He'd be a good person to talk to, and would be sure to have some ideas. We drove to Kington, over the Radnor Hills where the last mist hung in the morning, and walked through the town, dozing on a Tuesday. The grocery shop, called the Grapevine, was not the sort of shop you'd expect to find in Kington, which is small and sleepy: it was laden with the last fat Hereford strawberries and raspberries of the season, and huge dressed crabs and slabs of smoked salmon. I steeled myself buying fruit while the couple behind the counter served customers.

When I asked them, tentatively, if they knew of any musicians who lived out in the sticks and would talk to me, they asked me about my book and my whereabouts and, satisfied, nodded. They said I should speak to J, who lived nearby and was actually around at the moment. J was often on tour, and would be again in a week or so. They gave me his wife's name and his landline, which was an unusually trusting thing to do. I felt a bit like a stalker, and told his wife that when I called her, but she said he had a tattoo of the Green Man on his arm and would definitely be up for a chat, and so I found myself back in Kington at the same time the next day, sitting in a cafe opposite the grocers, and opposite J, and beside some elderly ladies having a deafening conversation that proved somewhat nerve-wracking, for I could barely hear a thing.

J didn't know when the first idea of the Green Man came to him, because his relationship with the land was a lifelong thing and his interest in Celtic art and folk traditions, which is what he saw as the Green Man's habitat, came to him over time as a result of that. He grew up on a council estate in Yorkshire, and his grandfather would take him off on moorland walks and instruct him to stop from time to time to memorise the scene. The memories stuck.

Later, a band coalesced around J while he was working as a teacher in Kent and moonlighting in the riotous Canterbury music scene of the seventies, where folk and punk existed side by side to the extent that their gigs would happen consecutively at the same venues, so that you might leave a folk gig at the art college just as the punks arrived for theirs, in a strange and peaceable flow between radically different aesthetics. It had never occurred to me that folk and punk could even meet, but upon further reflection there probably were similarities. There was the participatory nature of both scenes, so that, far from consisting of audiences consuming music as a commodity, spectating their idols from afar, everyone was somehow involved, by dancing or dressing outlandishly or performing some other less definable role.

They were each part of a counterculture at the edges of normality: one taking the wilderness and a sense of history as its aesthetic basis, the other a more urban form of wildness. The folk scene, like the punk scene, was tight-knit. Unlike the punk scene, it was involved in all sorts of wider local dances and rituals: the ceilidhs and the morris men, and the Whitstable Jack-in-the-Green, for whom J's band played. They were primarily a dance band, a ceilidh band, who existed to make the dance happen, bringing together the magic of the old folk gatherings and the movement of a whole English scene.

The Whitstable Jack-in-the-Green had been revived in the Victorian folklore fad. J described the Victorians as great recreationists: they were caught up in a romance with the past that you could say is being re-recreated now. In response to a request for people who saw themselves as Green Men, I had had an email from the organiser of the Deptford Jack-in-the-Green, which had Victorian roots and was rekindled in the 1980s, in a late wave of folk rituals that you could probably see as taking their inspiration, in turn, from that same revived folk scene. Speculating wildly, I would guess that both waves were also a response to urbanisation and industrial life, seeking rituals to embody a sense of connection with the land that was, in many other ways, increasingly lost.

The ceilidh band developed a scene in its own right and became a band in its own right. J was based in London and was otherwise on tour for much of the following decade, increasingly successful in a folk-rock scene labelled 'Celtic' by non-Celtic music journalists. At some point J realised that he didn't like the journey to gigs, the way he arrived stressed out and unwilling to share his space, and he began to walk to them instead. This turned out to be a far preferable arrangement. He liked it when people joined him, and the way they turned up with unreasonably large backpacks full of things they did not need, as though more stuff would save them;

he liked to lead them along the way and to stop from time to time to take in a view – a valley with no sign of human existence, a stoat, a red kite in flight – a phenomenon he called the 'pantheistic moment'.

Few people were able to get the pantheistic moment straight off. J found this a little disappointing, because it had always been with him, ever since his grandfather took him off onto the moors. You could say that he was doing what his grandfather did for him, taking people into the wilderness and making them discover a simpler way of thinking, an emptiness, a silence that did not exist elsewhere. He wanted to pass on what he called the 'spirituality of places' – a sense of being part of something larger, a sense of being the transient entity in a landscape that would always be there. The Victorians tried to master nature, he said, and we were doing much the same thing now; there was something about being out in the wilds that showed, wordlessly, that we were not succeeding.

I thought it all had a priestly quality to it, and liked the idea of musician as shepherd-cum-hierophant, leading his fan-flock into the wilderness for the greater good. It was a nice subversion of the idea of the untouchable rock star – the celebrity quality that, J acknowledged somewhat sheepishly, drew people onto his walks.

Sometimes words and lyrics would come to him on his walks, falling into place along the walk's natural rhythm. Sometimes musicians would join him, so that they were a wandering band of minstrels, and he would play in pubs and village halls, from the wild places to the small spaces where the folksongs began. The walking wasn't just about the music, though, and it was no longer about transport. Being in the wilderness was a metaphysical exercise for him.

He felt that there was something particularly wild about the border country, like the hills near here, the last English town before the empty wilds of Mid Wales. Perhaps it was the ungovernable nature of the people of the borders, with their fractured alliances, or the impenetrable hills, like the Black Mountains, that tended to form them. It was as though they retained their distinct local cultures for longer.

These local cultures with their breadth and difference were the lifeblood of folk. There was a more recent form of Englishness that was constructed by imperial values, a contained, uniform and subjugated Englishness. The ancient, regional Englishness that we needed to rediscover was based on difference, he said, one that celebrated the distinctive qualities of individual places, their landscapes and their dialects. To conserve one's heritage like this now had a radical quality in our uniform world, which seemed a strange, true paradox.

I had always assumed that folk music would have had a further anarchic function, existing outside the canon of church music and church stories, and challenging it as a sort of rival. The reality was more textured. You'd have the same musicians playing different music in and out of church, a village orchestra of sorts, musicians both skilled and uneducated, J said. You couldn't draw a particularly clear line through church and not-church music, either, for many of the hymns were based on old folk tunes, tunes whose words once evoked the sun and moon and gods, as opposed to God. 'The Holly and the Ivy', that most pagan of carols, and probably one of the most ancient pieces of music still in common use in this country, originally had the line 'the playing of the many gods' – now supplanted with 'organs'.

It wasn't so much that the Church suppressed folksong as

that it appropriated it, so that old songs about life and country were adapted to be about the godliness within them. This process happened in reverse, too, with biblical myth proving ripe material for folksong. Gypsy workers, who came from farm to farm to work in the hop fields of Kent or to shear sheep in the Welsh borders, were a source of songs and imagery that had taken fragments of the Bible into their own oral tradition and remoulded them over time, through centuries of Chinese whispers, into new vernacular forms. In 'Bitter Withy', Jesus gets a sound thrashing from Mary for going off to play with three 'of the finest children' who don't make it across his supernatural bridge over the river. Jesus curses the willow, or withy twigs she uses in chastisement, and this is offered as an explanation for the way that willow rots from the inside out.

I thanked J and agreed to meet for a walk one day soon, and then crossed the road to the Grapevine to thank the grocers, who had seen us talking across the street and smiled.

It was harvest time. At home, the grapes were weighing down the vines at the edge of the garden so that they nearly brushed the floor. We caught the train to London to stay with my parents for the weekend, and I took the children for a bike ride to my father's allotment, ostensibly to pick grapes there too, but really because it was a nice place to be, and a strange one.

The children ran off somewhere. I walked more slowly, along the middle path to the back wall where his plot was. The front plots were the neatest and most uniform, as though allocated to the most reliable allotmenteers, the showhomers. My father's bit was the wilderness, or as close to it as you could get on an allotment in Chislehurst. It was bounded on one side by compost heaps and on another by the corner plot, the largest and most wonderful of all the plots, tended by a bearded gay couple who made powdered peach tea in their shed, and who had a pond and wildflowers among the other, productive things. His neighbour to the left had fruit trees, and now the plums and apples were rotting on them, because his wife was dying. My father had trees too, and, controversially, brambles, the cultivated sort that made the most enormous blackberries. They were the allotment heretics.

The Committee, newly chaired by a retired head teacher, was clamping down on this sort of activity. Land was at a premium, now more than ever, and plots had to be tended and productive, or be passed on to someone else, someone who needed one more. Casualties of the regime included a mother on maternity leave, who couldn't quite handle the plot plus the toddler and the new baby. The squeeze on resources meant that to waste land was to steal it from more deserving hands, hands that would, in turn, squeeze every last productive inch out of it. The ever-tightening committee made sure that everyone was aware of this, and of new developments regarding correct bonfire protocol and risk-assessment systems.

In fact, there wasn't a long waiting list in this part of Chislehurst, the leafiest of leafy suburbias, where gardens were plentiful and Waitrose deliveries bountiful. The threat to productivity came as much from the Church of England, which owned the site and leased it on favourable terms to the Borough of Bromley, and wanted to build a new faith school on it. The other, existing faith school had an impeccably neat and empty plot, weeded but un-planted, immediately by the front gate as though to cement the connection.

A man, bearded, middle-aged, thin and wiry and wearing a green woollen cardigan and, weirdly, leggings, emerged from the compost heap. He asked me if the children were mine.

'Yes,' I said, 'I hope they're not bothering you.'

'No, no, not at all. They are very nice children.'

'This is my dad's plot.'

'Oh. I see. It's a good spot. His carving is well liked here.'

I wondered what he meant, and then I saw the carved oak stool that I'd given him for Christmas years ago sitting in the middle of the fruit trees. It was made by a New Age traveller who lived, from time to time, at the end of our track. He was obsessed with oak trees – not particularly in their living form, just for their potential to be carved into things. The stool was simple, with fat round ridges curving up its sides. It was the sort of thing you'd find in a tea tent or by the permaculture garden at a hippyish festival, not on an allotment in Chislehurst.

The man went over to it. 'I thought the children were looking for this. The other children do. They are drawn to it.'

'Oh, right. That's unexpected,' I said.

The man patted it. 'Climbing on it, hugging the trees. They are like little druids here.'

My father had never mentioned this – but then he was on notice for his patchy attendance under the new regime. He had never mentioned this man either: I knew the names of his immediate neighbours, and a few others he was friendly with. This one had evaded me. Now he stroked the cherry tree in a fashion reminiscent of the shaman, like stroking the hair of a child. I glanced round to see where my children were – by a water butt, soaked. I let them get on with it.

'She's lovely. She will become lovelier.'

'So – do you have a particular sort of relationship with trees yourself? What do you grow?'

He patted his beard and looked over the fence, where a shriek of parakeets had flown off the roof of a building. He asked me what I meant by relationship. Then, without waiting for an answer, he sat down on the carved stool and told me that he often had a deeply spiritual experience in the woods on the way home from the allotment.

It began when he took up running, and the thundering repetitive rhythm of his feet and the heat and endorphins altered his mind into a new state, a state able to comprehend the vastness and great age of the trees in the woods. These woods were old woods, beautiful broad-leaved woods, and as he ran through them, once he'd got himself worked up into the right place, he felt as though he could hear the things that the trees were saying, which were not words so much as vibrations, and he found himself extending his runs so that they looped around every track he could find, and off them, no longer seeing them as runs at all but as running meditations in which he found an eternal, inexpressible truth.

Sometimes, he said, he went round in circles because he worried that the magic would break if he crossed a road or some other unmagical, civilised entity. He could make it across the road so long as it was instantaneous, a leap across from Hawkwood to Scadbury, with no wait for traffic and unseen. Then he could go and go for miles. He was fifty-three and his knees were perfect. Proof, he maintained, that we were built to run in the woods rather than on roads. His running had started to make him think more critically about the rest of his life, which he increasingly saw as a threat to the running-magic rather than the main event. He owned his house and contemplated selling it, moving somewhere cheaper and living out the rest of his life in the woods. But the Chislehurst woods were special. He wanted to stay with them.

Over by the front gate I could see my father, back with the car to collect the children. We still hadn't picked any grapes. I left the runner and went over to apologise for the wet children. By the time they were dried off and in the car and I had returned to the plot with secateurs, he had gone. I looked all around, and couldn't see a soul – only the para-keets, moving noisily from tree to tree, stripping them of plums.

I cut the grapes down from the vines and packed them into ice-cream tubs and then into my rucksack. I decided to go home through the woods. I decided to run. The running-magic was impeded by the heavy load of grapes and the many Sunday dog-walkers who, I decided, were not magical. I ran an indirect route back, along the lesser paths, looping through places I had not been to since my child-hood: the cockpit, which once looked so huge when I was less than three feet tall; the clearing, which had once had a pond at its edge, long since dried, where my father made us bows and arrows out of beech sticks and where we learned to shoot them; the holly-bushes, hanging low with berries, where we'd hide in caves, pretending to be bears.

You couldn't call these woods wild, but they were won-derful. Once I got older and became aware of things that you could do apart from playing in the woods, I got sneery about the suburbs, yearning to live in the real city, preferably north of the river, in the sort of gritty concrete idyll that we over-romanticise in its own way as we do the hay-bales and wheatfields of English folklore. This rejection of the suburbs coincided with getting into music, which, at that time in the 1990s, was really a string of narratives about cities and their human peculiarities: my early-adolescent tastes, which were not edgy, were for Suede and Pulp and Blur, stories about druggy wastrels on council estates and concept albums about the Westway. I read and re-read *London Fields* and *The Buddha of Suburbia*, in which Chislehurst is fleetingly mentioned as the worst of all possible suburbias, dreaming of the urban wilderness in which an endless multiplicity of people and places made it possible to be an outlaw. It was no accident, I decided, that much of punk's Bromley Contingent was from Chislehurst.

This very English form of city-mythology was where I nailed my aesthetic colours while living, embarrassingly, in Chislehurst. It made complete sense then, offering a shared narrative about contemporary urban life aimed squarely at the suburban middle-classes. It would have been unthinkable to be into folk music then, idealising trees and flowers, as it would have been disingenuous to be into hip-hop.

Trees and flowers were what happened here, in this deeply unfashionable corner of suburbia that still yearned after being part of Kent, the stuff of Tory councillors and square parents, who, unlike parents north of the river, did not let me go to raves. Trees and flowers had been co-opted so deeply into the conservative suburban aesthetic, with its neat herbaceous borders and landscaped gardens, that they stood for the same tedious human authoritarianism that weeded in floral gardening gloves and went to church on Sundays.

It is possible to live in the south-east of England and go

to the countryside – the bit outside London and before the sea where the built environment is not entirely contiguous – and still think that there is something innately conservative about it. It may be countryside, but there is nothing especially rural about it. The value of Home Counties land is so high that the people who have it want it to be immaculate, and need it to be immaculate, for all living space is a financial instrument now, and even the remaining corners of agricultural land look like a postcard, as though the neighbouring millionaires-by-default might take legal action if the cows become untidy. The whole place is really suburbia, in a slightly leafier and more expansive form than Zones 4 and 5. Even the woodlands are managed, by people like my parents, who go out on Sunday mornings as part of a volunteer conservation team to rake the grass around the ponds, trim back dead branches and gather fallen debris after storms. Perhaps it is the new Church.

One of these Sunday woodland-tending trips invoked an email, forwarded by my father, which contained no fewer than three risk-assessment forms with requirements for protective clothing, including high-visibility jackets, and with a detailed breakdown of the potential catastrophes that await those who go into the woods. There were the physical hazards of slips, trips and falls; attack by members of public/ dogs; biohazards such as animal or human waste, for bears may no longer shit in the Chislehurst woods, but foxes still did; contact with micro-organisms such as tetanus or leptospirosis, one of which we are universally vaccinated against, the other vanishingly rare here; contact with plant sap; and weather conditions. Then there were the 'typical uncontrolled outcomes' which you could attribute to being in the woods, or perhaps simply to the state of being alive: cuts and bruises; burns; lower back pain; verbal abuse; contracting disease; blisters; sunburn.

At the edge of the woods, where a war memorial recessed into the trees gives way to the last thicket before a busy junction, I caught a glimpse of a figure running along the path on the other side. Still in the rural mode of assuming that you know or recognise most people you encounter out and about, I hoped it would be the allotment runner, and entered a brief reverie in which I would chase him through the woods and he would confess to being a dedicated Green Man worshipper or, perhaps, reveal in wild-eyed fashion that he was the Green Man himself.

Instead, I walked down the hill, unloaded the grapes by my parents' backdoor, and took the train into town.

I wandered around Borough Market and stood, watching, in one of the places where you could see sky, much of it obscured by the Shard, its tip fluffed by cloud. It was one of those fuzzy, low-pressure days when the air is slow and people move slowly in it. Even the market, which already teemed with people, had a quietness to it, as though the damp in the air absorbed sound.

The thing I had always liked best about Borough Market was the way it was intersected by railway lines that formed its constituent caves and ravines, the cathedral-like height of the arches and the streets cut into the ground by some giant carving knife. I liked peering down into it as a child on a train leaving London Bridge on the way to Charing Cross, the point where the train's wheels always shrieked on the sharp bend out of the station. It was different now, un-Dickensian with its sterile streets and smart restaurants, magic sapped by hygiene.

I wanted a coffee, but the queue for the coffee shop tailed along the street, so that the people at the end must have had a half-hour wait at least. Perfect herbs sat green in boxes, perfect fruit and cheese and meat: you could find all the fine fruits of the earth here, displayed museum-like and consumed as fetish items rather than sustenance. A glass-fronted restaurant had fake flames and glossy bulls' heads outside, like a plastic temple to Mithras.

Along the tops of the arches, growing boldly at the sides of the railway, were buddleia, big, thick buddleia, some still in bloom. You could see them sprouting out of the yellow brick, gravity-resistant, apparently rootless. They were everywhere once you started to notice them, lining some of the walls entirely. Were there butterflies, too, up above the city on the butterfly bushes? It was too late in the year, and London was probably too polluted, but there was something about the resilience of the buddleia that felt good, and made the weirdness of the market all the weirder. The drive for authenticity in food felt a bit like another of those displacement activities, a first-world problem, an authenticity that was not in any way authentic, with its air-freighted groceries and polished perfection. There were no farmers here.

But I wasn't there for the market. I walked on to Southwark Cathedral, where I saw the morris dancers getting ready and crept off to a quiet spot by the river. The yellow warning sign on the wall said 'Danger: deep water' – both ridiculous and true, for the river was higher than I'd seen it in ages, lapping at the tops of the bridge supports, silver-grey and nearly touched by the low cloud so that the city made a very flat layer of existence in-between. It was also empty, strangely empty in the same way that the day was strangely still, the whole strait clear of moving traffic, clear of anything apart from its own silvery surface all the way to Tower Bridge.

Through the gate, in the cathedral courtyard, more morris dancers were arriving and changing into their dancing attire, each side in its own distinct uniform. I could see the Green Man now, his tall frame hung with green rags, his face obscured with a mask. His side looked magnificently satanic, dressed in black rags and black masks adorned with Celtic tribal images in white, with red LEDs that could be switched on remotely to wink or glow. Here they were on the equinox, or as close to it as possible, on Christian ground – in the courtyard visiting clergy sat with pots of tea, observing the morris preparations, waiting for something. A vicar tottered by in impossible heels and a tight, dog-collared dress. The distinctions were collapsing all around us, and it all felt perfectly normal.

But then perhaps it was always normal. The north sides of those Herefordshire churchyards where the Whitsun Ales took place, all those folk celebrations adopted into the folk faith – perhaps there was nothing new or strange about any of it.

The music started. The Wild Hunt Bedlam Morris flung themselves to and fro in formation, rags flying, the Green Man weaving through them with his stick, whooping and jumping about like a possessed – well, like a possessed Green Man, I suppose. Sometimes he skipped across to a table of sedate people and waved his stick in pantomime menace. I moved closer. I was enjoying this.

The Wild Hunt disbanded and the other, more polite side, all knee socks and handkerchiefs, began. A black-clad figure approached me with a flyer. I mentioned that I'd been in contact with the Green Man. He told me various things about my other work interests in a vaguely prophetic fashion, which, along with the attire, was all quite Papa Lazarou. He said he was a journalist and gave me a brown envelope, winked his LEDs and went off.

I spoke to the Green Man, as we wove through Southwark past tourists taking photos of the strange people with their strange attire, and then hung back and watched the morris dancers walking together and talking together, their tankards swinging from their backpacks as they crossed onto Borough High Street to their next stop.

The Wild Hunt Bedlam Morris had been going for twenty-three years. They met weekly in Croydon to practise and took the Border style – the rag-costumes, masks and riotous energy – from the Marches. Bedlam was a description given to this form of morris dancing when it was reincarnated in the 1970s, for its wildness and whooping, and many reinvented contemporary sides use the label to set themselves apart from the gentle leather-and-willow reputation of morris dancing at large.

The original founder was a keen choreographer too, and had a bestiary of characters including a white hart, the sun and the moon, of whom only the Green Man remained now. The Wild Hunt was a democratic side, and if anyone wanted to write their own dance they were able to do so – it worked more like a band than a dance troupe. They took old pieces of morris dancing and old morris moves and filled in the gaps, reinterpreting them into their own style; the limited documentation of the Border style meant that it was impossible to prove authenticity anyway.

And morris dancing was never supposed to be formal or

correct. The blacked-up faces and figure-disguising rags of the old Border sides are thought by some to hail from the dancers' need to remain anonymous when morris dancing was an activity held in the same regard as mugging or trick-or-treating: the morris dance would take place after dark, in disguise and in menacing style with the waving and bashing of menacing sticks, and a cash donation would then be requested of the audience. If the payment did not come, a field full of crops might one day be found ploughed, or some other act of violence or vandalism might happen.

Others see the black-face tradition as indicating the dance's Moorish origin, with 'Morris' a corruption of the word. Whatever, the locations and dates chosen for the dances indicated a ritual connection – St Weonards, in Herefordshire, at the centre of the Border Morris tradition, would have dances around an ancient burial mound, and at all those times of year marked out in *The English Festivals*.

The Wild Hunt were youthful, cool sixty-somethings who had done things in their lives and continued to do so. Even their groupies were cool, milling around in black leather and tattoos. They named their side after a piece of Celtic pagan mythology, the Wild Hunt, in which Cernunnos, the Celtic Horned God and another suspected Green Man analogue, lead a pack of wild ghost-dogs across the hills at night. They didn't identify as pagans, but performed at the old pagan festivals – May morning, the solstice and equinox – and performed at explicitly pagan events like Witchfest and Pagan Pride alongside other paid, private bookings.

At the pub, in a lull, I chatted to the unmasked journalist and his wife, who stood at the entrance in her Wild Hunt Official Groupie T-shirt handing out flyers explaining what they were up to. They had been married for significantly longer than I had been alive, although you wouldn't have guessed it to look at them. They were avid walkers and youth hostellers too, and had worked their way across much of British history on foot.

She had taught folk-dancing and first got him into the morris. She told me about the misconceptions propagated by Cecil Sharp about how morris dancing was supposed to be the preserve of men, when that had never been the case, and about how the history of English folk music and culture had been discovered by men like Sharp and framed through their eyes into an all-male past, discarding many of the histories collected by his contemporary female folklorists.

When I said that I was writing about the Green Man she looked sternly at me and said that it would be a difficult thing to do, and for a moment I was worried because it looked like she knew far more about all of it than I did. Then I realised that we were in agreement. When I described the way the side respected the old festivals as soft paganism, her husband agreed. It was a relief: some of the ways that people understood these things were starting to fit with mine.

Anyone who knew their folklore knew about the bittiness of the Green Man and all about the controversy over Lady Raglan and whether he should even be called that. Anyone who knew their folklore just accepted the Green Man as a contemporary phenomenon that had come about of its own accord, and left it at that. There was no longer much to worry about on that front.

It was time for the last dance of the morning: the Beginning and the End of the World. The dancers began slowly, forming a circle that turned and grew as it turned. At some point in the dance the Green Man joined it and became present, and the circle formed and dissociated, and the dancers left the circle and the Green Man turned alone, slower and slower, until he collapsed and died.

The crowd applauded. The Green Man rose again, removed his mask and went into the loos to get changed into his black tatters. The Green Man mask lay on a bench outside a pub. I went off to look for a wilderness.

Once upon a time London had passed for one, or somewhere that contained them, because you could get lost in the vastness and chaos. It was big enough to be anonymous, and you could, if you wanted to, get on a bus or the Tube and go to a bit that you did not know at all, and wander its high streets and backstreets until it turned into another bit that you did not know, and there was something comforting about that, as though the world was still large and various enough.

Now, wandering back through sanitised Southwark, I wondered whether it was the mindset that I'd lost, rather than London having lost all its wild qualities. The wilder bits of it, the abandoned canals and industrial places of the city centre from here to King's Cross, had now been remodelled into public spaces that were grand and neat and full of people, and, whatever a wilderness was, it was not a public space. Now that the centre of London was so overstuffed with wealth and people, it seemed inconceivable that you would find a wilderness in it.

Wealth attracted order, or created it, as though to ensure that nothing wealth-threateningly anarchic could spring up. The backstreets of the inner suburbs that once bore a hint of menace – bad people and mad people prowling in the shadows as I wove my way unsteadily home from parties – were now uniformly smart. They'd priced out the crazies and the low-grade deviants, and I no longer knew where to look. I used to cycle along empty towpaths, overgrown with dandelions and thistles, and now they were bike highways and there was no longer much space for the plants, and even the graffiti was polished and planned. The disorder had moved on.

Waiting for the train home, gazing down the long straight track out to Bermondsey, I wondered where the wild edges lay now. All along the way, cranes hung across the sky, and new human spaces were marked out in skeletal towers, plots and poles and pylons, eating up land and sky that I'd never noticed before. Every so often another thicket of buddleia sprung up on a disused railway siding or a vacant square metre of land, and then ceded back to houses and gardens which grew larger and neater as the train pushed out to the suburbs.

I wondered what would happen if you left these spaces and their surroundings unchecked for a week, a month, a year – would they be consumed into buddleia forests, flitting with butterflies? Maybe one day all the teeming British cities would be new types of wilderness that we could not yet imagine, wildernesses so far as the lives weaving their way within them were concerned, lives that might no longer be human. Wildernesses of buddleia and knotweed, dock and thistle, sustaining new insects who, in comfort, would tie up their lives into new complexities. Wildernesses that would be fertile grounds for cockroaches and rats, who, amid the ease and richness of it all, would develop sophisticated cockroach and rat societies and self-actualise and have disagreements about the genesis of ancient cockroach and rat rituals.

I felt a sense of doom so far as our wildernesses were

concerned, back in our human sphere. We'd killed off half the planet's wildlife in forty years. There was little space to hide in now for any sort of life, at least the visible ones. Maybe new strains of E. coli would do well out of it. I felt as though we'd killed off our metaphorical wildernesses just as effectively: there was nowhere to hide in cities, either, with all the new shiny edifices that destroyed the old backwaters, and the visibility of everyone and everything, on CCTV and the panopticon of smartphone cameras. Where could you hide now?

On our overcrowded island, it did at least feel comforting to go home to Wales, where my father had promised to help lay a hedge to block out the noise of the traffic. I sat with the children, the three of us crammed into two seats, the small one dozing and the big one downcast at the prospect of leaving the paradise of Paddington Station with its cathedral roof and transcendent godly echoes and conveyor belt sushi outlets. Soon enough he was lost in a story enacted by three small plastic sharks and a stripy fish that came on the front of an overpriced magazine. He was lost to the train, where people shuffled up and down in search of non-existent space, and lost to the endless flying continuum of west-of-London. He was down, underwater, in his own invented wilderness. He was happy. Maybe that was as good as it got.

NINE

God, or Nature

It was an auspicious night to climb the mountain – more than usual, for it had become a habit, an indirect way through the domestic to and fro of evenings, a small way out of the trappings of comfort. The sun hung at the low edge of the sky, casting pink light across the valley, dusty with the beginnings of mist. Only the top of the sky was clear of it, white-blue and combed with cirrus clouds that promised a frost before too long, and as the sun sank into the pooled cloud on the other side, losing its roundness, streaked with fire, the dust or mist or whatever it was burned pink for less time than it took to reach the top of the hill.

I couldn't find the moon at first. It was supposed to be closer to the Earth today, and to rise at the exact time the sun set, so that celestial coming and going existed, moment-arily, in balance. Perhaps the mist obscured the horizon. The only thing for it was to scramble up the steep path to the plateau at the top where the sky could be seen in its entirety. I should have got there sooner.

The moon was still pink, lighter and higher than I had hoped to find it, somewhere above the Golden Valley, which laid itself across the land like a rippled blanket of woods and fields. The silence to the east of the mountain, composed of sounds too distant and too many to be heard, sat in the sky like the dust-mist, occupying it. I stood still, waiting for my heart to subside from the hard climb, watching it all,

263

listening to the nothingness, internally saluting the moon.

The dark crept in fast. I turned to go, dropping back down the north slope. The valley rang out with a multitude of sounds, perhaps because there was more in it than up on the open hilltop, perhaps because they were acoustically magnified by its shape, or some unfelt prevailing wind – for it was still, calm, the air warm for an autumn night. Sheep and bellowing cattle and quieter human voices somewhere down below all called, one over another in layers, under-scored with cars and other, unidentifiable things. Headlights crept along distant hills like glowing ants. Here, in the last light, I could see far enough to get a sense of the surface of the Earth as a single thing, its creases and folds, flats and channels, features that flowed into one another, merging in polymorphous unity.

At the side of the path, the last moths fluttered out of the long grass to find the moon. The first magic mush-rooms were up, matchstick-sized and pointing to the sky as if to indicate their function. I stopped for water by a stream and watched light fade. The evening resonated with life of all kinds, and the sounds attributed to it, human and non-human, although I was no longer sure I could demar-cate the boundaries now. Just as the surface of the land was shaped into its anthropocene form, with its patchwork of fields and winding lanes, the deviated rivers and clustered settlements, in a way that made it impossible to separate human intervention from nature, the sounds of nature – the farm animals and wild ponies, the sudden fluster of nightjars – lay across a bed of human sounds, the rush of larger roads like a gust of wind, or distant mountain brook, the fading babble of voices that might have been the murmur of birds.

We were of nature just as nature was of us, both made

up of the same stuff, of waves or energy or whatever metaphor seemed to fit in the moment. If you'd been up on the Bluff, at the moment when I wasn't, the moment when the sun slipped away to the north and the moon crept in to the south, a moment counterpointed in pink and red, you might have said it was all the work of God or gods, for how could you fail to see the holiness in that, whatever your inclination? Sometimes the world is framed in a way that makes its magic apparent on a gut level.

For months I had been thinking about Spinoza and pantheism, all wrapped up in his phrase 'God, or Nature'. I suppose I thought of the Green Man as inhabiting the same idea, as a point of intersection between the supernatural and natural, and felt that to know Spinoza's 'God, or Nature' better would be to know the godliness or nature of the Green Man. I had read the *Ethics*, page by slow page at bedtime, which was not entirely relaxing, while the moon, high and white and bright, moved across the big window to cast its light across the room, nearly but not quite enough to read by. Switching on the lamp felt transgressive.

I was all set for a grand pantheistic statement of God, immanent in Nature, but the more I read of Spinoza, the less I saw much God in it. Spinoza's theology, in both the *Ethics* and his *Theological-Political Treatise*, is so apophatic as to negate the idea of God existing as any kind of describable entity. It reminded me a bit of the end of *The Hunting of the Snark*, Lewis Carroll's under-read masterpiece of nonsense, in which the Snark, the object of the hunt, described only in nonsensical terms and notoriously slippery and unfixable, turns out not to be a Snark after all, but something else entirely, something defined only by its ability to 'vanish away' all who seek it:

265

In the midst of the word he was trying to say
In the midst of his laughter and glee
He had softly and suddenly vanished away –
For the Snark was a Boojum, you see.

Just as the Snark was the Boojum all along, Spinoza's God was only ever supposed to be Nature, Nature given a Godly tag in order to avoid inquisition at a time when both prospect and outcome of it were scarily real. 'God, or Nature' was a way of removing God from a description of the way in which things work, and from a description of what those things are made of at their deepest level, a way of calling for an entirely naturalistic understanding of the world untainted by divine agency.

Spinoza, a seventeenth-century Dutch Jew, was excommunicated by the Jewish authorities at the age of twenty-three and his books subsequently banned by the Catholic Church. His atheism was no secret in his lifetime. In the Dutch translation of the *Ethics*, even 'God, or Nature' was deemed too risky in evoking fits of pious violence, and so Nature is instead simply renamed God.

It is an ingenious strategy, harnessing the notion of God as creator of all things, and the notion that one must be awestruck at the divine hand at work all around, before quietly dismantling any possibility of describing what role God actually has in any of it. Spinoza sees any fixed or dogmatic description of God as a form of idolatry: the only valid way of seeing God is as the infinite substance that makes up the world.

There are points at which it looks as though Spinoza might be talking about God in some more conventionally understood sense, or in the sense of God as abstract moral

Good. But even here, the term can be accurately reduced to Nature or Existence or the Cosmos or some other analogue of being. Spinoza describes a state whereby a causal thread runs through all things propelled by the laws of Nature that may not be known in their entirety, but that are scientifically knowable.

Spinoza's determinism is shot through with a will to life, a striving to exist that characterises all living entities, rather than the mechanistic form of determinism advocated by Descartes, and you could see this life force as the essence of Nature, for 'striving is nothing but the essence of the thing'. It felt like much the same thing as the Nietzschean Will to Power.

In both cases, even if God was dead – which was absolutely fine as far as I was concerned, for what good did monotheism ever do us beyond perpetuating power in His image and making heretics of everyone else? – Nature was ferociously alive. If Spinoza's 'God, or Nature' turned out to be Godless, it was still possessed of will, a teeming of many wills, often in conflict, sometimes in harmony, all striving away to survive. Here, on this high hill that would soon become inhospitable, wild ponies moved into close clusters as night fell and errant sheep called out to find their flock. Nightjars followed moths out of the bracken towards the moon, orange now, unreasonably large and bright, and turned and dipped to eat them. A kite circled over the edge of the forest at the bottom of the hill, waiting for something. There was nothing supernatural about any of it.

It no longer seemed as though you could call Spinoza a pantheist, for the theism bit seemed a poor fit. The pantheist interpretations of his work sprung up, perhaps unsurprisingly, in the Romantic era, when the idea of God in Nature began to seem appealing as a way of depicting Nature's limitless magic. He was definitely onto something, though, and I remained convinced it was the same something that the image of the Green Man was concerned with.

The revival of the Green Man, the revival that I had had no hand in, for it or he had been there all along, was entirely metaphysical in the grand Romantic sense as well as the philosophical sense, of there being more going on with it than might appear at first glance. If you wanted to call this God, fair enough, but if you wanted to avoid all that you could call it something else instead. You could say that Nature had a soul, or a will, or consciousness. There were options.

The philosophical equivalent, or near-equivalent, of pantheism, panpsychism, was quietly alive in the edgelands of metaphysics and philosophy of mind, a tolerated eccentricity rather than mainstream view. In the Eastern religious traditions it had never gone away, so that in the Taoist and Buddhist and Shinto and Hindu worldview it was a given that everything in the cosmos – Nature in her broadest sense – was ensouled.

There were, and are, granular variations in the quality of the ensoulment. You could see it in crude terms, of speaking waterfalls and shamanic trees, or on an atomic level, of all matter being made of will. This last position was getting less weird. The panpsychists were creeping out of the woodwork again.

One of them had written a book, *Panpsychism in the West*, which I had discovered in the British Library a month or so before the floods, before the seed of the Green Man had manifested, and then bought in paperback so I could read it in the bath. There was something compelling about it, the way it demonstrated that successive waves of thinkers held the same coherent threads of thought, so that the history of ensouled nature and the extent of its dominance across all times other than our own were mapped out as neatly as it could be. It was written economically and without undue philosophical jargon. It told an alternative story of philosophical common sense.

There was also something compelling about the idea that its author was in correspondence with the Unabomber, and had edited the only existing publication of his work. My admiration for *Panpsychism in the West* had turned me into something of a fangirl, to the extent that, when the opportunity to interview its author arose, my voice cracked and wavered like an adolescent choirboy's and I sounded like an idiot, skipping all my best questions out of panic. He therefore sounded hesitant, or perhaps a little bored, although it may have been the slowness of the transatlantic phone connection, but eventually we found ourselves in conversation.

He said that it was starting to become less strange to take a panpsychist view in the academy. They were a small minority, but a growing one; things were beginning to shift. Younger philosophers seemed to feel more intuitively towards it, probably because the limits to materialism were becoming more apparent.

His own particular conception of the enminded quality of the world was rooted in a story about technology that was both radical and ancient. Technology, he said, was composed, both ontologically and in language, of the Greek terms *techne* and *logos*. *Logos* was the cosmic mind of the ancient Greeks, *techne* the process by which it was constructed. It was an ordering process, a natural law in much the same way that gravity was a natural law. I suppose you could see it as a force antagonistic to entropy, creating order from disorder, elevating the low-energy state of things in the world to higher energy and more complex forms.

Techne and *logos* were ideas as old as Aristotle, but the *logos* got lost along the way, so that our understanding of technology was specifically of human construction, and otherwise unminded. And yet technology, in its *techne-logos* form, was there across all scales, on scales we might be unable to access in our human-centred way of looking at things, a process driving ever-higher levels of structure that fed and grew off the energy processing of human society.

He was worried about technology in a way that most philosophers weren't – perhaps unsurprising for someone with a sympathy for Kaczynski. He was worried that we would be subsumed in its swell, and worried for the future of other life too. I asked him how far we would benefit from taking the primitivist line, handing in our creature comforts of electricity, pharmaceuticals, transport and retreating into the woods. In a way, he said, you couldn't do anything about it – the drive to technological order was a natural law. You could fight it and oppose it and resist it. You could try to delay it and defer it for some period of time. You could try to put limits on the process. Only retrograde actions were available to us now. We were past the sustainable point. Technological society was no longer benign.

If you were going to attempt hypothetical time travel to a better era, he thought that the ancient Greeks had a decent and sustainable quality of life, and that 1300 was probably the peak time when humans had the ability to construct the components of the good life without damaging the planet.

That was the time when the image of the Green Man flourished across the English churches. In the way he seemed to be understood today, you could read it as an understanding of the balance of man and nature; those earlier, happier Green Men of the early Middle Ages often seem to have that quality.

Animism, he said, was the functioning on an intuitive level of the same points he argued on a rational level. I had been nervous asking about it, suspecting that academic philosophers needed to police their discipline and keep metaphysics pure, away from the messiness of animism and its lack of intellect.

In an environment where Western academic philosophy sometimes looked as though it were fast becoming a sub-discipline of physics, in the wake of its submission to mathematics at the turn of the last century, perhaps metaphysicians had to be extra careful to de-woo themselves lest they be associated with dreamcatchers and unicorns and other such unrespectable entities. But perhaps the voice of the Logos was there within us just as Jaynes had described in *The Origin of Consciousness in the Breakdown of the Bicameral Mind*, there like the right-brained holism of McGilchrist, often edged out and shouted down by a world of things and concrete orders, but, quietly, there.

You could find it still if you walked up mountains and along rivers, and could find it in the flow of outdoor work – all those lesser meditations that we don't do enough. In the woods, I moved logs into piles ready to bring in for the winter, observing the growth of fungi and the holes where insects had made homes, technologising on their own scale, and I lost myself in it.

The farmer harvested the wheat in the next-door field, the tractor looping around it on its last tour of the year, and when it left I walked across it to the river, grubby and hot and after a swim. The slopes of the bank were soft and overgrown, and I clung onto a low branch to swing myself into the water, which was dark and cool. Insects skimmed the surface and weeds fluttered about beneath it. A dragonfly skimmed the insects, getting in a meal before its fortunes turned. British dragonflies can theoretically live for months, but rarely do, being killed before their time by accidents, predation or starvation – a few days of heavy rain that grounds them and their prey soon spells the end. And here, on this autumnal day, its wings beat furiously as it helicoptered in bumps and circles and strove in search of food, hanging in the balance of existence, glowing blue-green when it flew close to the ragged edges where the sun got in.

The river was small and low, but the force of the current was strong and swept me along so that going back against it was hard work. Wild swimming usually takes a few breath-less minutes to become lovely – perhaps less for hardier folk. I realised, as time passed, that on this occasion the river remained inhospitable. Swimming back around the bend, hard against the flow, I thought about the word inhospitable, and how humans use it to describe non-human things: the inhospitable landscape is often the wildest and most won-derful. I thought about the shaman and how she approached the tree for permission, and thought that it was time to get out. I was persona non grata here: it was a river for river-life, not mine, and time to go.

I had a friend who changed careers every seven years on the basis that they stayed interesting for a limited time. This phase was medical: he was an A&E doctor married to an acupuncturist, but had in previous incarnations been a man-agement consultant and a computer scientist. These various ways of seeing working life had led to ways of seeing life at work that he once wrote up drunkenly on his managerial stash of A1 flipcharts – a life in which water molecules possessed their own consciousness, a sort of hive consciousness that formed from the institution of its constituent parts, so that the individual will of each water molecule was incorporated into a new and larger will of the body of water.

Although eccentric, and the outcome of a late-night afterparty rant, this story had never seemed particularly crazy. The assumption that only humans could possess will, or mind, was, surely, more ridiculous – and there was an elegance to consistency.

Elegance was something that seemed to attract the panpsychists. They weren't so thin on the ground: I found another one in the UK, and collared him just as he was trying to leave for Budapest. The train ride through the Marches to see him was exemplary: winding valleys, high hills, dozing stone villages, all bathed in September light.

In Liverpool, early, I wandered through the warren of streets trying to work out where we were meeting, streets that were narrow and filled with bars and clubs and odd little shops in that second-phase regeneration mode of an urban ex-wilderness. No broken glass here, no sense of doom, just clean sunny streets, mildly fashionable, slightly dull. I had hoped to get lost in them but couldn't, or didn't.

I found a replica human skull in a junk shop and bought it for the woods, which were rapidly becoming over-adorned with all manner of things – toy planes, princesses, plastic musical instruments – by the children, who had started to call it the Disco Shed. Perhaps the skull would reappropriate it, although to what end I no longer knew. Perhaps I could get plants to grow out through its orifices, and in so doing create a living foliate head. If only the skull were a real skull, for then it would be truly authentic, but such authenticity would be hard to come by, and no doubt more expensive than the bargain price I paid for a piece of kit aimed at students of anatomy and dentistry, whose wisdom tooth kept falling out on the street as I dangled the inverted cranium from my right hand as I walked.

When I got to the vegetarian cafe where I was meeting the panpsychist, I put the skull beneath the table, worried that it might skew the conversation unfavourably. I don't think he saw it. We drank tea and he talked about physics, and how effective it had been as a description of how the world works, and about how all of the technological interventions made possible by it had impacted on metaphysical belief. Physics, he said, did a great job of telling us what matter does, but doesn't tell us what it is. All we do know about matter is that at least some of it is conscious, and it is therefore simpler and more elegant to assume that it is all conscious.

He described himself as a fictionalist Christian, which meant seeing the Bible as a metaphor, rather than taking it as fact, and using the Christian tradition as a way into accessing a God he saw as something glimpsed through mystical experiences, such as the experience of ineffable beauty.

This sounded far more like pantheism than Spinoza did. He described the Spinozist view of the universe as a singular fundamental thing, a whole prior to its parts, known philosophically as priority monism. Consciousness, too, was philosophically irreducible, and couldn't be explained otherwise; science could do neuroscience, describe networks of cells and areas aroused within the anatomy of the brain, and measure levels of neurotransmitters, but could not explain, and claimed to have no interest in, consciousness itself. You could elide priority monism with panpsychism to form cosmopsychism, which was my new favourite word. He hurried off to a last appointment, carrying a huge folded packing box under his arm, past the order and disorder of the city and the lives within it.

Talking to these two very brilliant men who wrote transparently about matters deserving a far greater audience, and who were very generous with their time, it was hard not to feel somewhat on the back foot. It felt as though talking about the structure of the world in a way that made sense outside the academy was a slightly heretical thing to do, and would alter it into something less valuable, something fluffy and childish. In our English-speaking world, philosophising was carried out by men in institutions and corrupted by stoned hippies in fields, and there was little to see in-between. Talking about the world's other lives was an exercise in cult-like religiosity if it veered too far from human interest; digging for the underpinnings of what people think about the world was a suspect exercise too.

If I'd thought it through better, I think I would have asked them about Schopenhauer's case for folk-metaphysics, concealed in the form of an imagined debate between two Neoplatonist philosophers, one of whom speaks here:

Philosophy isn't for everyone – as your friend Plato said and as you shouldn't forget. Religion is the metaphysics of the people, which they absolutely must be allowed to keep; and that means you have to show an outward respect for it, since to discredit it is to take it away from them. Just as there is folk-poetry, and, in the proverbs, folk-wisdom, so there has to be folk-metaphysics: for

275

men have an absolute need for an interpretation of life, and it has to be one they are capable of understanding. That is why it is always clothed in allegory; and, as far as its practical effect as a guide to behaviour and its effect on morale as a means of consolation and comfort in suffering and death are concerned, it does as much perhaps as truth itself would do if we possessed it.

Schopenhauer's other character goes on to cite the many abuses of religion as a counter-argument in favour of pure philosophy, perhaps a more accurate reflection of Schopenhauer himself, who was no fan of organised religion, and certainly not in its Judaeo-Christian form. Had Schopenhauer lived on to see the rising dogmatic faith in science and human technology as religion died, and the attempt by logic to kill off metaphysics entirely, perhaps there would be fewer value judgements to draw between philosophy and religion.

I had wanted to use the term 'folk-metaphysics' to describe the function I thought the Green Man had now, and in the end I didn't dare do so in front of the real philosophers. I sensed the Green Man would go down like a lead balloon. Secretly, though, if some neo-pagans saw the whole of the cosmos as a goddess whose attributes had the characteristics of other, individual gods, I didn't see that as wildly different to Spinoza's godless Nature manifesting in all her many attributes. Some things were timeless, perhaps because they worked.

Back in May, I had caught the end of a talk at the philosophy festival – encouragingly named 'Pagan Gods' or something like it – where I lurked at the back, earpiece in, phone on silent, wondering how long I had before my absence would become an issue. Two men spoke onstage, one taking a line that veered between doom and practical responses to it, or to delaying it – reducing fossil fuel consumption, stopping fracking, encouraging regulation – and the other taking a more unfashionable position. He was advocating a new religiosity in our dealings with nature and the world, talking about how humans had to get over materialism in its dealings with life, basically – I thought – advocating animism, or pantheism, or something like it.

When the questions started, I wanted to ask him lots of things, and waited impatiently as people asked questions that were not really questions, but demonstrations of their tribal status as doom-cult members. These events tend to select for their audiences.

Just as the lull finally fell, I got called back to the office, and so months later I went to find him at his home in Oxford instead, where we drank strong coffee and walked along the canal side past hops and honeysuckle and quiet boats disrupted from time to time by freight trains and light aircraft rumbling over golden wheatfields in a way that oddly fed the sense of baseline calm. It was as though the mythological English countryside was dependent on its proximity to industrial society, a quieter man-made structure of squared-off fields and hedgerows than the concrete shapes of cities, which were only ever a few miles away, as though to remind you that this was as good as it got.

He had started out as a biologist and then as a journalist specialising in farming. He had written a fascinating book about the ingenuity of trees, and was gung-ho about using terms like ingenuity that, to most of his biological contemporaries, strayed into the heresy of anthropomorphosis – the defining of all allusion to consciousness as human-like. He thought that people needed to think more philosophically about both biology and farming; he wanted to set up a School of Enlightened Agriculture, an exercise that was dependent on reclaiming a metaphysical understanding of life.

He had allies who were Christian and Muslim theologians, geneticists and environmentalists, and had the closest understanding I had found yet of all the things I saw entangled in the Green Man. He wanted to set up a School of Perennial Wisdom too, a way of teaching those threads of metaphysics that seem to persist through time, outside of today's silos of academic philosophy and organised religion.

In his most recent book, a refutation of the aggressive takes on Darwinism that he saw as yoked to neoliberal ideology – the bitter life-and-death competition for resources that propelled the clockwork of life – he argued for conviviality, in its etymological sense, the possibility of life alongside life, living peaceably, using its will to organise constructively. You could say, were it not for the anthropocentric pitfall of the term, that it was a humane vision of the world.

Spinoza made a similar case in his *Ethics*: that the institution of the State could and should be used to regulate the many wills of people in pursuit of greater harmony. He was a progressive too. All these ideas, good, workable ideas, never seem to die, but are reincarnated across time and place, and yet we never seem to be educated in them. C had a point. He invited me to be part of the School of Perennial Wisdom. I agreed. I suppose I joined his cult.

The next day, I took my car in for its MOT, and wandered about the garage yard in the bright morning sun, looking and waiting, inspecting the shells of former cars for signs of the lives that had once inhabited them with their roadmaps and thermos flasks, old horseboxes and ambulances decked out with bunk beds and curtains, an old-school booster seat that must have dated to my childhood. In the middle of it was a poured concrete ramp, and I climbed up to get more sun, standing at the top where my shadow fell across a patch of vegetation, slightly larger than life. Here were long grasses and vast docks with leaves bigger than my head, buddleia and little thickets of young mountain ash, ivy climbing an old lamppost and making its way into a nearby trailer.

A farm supply truck, consumed with rust, had a tiny, three-leaved oak seedling growing at its rear right-hand corner, leaves already turning at the edges. I felt a tenderness towards it and the likelihood of its survival that one might feel for the smallest puppy in the litter or a baby born too soon. Oaks are impressive survivors, in it for the long game, but the chances of getting a root stock through all that iron, despite the best efforts of the elements to dismantle it, looked slim.

Give it time, though, and anything was possible. Another truck, a glorious yellow Dodge twice my age, lay at the periphery of the yard with a dead tree inside its windscreen and sturdy brambles growing through the vent at the top of its bonnet, sprawling their fat fruit in a fan across its window like a harvest tableau. I climbed up a couple of dead tyres and ate my way through them, huge and firm and perfectly ripe. If the Green Man was consumed, in time, by nature, so too were van and truck and car, dismembered by rain and air and plants in less than a human lifespan.

It was time to go back to see them – the Green Men, foliate heads – whatever it was possible to call them. I went for the local triumvirate, to Abbey Dore, Kilpeck and Garway,

279

mostly because it was easy to do but also because I liked
those ones best of all.

It was good day for it: mid-September, still warm, hazy-
skied, the roads quiet on a Friday afternoon. Along the roadside, cow parsley faded next to willowherb fluffed with late
pollen and tall brown skeletons of hogweed. The fields were
shorn to stubby gold, some still host to round bales of hay that
seemed to wheel to and fro as I passed. Everywhere was hay:
the lane up by the mountain was strewn with the stuff after
some overambitious farmer had piled the trailer too high, and
a load of it sat dumped on the bank of a ravine. The sun had
shone for a week or so now, and hay had been made, and
barns at roadside farms glowed with it as the last bales of the
season were stashed away ready for the winter.

I wandered down to Dore Abbey, noting that the pink
flowers on the next-door garden wall had faded, so that only
one remained, noting the quiet in the air, the way the birds
seemed to sing sedately. I did not really know why I was
there, and just walked in, finding it empty, and seeing for
the first time the height of the ceiling and the colour of the
walls, and the signs requesting donations to keep it – I did
not know what the donation would keep it from. Falling
down, perhaps, or becoming deconsecrated and sold off?
I noticed how the transept at the back where the Green
Man lay was strewn with other fallen stones, and wondered
whether they fell or were removed. Next to the Green Man
was a woman of the same size, serene and lovely, an ideal
consort, and many other bits of ornamentation and idolatry,
all broken.

The reasoning behind Dore Abbey's demise was pragmatic rather than puritanical, with the abbey dismantled and its stone sold after Henry VIII's dissolution of the monasteries. Somehow, the ornamentation was saved, perhaps because it was not useful as a building material, perhaps because some inner sense or superstition prevented the images from being used in desecrated form.

When I touched the Green Man, ochre pigment came off on my hand, a pigment that dated to before Henry VIII and perhaps long before him, a remnant of the colour that lit up the Cistercian abbey in its original form. The Cistercians were renowned for their brightly painted monasteries. They also consecrated work and saw it as holy endeavour, breeding sheep at Abbey Dore to create the finest woollen cloth for export to Italy. When the Norman Conquest opened up passage across England and Wales, they sought out unobtrusive places to establish monasteries, places where an agricultural business could be run to sustain monastic life. God was in work, and the work of the land, the growing and making of things. It seemed pretty appropriate for an order whose spiritual practice lay in cultivation to have an emblem of man and plant overseeing the holy work, a smiling emblem, the golden colour of the harvest.

In the field behind the abbey, bounded by the low, slow Dore, ancient bits of farming equipment – harrows, ploughs: vast, rusting, useless things – lay in the long grass. A footpath crossed the river, fenced with uncharacteristic enthusiasm on the other side. Something in the woods above caught my eye: the red doors of an Underground train. I followed the path but couldn't escape it, and made my way back to the car. I drove a little further down the road to a layby where, if I clambered onto the car roof, I could see the train in its entirety, along the hillside, deep in the woods. I inspected the map.

The area to the west of Abbey Dore and north of Ewyas Harold was marked out with masts and had no footpaths crossing it. I remembered driving down the A465 at night and seeing the huge, bright masts lit up like an alien colony, and remembered the shadow of something S had once said when we driving down to Garway about a weird military base there where they mocked up terrorist situations and nuclear war and, probably, alien invasions too. Perhaps I should have brought her with me again for guidance: it felt as though she knew these places in a way I only glimpsed.

S's theory was that places with the greatest beauty, the places whose psychogeography drew people to them, the places whose energy, if you wanted to enter feng shui-type paradigms, was strongest, were a threat to imposed order. They offered a nourishment beyond material things, a nourishment that could be neither bought nor sold. They had a dissidence about them.

There seemed to be a pattern, she said, at least in Herefordshire, a county unusually rich in places of ancient spiritual significance, of building big, bleak, soul-destroying things beside the beautiful places, as though to make a stamp of authority upon them. You could think of loads of examples if you put your mind to it – the huge satellite observation station along Watkins's first ley down the Golden Valley, or the way Llantwit Major, the site of St Illtyd's first Welsh monastery, got turned into an RAF dormitory town. Maybe the MOD had a ley-only building policy. Maybe you could make anti-leys from lines of missile storage facilities or out-of-town business parks if you put your mind to it.

I drove down the lane at the end of the housing estate at

the edge of Ewyas Harold, past the man in dark glasses standing still on the pavement carrying a black carrier bag, past the
end of the speed limit to where the fences began. High, steel
fences on both sides, and behind them tall trees – leylandii
or something like it, dense and tall and perfectly uniform,
blocking all view of what lay behind them. There was a gap
to get to the staff car park, but only cars and a Nissen hut
and a sign stating MOD property were visible before the
high trees resumed. A man in a fluorescent jacket walked, or
patrolled, the lane with a big dog. I passed a mast, an enormous thing with a big head made of arcs of steel, indescribable
from memory – there was no way I was stopping to get a
closer look, or take a photo, for I had the sense that it would
be noticed, and would not go down well. Further along, two
high gates were blacked out in polythene, like giant barbed-
wire bin liners, labelled GATE 5. I could only speculate. On
the right, a farm piled high with hay and sleepy cows materialised. It was the end of the road. Just beyond the T-junction,
a black car waited with a man in it, also in dark glasses, who
may or may not have been a farmer.

The lane to Wormelow was marked out with gold-edged
oaks, fields sleepy with cows, the whole place in a hazy
slumber. It was reality as nostalgia, a corner of England little
altered over centuries, dozing next to the strange and secretive technologies of power. It would all change in time: the
human tracks of roads and cables would grow or move or be
overcome by some other trace of life. It was as though *techne*,
the cosmic drive to greater order, would change this last bit
of land into some other form eventually, yoking it into some
new and unimaginable power, human or not.

On to Kilpeck, where sheep grazed the castle mound and
nestled in the crook of the ruins, one of which I climbed in

a vain attempt to get a better view of the masts. The ruins of a Norman motte-and-bailey castle, once the edifice of a new and technologised military force, now crumbled into land again. The Normans conquered England and made their marks on Archenfield, but beneath it all along were other ways and lives, lives that, unsubsumed, flourished in the edges and the woods. No power was omnipotent, even in its own time, for even suppressed things seethe beneath the surface, and rise and bring about falls and revolutions. Change, as Heraclitus never really said, is the only constant.

Past the holly and the hawthorn, hung with berries, past the yew, its deadly fruit and ivy-covered base, past the twisty oak whose leaves were gold and going. The Green Man above the door did not stand out to me now, but existed within the interconnected Celtic knot of creatures that formed the doorway in their interconnected lives. Life – being tied into the knotty continuity of it – was his function, taking part in the grand bestiary of existence.

At Garway, where, for the first time, I took the correct road without getting lost, smoke rose from a woodburner somewhere and the sides of the lane to the church were thickly garlanded with blackberries and haws. I didn't know what to think about Baphomet, so I climbed onto a chair with a cross-stitched Silver Jubilee cushion on it and embraced him, hoping for a sacral rush of magick, which never came. My small act of cushion-desecration seemed trivial in the grand scheme of things, given all the bad PR endured by both Horned Beast and swastika in the religio-fascist Common Era.

The woman, and I am certain it was a woman, who painstakingly cross-stitched the cushion would no doubt have been horrified at the defilement of her pure intent, but what of the intent of the stonecarvers whose own spiritual intent, unknowable now, had been relegated to heresy for centuries? If I'd been more organised I could have done a proper Crowley sex rite, but I wasn't in the mood, and needed to get back and take the washing in before it got dark.

At home, the vines hung heavy with grapes I hadn't picked and hop bines brushed the washing line. I took the laundry down and folded it, sitting on the edge of the path at the top of the garden as the bats swooped at mosquitoes in the dusk. I went inside, where I found an email waiting.

In the spirit of research, I had put a message out to The Company of the Green Man, an organisation that brought together Green Man enthusiasts of all kinds. Here was a reply:

> I saw your request for information about the concept of the Green Man and how it fits in to modern people's lives.
>
> I thought I would tell you what it means to me. I have a Green Man image in each room of my house and a half sleeve tattoo of a Green Man on my arm.
>
> It may seem that I am a bit odd, but to me the Green Man is a symbolic link of man to his origin as a natural animal, with trees and foliage being the symbol of nature and its all-encompassing presence. The general assumption that we are the highest order of animal is tamed by being drawn back to nature's stages of life: birth, youth, fertile adulthood, self-sacrificing to our offspring, old age and decay, then death.
>
> From here, I like to think we will be like other forms of nature and are reborn anew in the next season or cycle.

The image of a man formed from foliage is a blend of him as an animal but still strongly part of nature.

The reason for so many images around the house is to hopefully remind us of our origin and not to be so arrogant to assume we are superior to all other forms of life. Also, I like the images of the Green Man and if I am way out it does no harm as it is a positive feeling towards nature.

I am not sure if this rambling makes any sense or is of any use to you but as the idea is wishful thinking on my behalf, I just thought it may be of use.

All the best with your work,

G

In the end, it turned out that the cult of the Green Man had meant exactly what I had hoped it would. It had needed no further intervention. It had been there all along, hidden at the edges, doing its own thing, like a wild man of the woods.

And in the woods, at the end of the woods, I found my father, who found new reasons to be there: investigating the drainage of the ditch beside the embankment, examining the trees, clearing old bits of brush. I wasn't sure that there was any need for him to rationalise it. In the woods, as the nights drew in, my son would insist on lighting bonfires at the end and gather around them, alone or with other small boys, moving between the shadows of the trees in search of sticks and climbing onto log-piles to see the newly risen moon. It was often difficult to convince them to come back across the road into civilisation.

Acknowledgements

Thanks to all who made this happen: to Rupert Heath for developing it into an idea that worked, to Dave Watkins for tireless patience and inevitably being right, and to Lee Brackstone and the team at Faber Social for their enthusiasm and assistance. I am indebted to Luke Brown and Sarah Barlow for excising inaccuracies and grammatical howlers; to Eli, Sarah, Ian and Niklas for reading drafts, being appropriately rude about them, and coming up with a long-elusive title; to Jeff Barrett and all at *Caught by the River* for creating a space to air early versions and ideas.

This book would not exist without the various adventurers and interviewees, who are all Green Men and Women of a fashion: thank you for your time, hospitality, wisdom and good humour, and for staying up late and bearing strange lines of questioning. I am enormously grateful to the Society of Authors, whose Authors' Foundation's generous provision of the Roger Deakin Award gave the project room to breathe.

And thank you to my parents, Ben and Crista, and assorted family and friends for your help and support, from the provision of information and allotments to the occasional removal of children, who were more instrumental to the story than they or I knew.